STAGE MANAGEMENT
for the
AMATEUR THEATRE

STAGE MANAGEMENT
for the
AMATEUR THEATRE

WITH AN INDEX TO THE STANDARD WORKS
ON STAGECRAFT AND STAGE LIGHTING

By

WILLIAM PERDUE HALSTEAD

UNIVERSITY OF MICHIGAN

Drawings by

HENRY HARLAN BLOOMER

UNIVERSITY OF MICHIGAN

1937

F. S. CROFTS & CO. NEW YORK

EDITOR'S FOREWORD

While there are many excellent books on play production, and on even the technical phases of this subject, there is little material available on stage management. Instructors in college courses on dramatic production, as well as directors of Little Theatres, will welcome this comprehensive treatment of the subject.

I have been very favorably impressed with the author's practical knowledge of the field, and the thoroughness with which he has dealt with it. He gives us specific and detailed suggestions with many valuable illustrations drawn from his own experience as a teacher and director. For this reason the book will prove especially useful in courses in technical practice where the instructor must carefully organize and plan the work of each student.

While Dr. Halstead presents an organization chart calling for an elaborate backstage staff, he also suggests a simplified plan for small groups who find it necessary to assign more than one backstage job to a single individual. The diagrams seem to me admirably designed to meet the practical needs of the student.

A special feature of the book is an exhaustive bibliographical index. The technical director often remembers vaguely that some book he owns contains useful information on papier mâché, on the paste method of painting scenery, on shoe risers, on fluorescence, on advertising contests, on shrinkage of fabrics, on supporting tights, on expressionistic or idiot make-up, on a collapsible run of stairs. It takes valuable time for him to search through all his books for it. Many of them do not contain indexes. Worse still is the plight of the student or inexperienced technical director who is not familiar with stagecraft books. Dr. Halstead's composite topical index will be a great boon to both by providing them with book and page references on all staging subjects.

FREDERICK H. KOCH

v

FOREWORD

The unique feature of the system here presented for handling the backstage work in amateur theatrical productions is the division, the breaking up, of such work into many separate tasks or projects for individual workers and small groups, with comprehensive descriptions and detailed directions for each project. Other phases of the preparation, such as theatre organization and management, scene design and construction, costume design and execution, make-up, stage lighting, directing, and acting, adequately covered in the textbooks on the theatre, are discussed only to the extent that they are related to the backstage work at the set-up, at dress rehearsals, and at performances. These texts also contain chapters and passages sketching the work to be done by each major division of the backstage staff, but this treatment of the subject offers for the first time, it is believed, an exhaustive discussion of stage management. A method is presented by which this phase of a production may be carried out with less lost motion, less confusion, less excitement, and fewer mishaps, oversights, and blemishes to the performance than are customary. The system is especially applicable to school theatres and Little Theatres.

When a worker, especially a beginner, is given opportunity to do, and personal responsibility for, even a minor project, he much more fully appreciates his significance as one of the essential cogs in the producing machine and, in consequence, is more attentive, accurate, and punctual. Just as in my shop work, where I have made it a practice to assign work by the piece, the worker is more enthusiastically interested than if he were merely told to "just make yourself useful." The importance of the task is magnified in his estimation when he can foresee a concrete end-result to his personal activities. Written instead of oral instructions increase this effect.

vii

So far as is possible without limiting their range to some individual production, detailed instructions are provided here for all projects. General directions for all the members of a division are contained in the section addressed to its head officer. When the workers are once made familiar with the general duties of a department, they will readily understand the directions for their individual projects and will require little additional instruction except specific directions on the staging requirements of the particular production on which they are engaged. It is anticipated that the book, or sections of it, will be put in the hands of the workers individually.

In order to create enough separate projects for all the members of a high school or college class in play production or of similar groups which present plays, and to permit any arrangement of them the Technical Director desires, the number of projects given is greater than is likely to be needed or than will be found practicable for any single production other than an elaborate show or pageant. Nevertheless, in some of the plays I directed or staged at the Sacramento (California) Junior College, where the system was originated and developed, I found it advantageous to assign the full list of projects as separate tasks. The entire plan was evolved in the course of staging a wide variety of productions.

It is assumed that those who will read or use this book already know general stage terminology, so only the less familiar terms are defined. In instances where the use of common words in a special stage sense might cause confusion, quotation marks are employed to show the distinction.

An elaborately equipped stage calls for more system and a larger staff of workers than does a simply equipped one. Therefore the plans given are for an elaborate production on a fully equipped stage. On simply or poorly equipped stages and with small backstage crews, the same methods, modified accordingly, may be successfully used. Suggestions are made for this simplification and for special methods of handling scenery under those conditions.

I have long felt the need for topical references to the standard works on stagecraft. Much time is consumed by instructors and directors in finding textbook citations for the workers. Accordingly, an appended special index provides them by book and page for all construction and backstage work. The references to the one hundred and thirty-five texts are confined to those sections and passages which are of immediate value in the actual performance of such work.

ACKNOWLEDGMENTS

I wish to express my appreciation to the authors and to Samuel French, Inc., the publishers, for permission to reprint speeches from *Alison's House* by Susan Glaspell, *Berkeley Square* by John L. Balderson, *The Royal Family* by George S. Kaufman and Edna Ferber, and *Three Cornered Moon* by Gertrude Tonkonogy.

I am heavily indebted to Mr. Alexander Wyckoff and Miss Evelyn Cohen, professional theatre artists and technicians, who read the book in manuscript and made many valuable suggestions for its betterment; to Dr. H. Harlan Bloomer, a colleague at the University of Michigan, who made the drawings; to Professor Frederick H. Koch, who edits the series of books in which this volume appears; and to Mr. William L. Halstead, my father, who gave me much help in the preparation and revisions of the manuscript.

WILLIAM P. HALSTEAD

Ann Arbor, Michigan

TABLE OF CONTENTS

TABLE OF CONTENTS

ILLUSTRATIONS

STAGE MANAGEMENT

for the

AMATEUR THEATRE

CHAPTER I

INTRODUCTION

To the entire backstage staff:

Producing an amateur play is a nerve-wracking business at best, and the general dread of "what might happen" usually gives everyone the jitters as the opening night approaches. Some directors regard this condition as desirable and one to be fostered because it "keys up" the actors to give a better performance. But many directors now realize that this desire for tension is an evidence of their own weaknesses. If a director has had sufficient time to train his actors to the peak of their abilities, he does not need to rely upon a form of nervousness which is supposed to cause the performers to "outdo themselves," but which, just as often as otherwise, will cause them to undo themselves through over-acting and shrillness of voice. The cast will respond to the reactions of the audience just as well or better when its members are free from this strain as when they are worrying about the possibility of onstage and backstage errors.

The sight of stagehands running about doing last minute tasks has a strong tendency to aggravate the nervousness of actors preceding the rise of the curtain. They hear whispered conferences about whether the horsehair sofa belongs in the first or second act, who is to ring the chimes, what the cue is for the explosion, and what can be substituted for the cuspidor that has been mislaid. "If those guys are uncertain about these things now," think the actors, "what may not go blooey during the performance!" This, naturally, makes them worry about the placing of the furniture in the setting and whether its doors will open and shut properly, and they seek, in their distrust, windows and cracks through which to examine the setting in order

3

to make sure that they will not be the victims of misunderstanding or carelessness on the part of the backstage people.

On the other hand, actors have an entirely different feeling, even if they are apprehensive about their own performances, when they have confidence in the backstage crew, and are certain that they will find "the papers" hidden in the davenport, that the door to be closed will stay closed, that they will be handed the properties they are to carry on, that the call boys will have all of them onstage for their cues, and that the lights on the stage will go out when the dummy switch is touched. It is soothing to their jangled nerves to see the stagehands at ease, to observe the stage manager coolly wait for his wrist-watch to show the second for the curtain, and to hear the proverbially excitable director wish the cast well before he calmly goes out-front to watch the performance.

Yet this serene backstage atmosphere can be obtained. Nor does it require a crew of long experience. An efficient person to plan the production painstakingly is the one indispensable requirement. Even he need not have had extensive experience. Planning and supervising are only relatively simple matters of method, calling for no such technical knowledge and sensitiveness to characterization and dramatic effects as a good director of acting must possess. Anyone who has a flare for system, and who knows how scenery and equipment are handled backstage, can formulate the procedure and manage the activities.

It is this element of system that is most often wanting in amateur productions. There is an abundance of good intention and a flood of enthusiasm, but a dearth of thoughtful planning of the preparatory work. The standard plaint of the amateur stage manager is: "If you want a thing well done, do it yourself." When, in the stress of dress rehearsal, he says to an assistant, "Mask that entrance with an eight-foot book!" and the response is, "What do you mean 'mask'?"—"What is a 'book'?"—"Eight-foot which way?" it seems easier to him to do the thing himself than to take the trouble at that belated point to show someone how to do it. Doing it himself does save time at that dress rehearsal, but he is then burdened with it for all subsequent dress rehearsals and performances, and it follows also that, when there is a quick change, it is actually the stage manager himself who must delay the curtain. The same condition prevails in all the other departments of the backstage work, with the various supervisors prone to think that it is inevitable.

The condition has been and can be avoided, however, even with inexperienced workers. The backstage may be a romantic mystery to outsiders, but those familiar with it know that there is no task in the setting up or changing of scenery that cannot be done by a novice at the end of five minutes' or less training. In one scenic and two dress rehearsals, the author taught inexperienced members of a stagecraft class to run a performance of *Macbeth* containing twenty-eight changes of scenery each involving almost complete rearrangement of flats and wagons. No single change during the performance required more than one minute.

While the methods provided are for the management of an elaborate production such as *Macbeth,* similar ones are also necessary to the highest efficiency in a one-set play. The principle is always the same; the scheme varies only in its elaborateness.

Plays are produced, and are well produced, without so much system. In fact, most amateur plays are put on with a minimum of system. But the author's observation has resulted in the conclusion that, in its absence, not only are scene changes of longer duration, but that at the early performances the backstage workers make mistakes, and are in constant dread of making many more.

At the dress rehearsal each scene shift is spread out in leisurely fashion over ten minutes to half an hour. At the first performance the crew must speed up the shifts. They try, in their excitement, to gain speed by undue haste. So they run and jump, and not infrequently collide, drop properties, and tear flats. Then, typically, just as the curtain is about to be pulled, the stage manager discovers that the grand piano has not been placed. Only after this has been frantically done can the curtain go up and the scene start.

By the third or fourth performance much of the false haste and dangerous tension may be gone. The changes then go much more rapidly and smoothly. A sort of system has been evolved instinctively by the workers themselves with the individuals doing much the same tasks each night. There is still hampering inequality in the division of the labor and much needless jumping from one task to another, although the settings may then actually go up well enough.

Nevertheless, the first strained rehearsals and uncertain performances can be eliminated by a systematized scheme for the changes. The first rehearsal, or the first scenic rehearsal, will be a lengthy one still, because each worker must be shown the exact points on the stage for the scenic elements and properties he handles. Their positions can be only roughly indicated in the scene shifting plans. But the stage will no longer be a madhouse at rehearsals, and all the performances will run "like clock-work."

Methodical planning will also lessen the time consumed at the set-up. If, for example, fifteen workers are present without individual assignments when the technical director decides to hang a drape cyclorama, only one or two of them are needed to find the correct set of lines, to lower the batten, and to adjust the leg-arms, while the rest must merely look on. A considerable number of them are needed for five minutes or so while the drapes are being attached. Nearly all must remain idle while the cyclorama is being raised and trimmed, and must wait again while the technical director wanders around the stage in search of the various flats with which to form the back-wall. After these flats are laid together on the floor, because, curiously, there are never more than three hammers to be found at one time on any stage, twelve workers must watch three workers batten the wall, tie it to a batten, and then only two more are needed to raise it. Five people at the most can be kept busy continuously and the other ten present can only be used conveniently at odd moments. So it goes everywhere. Oftentimes it is advantageous to have many people present at the set-up because of their usefulness on certain jobs, but when people are summoned to help, they expect to be kept busy. If they are not, and thus are given the impression that they aren't really needed, they will not come the next time.

It is sometimes possible to assemble a crew of thirty or forty people, but the technical director, without a system of distinct units for the work, cannot use them all at one time, and so does not call them. He realizes that he will be confronted continually with, "What can I do now?" Yet, if by means of individual tasks, he could put them all to work at the same time, calling them together only for something requiring a large group, his settings would be erected in a third of the usual time, and he would have extra time for rehearsals and for lighting adjustments.

A multiplicity of minor executive positions, even though the specific functions are not essential to satisfactory organization, will be found beneficial to morale, since more persons will then have definite obligations and responsibilities. Workers like this. It provides the director and technical director with opportunity, otherwise lacking, to watch them in minor supervisory capacities before trying them in major ones. The experience is excellent training for prospective stage managers, property masters, and the like. It is good training for teaching dramatics, for Little Theatre producing, and for the work in stage management a beginner in the professional theatre frequently is required to do, as well as for administrative activities apart from the theatre.

RESPONSIBILITY

Clear individual responsibility is an essential element of organizational efficiency. Greater reliance can be placed in one person to whom a definite task is assigned than in half a dozen who are told collectively to "see that it is done." By the same token, the stage manager should delegate the full responsibility of supervising various branches of the work to his assistants. In an elaborate production, these assistants, in turn, should delegate part of their duties to subordinates. The more complicated and elaborate the enterprise, the more people there should be at the top of the staff with, seemingly, nothing to do. In a one-set play the stage manager may help make the changes and do other similar work. When there are several changes to be made, during them the stage manager should have nothing of a specific nature to do. In the production of a very complicated play or a musical show, the stage manager, the property master, the assistant stage manager in charge of scene shifting, and possibly the electrician, the effect master, the head call boy, and the costume master, should be relieved of all specific tasks except checking. Their sole responsibility should be to watch and to verify the work of others, and to help them in emergencies.

Lines of Responsibility

The lines of responsibility should be made clear to all workers and they should be required to adhere to them.

The stage manager is responsible for every phase of the work behind the footlights except the interpretation of the lines by the actors. In the absence of the director he is responsible even for this. If the director, manager, or other executive ordinarily his superior in the organization, should be backstage during a dress rehearsal or performance, he is under the stage manager and is subject to his orders. During the performance no one may dispute him. As Alexander Wyckoff puts it, "When the curtain is up, the stage manager's responsibility is solely to the audience."

Directly responsible to the stage manager are the heads of departments, such as the electrician, the assistant stage manager in charge of scene shifting, the property master, the head call boy, the costume master, the effect master, et cetera. Their assistants, in turn, are responsible to them, and only indirectly to the stage manager. Within the departments there may be any desired divisions of the work, with appropriate authority delegated to assistants. All this depends upon the size of the crew and the elaborateness of the production.

In a strict sense, the director and technical director ought to give orders only to the stage manager, who should relay them to individual workers through the fixed channels of authority. The director should never give directions to an individual crew-man without the knowledge of the stage manager and the worker's other direct superiors. To do so will lead inevitably to confusion, misunderstanding, and hard feeling. If there are many such unreported changes in the directions, the stage manager gets in such a state of mind that he does not dare to correct any error for fear it is another of these unreported changes.

In the original instructions and assignment of tasks, and in the criticisms and changes at dress rehearsals, these channels of authority should be strictly observed because only in that way can changes be noted in every written record where they should appear. Questions, complaints, requests for assistance, and the like, should go through these channels in reverse order. One important advantage of such a practice is the feeling of responsibility it arouses all along the line. Another is that many problems will be solved by assistants without bothering the overburdened director and stage manager about them.

In an emergency during performance, of course, all questions of precedence should be cast aside for the moment. For example, anyone on the stage should tell the stage manager of an error or accident that ought to hold the curtain, and the stage manager should commandeer anyone present to remedy such a condition.

Previous to the hour of dress rehearsal, the heads of departments are directly responsible to the technical director, excepting those who work only at the performance.

ORGANIZATION CHART

The chart that follows shows by successive indentations the interrelation of the backstage positions.

PRODUCER (Director of a school theatre, Board of Management or Executive Secretary of a Little Theatre.)

DIRECTOR
  Assistant Director
  Actors
  Prompter
  Director's Rehearsal Secretary

TECHNICAL DIRECTOR (and Chief Technical Assistant)
  Designer
  Assistant in charge of scene shifting plans
  Superintendent of moving and the set-up
    Assistant in charge of making the moving plans
    Assistants in charge of shop and stage
    Group Leaders
      Set-up crews
    Assistant in charge of tools and supplies
    Superintendent of flying
      Flymen
      Performance Flymen
      Curtain Man
  Stage Manager
    Assistant in charge of scene shifting
      Assistant in charge of stage marking
      Grip Crew or Stage Carpenters
    Effect Master and Staff
    Head Call Boy
      Assistant Call Boy in charge of cue-sheet
      Performance Call Boys
    Signal Board Operator
    Assistant in charge of checking
    Reader for scene shifting rehearsal
    Timer
    Additions at the time of performance:
    Curtain Man (for initial cues)
    Superintendent of Flying and Staff
    Property Master and Clearers
    Electrician and Operators
    Costume Master and Staff
      Make-up Master and Staff
    Musical Director and Staff

Actors
Prompter
Property Master
  Assistant in charge of borrowing and renting
  Assistant in charge of buying
  Assistant in charge of property cue-sheet
  Performance Property Master
    Clearers
    Hand Property Master
Head Electrician
  Assistant in charge of planning
    Electrical Draughtsman
  Assistant in charge of cue-sheets
  Assistant in charge of construction and supply
  Set-up Electrician and Assistants
  Performance Electrician
    Switchboard Operator
      Reader for Switchboard Operator
    Floor Operator
    Bridge, Tower and Balcony Operators
    Reader for lighting rehearsal
Costume Master
  Assistant in charge of borrowing
  Assistant in charge of renting and buying
  Performance Costume Master
    Wardrobe Master
    Valet
    Dressers
  Make-up Master
    Make-up Designer
    Superintendent of Make-up Rooms
      Make-up Supply Master
      Make-up Assistants (or Actors making up themselves)
Musical Director
  Assistant in charge of music cue-sheets
  Orchestra Leader
    Pit Musicians
  Backstage Musicians
    Reader for Backstage Musicians
  Onstage Musicians

The elaborateness of this chart need not frighten the reader. Some of the tasks can and should be combined. In many productions the stage manager can serve also as superintendent of moving and set-up, superintendent of flying, curtain man, call boy, and timer. There will be productions, however, in which one man cannot handle all these tasks. If, for example, the play has twenty changes of setting, the stage manager cannot leave the stage, and so cannot serve as call boy. If half the scenery is hung on lines operated from an overhead fly gallery, he will need an assistant to direct the flying. If he has many tasks to perform, he may be too busy to note the time the curtain rises and falls, and so needs to have someone else make this record. In a complicated production it is advisable to divide these tasks between the stage manager and one or more assistants.

To make the distribution easy, each distinct phase of the work has been treated as though it were to be assigned to a different worker. The duties of the property master, the costume master, and others, have been similarly divided. It is hoped that this will permit and suggest efficient combinations of tasks, and not necessarily increase the size of the backstage staff. A few officers have been described that do not usually appear in an organization, but which the author has found helpful in increasing efficiency and assuring accuracy. Except for these, all the work described can be done, if so desired, by the usual staff, whatever its size.

As a suggestion of the possible combinations of tasks, there follows a simplified organization plan for a fairly complicated play. Only such executives are listed as are active at the time of the set-up, dress rehearsals, and performances. The number of crew members working under each executive will vary with the staging requirements of the play.

DIRECTOR
  Prompter (Maker of call-sheet; reader for technical rehearsals; timer)
TECHNICAL DIRECTOR
  Stage manager (Superintendent of moving and set-up; superintendent of flying; stage marker; curtain man; signal board operator)

First assistant stage manager (Maker of scene shifting plans; maker of moving plans; stage assistant during moving and set-up; director of scene shifting)

Second assistant stage manager (Shop assistant during moving; tool assistant during set-up; call boy)

Group leaders (Performance grips; flymen)

Property master (Effect master)

Electrician (Assistant in charge of cue-sheets, planning, and set-up; switchboard operator)

Assistant electrician in charge of draughting, construction, and supply (Assistant at set-up; floor electrician)

Costume master (Assistant in charge of borrowing, renting, and construction; performance costume master)

Wardrobe master (Valet; dresser)

Make-up master

Musical director

The staff of executives can be reduced still further. The minimum staff usually found practicable consists of the technical director (often also the director), prompter, stage manager, director of scene shifting, property master, electrician, costume master, and make-up master.

THE ELEMENT OF SPEED

Speed is not the most essential consideration in making scene changes; nevertheless it is a very important one, because the audience consciously or unconsciously compares an amateur production with one given by a professional company. For the changes during an act, even the professional theatre seeks to approximate the instantaneous ones of the motion picture. The Little Theatres were so slow in their scene changing at first that fast scene shifting, when achieved, is still a surprise and delight to their audiences. Nor should the handicaps of a small stage or inadequate equipment be any excuse for slow changes. It is the duty of the designer to take such conditions into consideration in planning the scenery, and to overcome them.

No single scene change involving the redecoration of a unit or a permanent setting should take longer than one minute, and it can be reduced to thirty-five seconds by proper planning and rehearsing. It is possible to change from one box-set to another, or to an exterior, in not more than three minutes. Only the most elaborate platform settings should take more time, and such settings should be used only when they can be changed at intermissions. No scene change between acts should be attempted which will not be completed two minutes before the end of the stated intermission.

When there is only one intermission, it should be at least eight minutes in length, and may be as long as twelve minutes if that is stated in the program, if there are comfortable lobbies for smoking, and if an orchestra is present for the entertainment of the members of the audience who remain in their seats. When there are two intermissions, the combined time should not exceed sixteen minutes. Twenty minutes should be the maximum aggregate time allowance for three intermissions. Current practice is against the use of more than three long intermissions, two or more acts of a five act play usually being treated as scenes in a single act, with only a very short pause between them. Intermissions may be of equal duration or some long and some short. The length of the intermissions should always be indicated on the printed program.

A three or four minute pause during an act, with the curtain rising on the same setting, is especially irritating to an audience. There is no justification for it. There are few plays which do not provide sufficient offstage time for costume changes. If a very quick change is called for, the costumes can be planned with under-dressing and over-dressing so that, when the change is made in a dressing booth backstage with the assistance of dressers, it can be completed in from thirty seconds to one minute. Only a change into a tuxedo or full dress suit, or a change such as that of Peter Standish in *Berkeley Square* from modern to eighteenth century clothes, should require more time. As a matter of fact this particular change has been made in one minute, while Mr. Balderston provided a little over two minutes for it, counting the offstage time of the actor and a thirty-five second scene change. (See Figure 32.) Quick changes require careful selection and arrangement of garments, a detailed plan of every movement of the actor and the dressers in connection with the clothes, and enough rehearsal—that is all.

WRITTEN REPORTS

The importance of written directions and reports in planning and executing a production cannot be over-stressed, because of the opportunity they afford the technical director and other members of the staff to check all work and to refer to the data instantly throughout the progress of the enterprise. But they should not be allowed to become burdensome or to involve needless red tape. Only such written material should be required as will save effort and prevent delays during the set-up and dress rehearsals. The saving of an hour for the entire crew at the time of the set-up justifies many hours of planning in advance of it. Moreover, it will be found that much needless hunting for scenery and moving about of flats and properties will be eliminated by planning, and that a much larger crew can be handled without loss of efficiency. Some technical directors say that fifteen people is the greatest number that can be successfully kept at work during a set-up, and that, in consequence, it is necessary to spread the work of an elaborate set-up over two days. The author has used as many as sixty workers at one time, and invariably in such cases has erected the production in from two to six hours, leaving undone only such small matters as retouching the painting and adjusting the lights.

In the instructions which follow, the maximum of reports and written plans are called for. In a simple production, or where the technical director is a full time worker in constant touch with all phases of the work, oral reports are often sufficient, provided he makes complete memoranda of them. Inventories, the schedule of tasks at the set-up and in performance, and the cue-sheets and scene shifting plots should always be in writing.

One purpose of the report system is to eliminate, in part, the carelessness and lack of definiteness more or less common to high school and college students, and to improve not only the preparation of plays, but to add to their training for later business and professional life. In some cases this may lead to a multiplicity of reports which would be over-formal in other circumstances.

Written reports, and plans typed in duplicate, have the further advantages that they allow lost papers to be replaced, and, in emergencies, enable other persons to take up the work without delay. For a similar reason, every task in a production should be so thoroughly learned by an understudy or supervisor that an immediate substitution can be made at any time—even at the performance itself. This provides for such accidents as may make it impossible for a worker to finish a performance.

A reduction in the amount of double checking called for in many places can be made with workers who have proven their dependability. Double checking is especially necessary with organizations making use of inexperienced volunteer workers and beginners in stagecraft courses.

Dress Rehearsals

The stage manager and all other members of the crew should make definite written reports of everything which goes amiss in any way during dress rehearsals or performance. These notes should be assembled by the stage manager, and steps should be taken to prevent the recurrence of the mistakes. It should not be considered tale-bearing to report that a certain chair was not brought on the stage by the proper person and had to be placed by another, or that the fireplace was left in the way backstage when it was taken off. These things will continue to be neglected in performance unless they are reported and an investigation made to reveal whether they were mere oversights that will not recur, or whether there has been improper distribution of tasks that necessitates a reassignment of them.

At dress rehearsals, a rule would be rigidly enforced to the effect that no one, under any circumstance, should do anything to which he has not been assigned. This is essential in order to discover inaccuracies in the scene shifting plot and errors in interpreting it by crew members. No private arrangement to transfer a task should ever be made between two members of a crew. The reassignment may be satisfactory, but it must appear in the records of their superiors so that an absent worker may be replaced without the possibility of a task being omitted. If a member of the crew gets volunteer assistance at the dress rehearsal on a task he finds he cannot do alone, and this is not reported and definitely recorded on the list of the volunteer's own tasks, it may be forgotten, and the original crewman may find himself without a helper at the performance, and so delay the curtain.

Absolute silence must be enforced backstage during dress rehearsal and performance. It does not suffice that conversation in low tones cannot be heard by the audience. If it can be heard by the actors on the stage, even as a murmur, it will injure the performance. Greenrooms, or other isolated places where conversation can be held, should be provided if possible for actors and crew in order to keep them off the stage. Ideally, there should be two automatically closing doors between such a room and the stage in order to shut off a burst of sound when the door to it is opened.

It is amateurish in the worst sense of that term for an actor or a member of the staff to peek at the audience through the curtain, or through any opening near the stage. Doors which obviously lead from the auditorium to the stage should be used in emergencies only. An actor should never allow himself to be seen in make-up by a member of the audience before or during the play, and he should avoid it after the play if he can. Make-up must be removed before the actor leaves the theatre.

CHAPTER II

GENERAL STAFF

To the Technical Director:

As is customary, and unless altered by special conditions, you have charge of the building and assembling of all scenery and of all other technical phases of the preparation of the production. The stage manager usually directs the actual performance while you view it from out front.

Prior to the performance, you have equal authority with the director who is in charge of rehearsing the actors—he in relation to the acting, and you in relation to all technical matters. But, since scenery is only background for the actors, it is necessary for you to make the physical elements of the production completely meet the actors' needs. The director will be the best judge of this. To that extent you are subordinate to him, for your completed work must meet with his approval. He owes it to you, on the other hand, to have the actors utilize your scenery in the way that will produce the best effect and will most enhance their performance.

You are obligated to plan, assign, and approve or disapprove every part of the production except the acting. Thus, you should scrutinize every other activity. You may have assistants doing parts of your supervisory work or an assistant in entire charge of a single production. In the latter case the position may be named chief technical assistant for that play. The duties, responsibilities, and powers of such assistants in relation to their special phases of the work are the same as yours, but they are responsible to you instead of the head of the organization, such as the manager or producer. The stage manager is one of your assistants.

18

Your assistants may not be as well informed as are you, and they may have to come to you for answers to questions that their workers ask them. It is helpful in establishing the authority of these assistants, to allow them to report your answers to their workers, instead of making them directly to their subordinates yourself. For the same reason, all suggestions to subordinate workers are best made in the same way. If you once comment directly to the workers, you will always be besieged by those of them who want your personal approval or criticism of their individual work, and they will then be likely to ask you many needless and time consuming questions. Judicious commendation of satisfactory work from time to time does not produce this annoyance, and helps immeasurably to show that you have observed their work and that you appreciate it when meritorious. Necessary criticism of the work of an individual may be softened by commending at the same time parts of it that are satisfactorily done.

Especially in dress rehearsal and performance is it best to give instructions to individuals only through the entire chain of officers in proper order. Clear and well recognized authority is essential to the smooth running of the organization. Always bear in mind that while the curtain is up the stage manager is superior in authority to all other executives, including the director and technical director.

At the dress rehearsals you should be out-front, notebook in hand, perhaps accompanied by a secretary, making notes on corrections and changes you want made in the staging, on things that are remiss, and also on conditions that are praiseworthy. You will find it extremely valuable in arousing good feeling on the part of your staff to review orally, on some opportune occasion, every piece of work that has been done, always making it a point to commend those that are satisfactory. If a suitable interval can be found at a dress rehearsal, it is wise to do this in the presence of the actors in order to impress them with the magnitude of the preparation that has been made to display them and their work, and in order to have them understand that there are other parts of the whole enterprise which are nearly as important, through not so conspicuous, as their own roles.

After the dress rehearsal, the director should allow you, if possible, to make your comments to the technical staff in advance of his observations to the actors. This period can be used by the actors to remove costumes and make-up. This arrangement will not delay the departure of the actors, and it will allow the technical workers to leave the theatre earlier than otherwise. Also, it will allow the director to comment to the actors in semi-privacy. The nature and order of these comments are outlined in the suggestions to the director in Chapter XI.

An effective means of forwarding the preparation of a production is to have frequent conferences between yourself, the director, and the heads of departments. The assignment of individual work in construction and in scene changes can best be done at such times.

The technical director or chief technical assistant should set definite dates for the completion of plans for the various tasks. The tasks of other people on the staff are contingent on them, and they are necessary for the completion of cue-sheets and scene shifting plots. The dates should be well in advance of the performance, and the dead-lines should be enforced rigidly.

Many of the foregoing comments apply to the handling of the shop work as well as to the backstage work.

Production Prompt Book

All plans should be fully recorded in writing. Copies of them, together with all other memoranda on the production, should be kept in a loose-leaf notebook, known as the production prompt book, which will remain during the production in the custody of the technical director or the chief technical assistant. In addition to the final plans, the preliminary drafts of all plan material should be so filed. Thus, any errors made in copying and rearranging the cue-sheets and plans can be readily corrected when discovered.

The production prompt book will, of course, contain the plan material on scenery construction as well as that on stage management.

It should contain a summary of the plot of the play, any special comments and suggestions by the director as to the interpretation of the play, and any general notes on the scenery the technical director wants to make. It will include floor plans of the settings, or the designs, if they are of convenient size for the book.

This not only allows the technical director to keep himself fully informed on the progress of all work, and to have all plan material available for the use of any worker, but also constitutes a reference book that will considerably lessen the work of repeating the play later in the season or in after years, should that ever be done.

All important reports should be in writing, and the technical director should make a permanent record of all others that are accepted orally. So that all records may be kept in one loose-leaf notebook, reports should be made on 8½ inch by 11 inch paper, because that is the size which will be used for correspondence in connection with the production, and consequently the letters and the carbon copies of letters can be included in the same book.

The section of the production prompt book covering the stage management, or a copy of it, should be in the hands of the stage manager during the performance, and should contain not only the combination cue-sheet and scene shifting plot for his use, but also copies of every individual instruction sheet, so that if one is lost, or the worker fails to appear, the copy can be supplied and the work performed by someone else without a hitch.

PHOTOGRAPHS

The intended use of photographs of the play, if they are made, will determine when it is best to take them. If they are to be used for publicity, they must be taken at an early dress rehearsal, though this will add considerably to its length. If they are merely for record, some other time is to be preferred. When there is only one setting they can be taken after a performance; but when there are a number of setting and costume changes, the photographing should be done during the progress of one of the dress rehearsals, thus obviating the necessity of resetting the scenery. When there is only one dress rehearsal, pictures should not be taken at that time. High-speed photographs taken during the action are becoming increasingly popular.

In taking the pictures, the timing of scene changes at dress rehearsals must not be disturbed, because it is vitally important that both the crew and the actors learn the cues and the timing so well that they will be prepared for cues in performance. This makes it inadvisable to take pictures before a scene begins or just after it ends. It is good practice to have the scene change proceed just as if no pictures were to be taken, allow the actors to start their scene, and then stop them after half a minute or so of action. A check should be made at this time in order to be sure that actors who have costume changes will have completed them in time for their entrances.

The pictures taken, the scene starts again from the curtain. The performance continues without interruption through the first minute or so of the next scene in which pictures are to be taken, when the action is again stopped and photographs made. So on through all the scenes. This method permits all timing elements to be tested.

The presence backstage of friends of the actors may make it difficult to take pictures after the first performance. Pictures should not be taken following the last performance, if the scenery is to be taken down that night.

If there is a matinee, and it is possible for the management to provide a supper, or to have a community meal served between the matinee and night performances, this intermission is an excellent period in which to take pictures, for no one is then in haste. This will have the further advantage of converting the occasion into a recreative one, when otherwise the actors would be put to the trouble of removing costumes and make-up, rushing out to dinner and then back to the theatre, only to put them on again. With amateurs such a use of the interval helps to prevent the "let-down" night performance that often follows a matinee.

STAFF MEMBERS

It usually is easy to get people to work backstage in supervisory capacities, for most young people find such tasks interesting to perform. Every backstage executive can bring one or two personal friends to help him. This augments the staff, with the result that there is rarely a shortage of help. The more elaborate the production, the easier it is to get an adequate number of people for the crew, because a difficult and complicated production that runs smoothly and swiftly gives a joyous thrill to everyone connected with the production.

Women usually are assigned to properties, costumes, and the prompter's chair in the amateur theatre, but there is no reason for such a limitation. Nor is there any reason why these tasks should be considered as suitable only for women. In the professional theatre, all backstage tasks are done by men, because the only women who are members of the universally established stage union are designers. Occasionally a woman serves in the professional theatre as stage manager because this is a position requiring an Equity card rather than a union card.

A woman can perform almost any backstage task. Any of the directing tasks can be assigned to her. If the fly-lines are properly counterweighted, she can serve as a flyman. When taught how to hold and handle them, she can move flats, for this is largely a matter of skill rather than of brawn. Because she is put on her mettle to prove to the men that she can do the work they normally consider theirs, a woman frequently will make an even more capable stage manager than a man.

Discretion should be used, of course, in the selection of a woman to be put over men workers. Make sure that the one you select has proven to the crew by her work in the shop or previous good results on the production staff that she is capable of doing the things she is directing others to do. There is now no other valid criticism of such a selection, inasmuch as women are holding executive positions today in all lines of business and industry on a parity with men. The author has successfully used college girls in every capacity from stage manager and electrician down the scale of positions to the bottom ones, as well as for almost all actual and supervisory work in the shop except the heaviest of carpentry. At the college age, women frequently are more methodical than men, and hence are superior to them for tasks calling for extreme accuracy in detailed work, while men of the same age are better adapted than women to advance planning and designing, as, for example, in the case of stage lighting.

No actor with a major part in the play should be given backstage responsibility. A major backstage position, however, can be held by an actor who has a one-scene part, or a walk-on. It also is possible to use almost any actor for scene shifting or property work, if consideration is given to his costume, make-up, and the relation of such work to his appearances on the stage. The author has repeatedly used actors in this way with satisfactory results. Care must be taken that the tasks can be done without anxiety. An actor who is on the stage at the fall of the curtain should never be asked to rush immediately to do some task, but he can, for example, carry off the chair in which he was sitting. It is especially useful and appropriate for an actor to place a property that he is to use in the scene, and for one who is to be on the stage when the curtain rises to carry something to its place in the setting.

It is even desirable, frequently, for the actors in an amateur organization to be required to assist the crew in scene changes, for the sake of the spirit of co-operation thus developed between them and the crew members. The extra activity often relieves the actors' nervous tension by giving them something other than their acting roles to think about and to do. Nor should this assistance be limited to those playing minor parts. If many members of the cast are used, no one should be exempt, although equal division of work is not essential. There are few better preventives of "temperament" and "the swell-head" among leading actors than for Hamlet to place the bench on which he is to sit while delivering a soliloquy, for Queen Elizabeth to arrange the draperies on her throne, and for Peter Standish to place the spotlight which is to shine on him. A lowly prop man feels much more essential if he is assisted by Juliet herself in placing the ladder which leads to her balcony.

Rehearsal Secretary

If an assistant is to record notes during dress rehearsals for you, instructions for him are to be found in Chapter XI.

To the Chief Technical Assistant:

If the technical director is a permanent staff member, and you are appointed chief technical assistant for a single production, you have the same duties, responsibilities, and powers for the one production as the technical director, but are responsible to him rather than to the head of the theatre organization. In the producing group of a university or college, the technical director is usually a faculty member, while the chief technical assistant is a student. If the director also supervises the stagecraft work, and there is no permanent technical director, the latter title can be given to you for the single production.

You, as chief technical assistant, supervise all preliminary construction work and also the performance. For a discussion of your duties, see the instructions to the technical director immediately preceding. You must, of course, know completely every phase of the work you are directing.

CHAPTER III

SCENE SHIFTING PLANS

To the Assistant Technical Director in charge of scene shifting plans:

The entire work of planning and supervising the scene changes in compliance with the directions of the designer, normally is one of the stage manager's tasks, but if he has many other tasks, and especially if he is working on the construction of scenery, this work can well be assigned to an assistant stage manager or an assistant technical director. The plans must be made well in advance of the first dress rehearsal, so this work will not interfere with any performance task to which you are assigned.

Greater accuracy is assured if plans of this kind are checked by a second person. It therefore is an advantage to have the plans made by someone other than the stage manager, and then have them gone over very carefully by him. At the same time, you acquire such a complete knowledge of the plan of the scene shifts that you will be prepared to substitute for the stage manager in performance if the latter is unavoidably absent.

Two directors working in harmony are desirable at the early rehearsals of scene changes, for the individual workers will require a great deal of personal instruction at that time on the exact points at which to place properties and scenery, and in the methods of placing them. One, of course, will be the stage manager or his assistant in charge of scene shifting. The other is referred to herein as the checker. He also is an assistant stage manager. This task, however, may well be assigned to you, since you have made the plans for the scene shifting, and, in consequence, are thoroughly acquainted with them. After the first rehearsals the stage manager or director of scene shifting should take sole charge, while the checker double-checks his work during the scene shifts, sees that all the backstage effects are on time, and verifies the arrangements for the next scene shift. The latter is an especially useful function. After the first dress rehearsal, errors should be reported to the stage manager and corrected by him. These duties are explained in greater detail in Chapter VI.

The duties of stage marker can also be combined with those of maker of scene shifting plans and checker, for these tasks have much in common, and separate individuals will be needed for them only in the most elaborate productions or when it is decided to have extra tasks for the purpose of training the staff in responsibility. This task is also explained in Chapter VI.

Compiling Scenic References

This part of your work is preparatory to that of planning the scene shifting, and may be preparatory to that of designing the scenery.

You will first read the play to familiarize yourself with it generally. You will read it again, copying out every reference which may be related in any way to any phase of the technical work—scenery, properties, costumes, make-up, lighting, and the like. This is material for the use of the entire technical staff. You will copy the statements, wherever possible, directly from the text of the play, giving the page reference. Enclose speeches in quotation marks; enclose author's stage directions in quotation marks and parentheses; omit quotation marks and parentheses from any summaries or remarks of your own in order to distinguish them from the other material. Include cues and page references for any backstage effects—sound, light, movement, curtain, and the like. This will be helpful in compiling the combined cue-sheet and scene shifting plot.

Following your quotation of the author's description of the setting, you will add such comments as:

"(Carries in a teapot and sugar bowl.)" Poems in a wallet are supposedly hidden in the teapot. p. 19

"What a beautiful chest!" Pepys later hides in it. p. 46

"Ramshackle old place." Spoken by Mr. Hodges. p. 6 [1]

"Needs that new wall-paper that's more lively like." p. 8. Mr. Hodges speaking.

"Woods all around." p. 12

"My dear, did you see the disgraceful dress she is wearing?" Lady Folderol speaking of Hortense. p. 75

"(Hedda goes to the fire and stirs it.)" p. 42

"I'm too fat for games." Conrad speaks. p. 18

"Ready to go swimming?" John, Arthur and Susan are dressed for swimming. Mrs. Pastor and Dr. Johnston dressed to sit on the beach. p. 37

"You are pale from too much brooding." To Bob. p. 99

"How dark it is!" p. 14

"The sun seems to have gone under a cloud." p. 38

"Out of my house forever!" WARN CURTAIN p. 27

"My daughter! (Staggers across the room, clutches at the handle of the door, stands undecided a moment, and then sinks to the floor.)" CURTAIN p. 28

When this compilation is finished, submit it to the director and ask him to make any corrections, additions or special comments. All the stage directions must be very carefully checked for changes with the designer and the director. Few designers use the exact floor plan given by the author or the one used in the original production, and few directors use the exact business specified in the printed script. This frequently will necessitate revision of your notes.

When your scenic references are completed and approved, you usually will make a number of copies of your compilation—one for the technical director and each of his assistants, and several extra ones for posting at convenient places in the shop and on the call boards. Reserve one for your own use in making the cue-sheet.

SELECTING CUES

Be most careful in selecting the cues for lighting changes, noises, and the like. The cue given in the reading edition of a play is not

[1] Include the name of the character in such cases, for it is not the opinion of any other character in the play.

always dependable, for frequently the author inserts it where it least interrupts the dialogue. The actual backstage cue may be either earlier or later. The play may read, for example:

PETER STANDISH: But I can't; you'd—no, no—you mustn't ask it— (Stops, listens. Noise of coach. In a low tense whisper.) What's that?

Naturally Mr. Balderston did not insert the stage direction, "Noise of coach," in the middle of Standish's line, "you mustn't ask it," but that is obviously when the noise must begin in performance.

In recording cues, indicate carefully those which must be taken from the action rather than the spoken lines as, for example, the foregoing curtain cue cited. If the worker will not be able to see the action on the stage, give him a "counting cue." If the time of the count is given in seconds, the worker can time the cue by a watch, or for each second that is to elapse he can count in a whisper, "One, two, three, four, five," as fast as it can be done distinctly.

Make a note of any line used as a cue which is spoken more than once in a scene, and include with the cue to be used the line preceding it. A cue consisting of a much used phrase such as "Thanks," "Yes, sir," "Hello," or "That's right," would make the effect master delirious before the performance is over. Absolute cues must be predetermined by the director, irrespective of the nature of the line. But for warning cues, the purpose of which is to obtain the attention of a worker after a break in his work, a distinctive, easily remembered, and loudly spoken line can be chosen. A warning cue should be given thirty to sixty seconds in advance of the actual cue, and the time interval between the warning and the cue should be constant throughout a performance.

SCENE SHIFTING PLOT AND MASTER CUE-SHEET

The scene shifting plot is a detailed plan for a change of setting or a series of them, including assignments of the individual scene shifting tasks. A departmental cue-sheet is a compilation of all the warning cues and absolute cues that control the movements of the backstage workers in that department. The master cue-sheet is the combination of the departmental cue-sheets with the whole set of cues arranged chronologically. Usually the scene shifting plot and the master cue-sheet are combined. If they are not, the cue-sheet will contain only a record of tasks to be performed during the action of the play, while the scene shifting plot will outline the work involved in the scene changes.

You will obtain a detailed plan of each setting, and the plans for any special methods and devices to be used for either speeding or simplifying the changes. It may be part of your task to plan these methods and devices. Among those which you may provide are: flying the backwalls and the furniture which can be attached to it; flying complete settings; pivoting side walls and the halves of the backwalls to posts placed at the upstage corner of the settings; erecting one scene inside another or inside part of another; putting part of the scenery on tracks or runners; attaching casters or skids to heavy pieces; flying properties; repeating scenic elements in more than one setting; hinging entire walls or settings in screen fashion, or with dutchmen; building wagons or island stages (both being rolling platforms); and using revolving, sliding, pivoting, elevator or double-deck stages and other built-in stage devices. If the designer has not planned his scenes to include these aids, you may add them provided they do not alter his designs. You may be able to get permission from him to make slight changes in the designs in order to secure faster or easier shifts. When a wagon is used, attach everything possible to it— adjacent flats and the like. Combine other such elements wherever you can.

From these plans you will make up a series of lists and charts as follows, and in the order given:

1. All items on the stage at the rise of the curtain. Arrange this, and all other lists which permit of it, in a convenient form for checking, by starting at one side of the stage and circling it, by starting backstage and coming toward the footlights, or by enumerating scenery, large properties, small properties, lights, et cetera, under

Flats
Y
F
Window unit
Wagon E
C-D
Hood
X
A
Large Tapestry
B
Z
Act III props

(HALL)

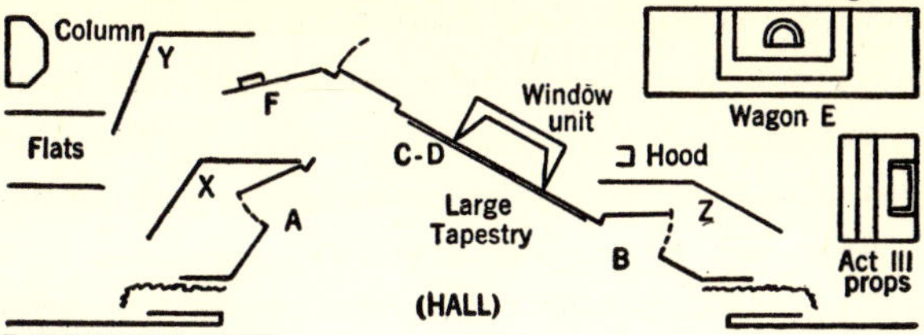

SET BEFORE THE PLAY:

FLATS:
   Onstage: A B C–D F   Backings X Z
   In scene-dock rightstage, and packed in this order, start-
  ing from the bottom:
      K (hinged sky-flats)
      L–M (one-foot jogs)
      G (extra door flat)
      D-inset plug
   Against right wall: H (column)
   Offstage right, ready for placing: Y (backing)

LARGE TAPESTRY hung

WINDOW SEAT UNIT in place behind D, already attached to D:
   Platform   Large book
   Cushion   Flood placed behind
   Windows   Drapes hung
   Ceiling

OFFSTAGE RIGHT, just behind A, ready for first shift:
   Step   Green door drapes
   Chest   Study chair
   Tapestry

ON WAGON (Unit E) Offstage back left
   Draperies   2 pillows
   Platform   Orb and sceptre in throne-chair
   Steps   5 stools
   Throne   Shield hung
   2 spears

OFFSTAGE LEFT out of way; Act III platform, drapes, throne

ALSO CHECK THE FOLLOWING:
   C is so lashed in front of F that it will swing free
   without moving F, and will exactly meet A.
   Lashing arrangement on front of D for L–M lash in Act III
   Nails for curtain poles on A, B, and C.

FIGURE 1. Part of a scene shifting plot for the stage manager. The letters A, B, C, D, X, Y, et cetera, referred to flats or wall units composed
of two or more flats. The letters were painted on the back of the flats.

headings. This list or chart is to be made for each setting of the play.

2. The detailed set-up of the lights.

3. The location backstage of every object not in the setting at the rise of the curtain.

4. A résumé of this list in a floor plan of the stage and the backstage in a form that can be readily checked.

5. A minutely detailed plan for each change of scenery. In the order in which each action must be performed, record the removal of each object of scenery, lights, heavy properties, small properties, flied material, et cetera. Then, in the order in which they should be placed, list the materials to come onto the stage for the next scene. Include directions for the disposal of objects removed from the stage. Remember that objects sometimes have to be handled twice in the same change—it may be necessary to carry some object into the setting before the walls are placed, leave it, and then place it exactly after the walls are erected. Similarly, it may be necessary to move a piece of furniture away from a wall to prevent its being injured in removing the walls when a setting is struck. In some professional companies all properties are moved to the center of the stage, the scenery is removed, the properties are removed and are replaced by those for the next scene, the new walls are erected, and then the new properties are moved into place. This is probably a safe practice, but a needless time killer if, instead, the moving is carefully planned so as to prevent the "clearers," or property assistants, from getting in the way of the "grips." In other companies, the downstage flats are removed first and old and new properties exchanged somewhat in the manner suggested here.

6. The movement of scenery and properties, and other backstage rearrangements during a scene.

7. Alterations of lighting in scene changes.

8. A compilation, in chronological order, of all the scene shifting, including the lighting changes, with warning cues and absolute cues for all the scene shifts.

CHANGE FROM ACT I, SCENE II TO ACT I, SCENE III (Study to Council)

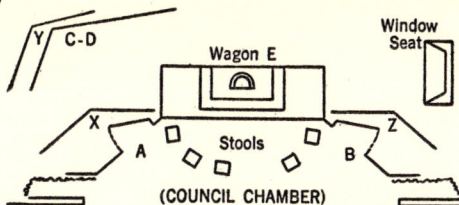

(COUNCIL CHAMBER)

(Griffith, Pliss, Hirt, Frink, Morgan, Chase, Saunders stand
  ready down left and enter there. Exit with props up right)
(Actors ready down right: Funk, Harrell, Zimmerman, Nelson,
  Crandall, Pozz, Auble, Light. Take places as soon as
  wagon is in place)
(Elizabeth goes directly from her exit, sits on throne, and
  rides into position: Pierce)
Unlash C-D and pull off-stage back right (Cherry unlash C-A;
  Eskowitz remove stagebrace; Brimmer unlash D-B)
Remove masking Y and pull to right (Pick and Baird)
Unhook window unit and pull far left (Lester and Dillon)
Remove flood (Geisinger)
Swing B to new position (Lester and Dillon) Door closed
Move Z backing to new position (Lester and Dillon)
Swing A to new position (Pick and Baird)
Remove tapestry down right (Griffith)
Remove chest down right (Pliss and Hirt)
Remove drapes down left (Frink)
Remove chair down left (Morgan and Ferris)
Remove step from windowseat (Saunders and Chase)
Place wagon (Brimmer, Cherry, Eskowitz, Brodkin, Schurz.
  Lester and Pick help lash)
Remove stools from wagon (Funk, Harrell, Zimmerman, Pozz,
  Crandall)
Guards pick up spears from corners of wagon (Dillon and
  Hirt)
Spears handed to soldiers at doors (Saunders, right; Chase,
  left)
See that door left is closed (Griffith)
See that door right is closed (Frink)
(CREW EXITS UP RIGHT WITH PROPS; DOWN LEFT AFTER WAGON IS
  SET)

DURING ACT I, SCENE III

Check that tapestry, green door drapes, chest, chair and
  step are ready behind A (Ferris and Morgan)
Check presence of book on window seat (Ferris and Morgan)

FIGURE 2. Another page from the scene shifting plot illustrated in
Figure 1. The lighting changes from the switchboard were not included
here, as is often the case when the switchboard operator is sufficiently
reliable to make a check on his work by the stage manager unnecessary.

9. Names, titles, or numbers of all the members of the crew, with a record of their departmental type of work.

Insert the name of the worker after each distinct task he will perform in scene moving, property moving, lighting alteration, and the like. For changes in which there is ample time, you will give each worker the same kind of work he performs in other changes; but for quick changes you will estimate the greatest number of tasks which can safely be done by one individual in the time given, and assign him no others. When you are authorized to do so, you can recruit workers from other branches to assist a department whose group cannot do all of its work in the time allotted. In the same circumstance, you will enlist the help of the actors. In planning to use actors, as has been explained in Chapter I, be careful not to use one just leaving a scene, except for an object which falls directly under his hand, such as the chair by which he was standing or a property he will pass on his way; not to give an actor who will open the next scene any object other than one which will bring him into approximate position for his action; not to use him for anything for which his costume or make-up will be a handicap, or which is dirty; and not to use him for anything that will tire him. This will result in actors being used chiefly for furniture and other properties. The smaller in size and weight these objects are the better.

Assign no tasks to the stage manager or to departmental heads and supervisors without asking their permission or that of their superiors.

In the assignment of tasks, attention should be given to the past dependability of the various workers. Objects which have to be placed precisely should be given to the more dependable ones. If it is necessary to use an unreliable worker, objects should be given him which require two people to handle, or objects the absence of which would be obvious to the stage manager.

If an object is to be placed more than once, but in a different position each time, it will obviate the possibility of mistake if a different worker is chosen to place it each time.

SCENE SHIFTING--ELIZABETH

LESTER

Change to Act I, Scene II (Study)
 Turn C to place and lash (with **Dillon)**

During Scene II
 If necessary, remove window flat F (with **Eskowitz)**

Change to Act I, Scene III (Council)
 Unhook window and pull far left (with **Dillon)**
 Move Z backing to new position (with **Dillon)**
 Swing B to new position (with **Dillon)**
 Help lash wagon, if needed

Change to Act II, Scene I (Study)
 Move B to study position (with **Dillon)**
 Place window group (with **Dillon)**
 Move Z backing to position (with **Dillon)**

Change to Act II, Scene III (Council) (Same change as
Act I, Scene III)
 Unhook window and pull far left (with **Dillon)**
 Move Z backing to new position (with **Dillon)**
 Swing B to new position (with **Dillon)**
 Help lash wagon, if needed

During Act II, Scene III
 Place plug in D flat (with **Eskowitz)**

Change to Act III (Tower)
 Remove Z backing and place in leftstage dock (with
  Dillon)
 Swing B to new position (with **Dillon)**
 Lash L and M to B at three feet from the front;
  use a stagebrace (with **Dillon)**
 Place steps behind up left door (with **Dillon)**

FIGURE 3. An individual instruction sheet from the set used with the scene shifting plot presented in Figures 1 and 2. There were seventeen stage-hands. All the men except two electricians were actors or extras. When first made, the plans called for only two women not members of the cast, but enough other women volunteered so that no actress was put on the crew. Cues for scene changes were not included in this instruction sheet because the crewmen were called to place by the call boy.

Relate and couple the tasks to be done, as, for example: "Enter down right, remove Queen Anne chair through up left entrance and place in storage bin 2; get Louis Quinze straight chair from bin 3, carry in down right and place down right, 7 feet from side wall, 4 feet from curtain, facing slightly center; exit up right," and, "Enter down right; with Parker move Queen Anne sofa to up center, 3 feet from back wall; remove secretary through up left entrance and place in storage bin 2; get library table from bin 3, carry it on down left, place between doors of left wall; exit up left."

10. Cues for every backstage worker during the action of the play. This will include those for the effect operators (sounds), electricians, property masters of both general and hand-props (those to be carried on or off the stage by actors), dressers (costume changes, for which the re-entrance cue should be given), pit and backstage musicians, grips, call boy, signal board operator, curtain man, and all special helpers.

11. A master cue-sheet, containing these action cues and instructions in chronological order. Or you may arrange for the head of each department to make out his own cue-sheet. You will then check all these sheets for accuracy with the script, and compile them into the master cue-sheet.

Both the master cue-sheet and the scene shifting plot must be checked by the stage manager or someone else qualified to do so. It must be double-checked because of its complex nature as well as the imperative necessity to have it accurate and complete.

12. With the tasks listed chronologically, and the cue-sheet and plot inter-related, a final form for the stage manager and other supervisors of scene shifting. This is the combination cue-sheet and scene shifting plot. Mimeographed or multigraphed copies of it may be given to the workers with their tasks underlined in red; other forms may be made up with their names arranged in alphabetical order and their tasks for each scene change collected and listed after their names; or individual sheets may be made out for each worker. The

CURTAIN (on Act II, Scene IV)
  WARN: "Where's Duncan's body?"
  CUE: "Make good of bad, and friends of foe." Fast curtain

CHANGE TO ACT III; SCENE I

WAGONS AND PORTAL FLIPPERS
  Roll Wagon 2 back--Page, Pedder, Milton, Henderson.
  Roll Wagon 1 down. Revolve once to right.
    III-I corner-- 6 feet onstage from right portal at por-
      tal line--Pedder (see below).
    Sleep corner--directly upstage of III-I corner--Page
      (see below).
    England corner--directly upstage of cavern--Milton.
    Cavern corner-- touching left portal with flipper down-
      stage of it--Henderson.

    Right flipper--unlash and lash to EE, 180 degree angle--
      straight across stage--Davis.
    Left flipper--unlash and lash to LL, 180 degree angle--
      straight across stage--Muncey.

ALPHABETICAL
  Azzara: @ Duncan's room--armour, sword, no helmet or
    shield. Possibly change cloak for Duncan's.
  Callnon: with B. Speak block off backstage from kitchen
    at right with QQ-RR.
  Conard: @ Duncan's room--fully dressed.
  Drollet: @ Duncan's room.
  Eichenberger: with Ryan bring right banquet benches down
    right.
  Greene: with Silva, bring left back banquet benches down
    left.
  Hoffmeister: @ Duncan's room.
  Hunter: with Kister place throne on dais backstage.
  Kister: with Hunter place throne on dais backstage. Place
    tapestry above dais.
  Lynn: hang shield on left flipper, then with Smetherham
    bring right banquet table downstage right.
  Moller: @ Duncan's room--fully dressed except shield and
    helmet.
  Morford:@ Duncan's room.
  Nash: with Harry Tyler bring left banquet benches down
    left.
  Page: @ Duncan's room.
  Parker: with J. Wilson bring right back banquet benches
    down right.
  Pedder: @ Duncan's room.

CHANGE CONTINUED ON NEXT PAGE   II-IV, III-I

FIGURE 4. A portion of a mimeographed scene shifting plot for an elaborate production, in different form from that shown in Figures 2 and 3.
The crew was composed of fifty members of the cast, plus about ten other
people. Each had a copy of this plot. Departmental cue-sheets were used
by the effect master, the checker, the reader for backstage musicians, and
the call boys and electricians. Wagons I and II were island stages riding
on casters. The symbol @ indicates that the actor involved had an entrance during the scene from the position mentioned.

last method is probably the most satisfactory, although a little more time is required to prepare it.

Leave a liberal amount of blank space in the cue-sheet and scene shifting plot at points where a new act or scene begins, and indicate plainly any scenes in which there are no cues or changes.

If your scene shifting plot is long, divide it by scenes, either a page for the cues in each scene followed by the instructions for the scene shifting afterwards, or a separate page for the cues during the scene, and one following for the shifting. Plan the cue-sheet for its usefulness in performance, not for its ease in making.

Arrange the data in columns, listing cues and warning cues, the object to be used, what is to be done with it, and the name or title of the worker who does the task. These columns may be in any order desired. Usually the cue is placed in the first column and the worker's name in either the next or the last column to the right. (See Figures 1 to 5.)

If the master cue-sheet is to be separate from the scene shifting plot, construct each separately, but compile them identically in all other respects.

The master cue-sheet and scene shifting plot may be assigned to separate individuals for compilation. Assistants may be secured to do single steps in the preparation of either of these forms.

Obviously, after one is once familiar with the technique of making up these plans, several of the steps can be combined. A technical director making such a plot and also supervising the construction work, would carry much of the information in his head instead of writing it out, but such a course increases the chance for error.

Planning the Backstage

The shape of your particular stage will determine the exact plan for the distribution of scenery backstage. In professional practice the stage is theoretically divided in the middle, with the scenery on stage left stacked on the left side, and right-stage flats on stage right.

(DURING ACT IV, SCENE I-- continued)
    "Come like shadows, so depart"---
        Take crowns and sceptres from kings, left portal (Haas)
        Capes from kings in left portal (Eichner)
        Torch for Lennox at postern gate (Petersen)
    "blood-bolter'd Banquo smiles upon me"---
        Dim out left portal spot, fairly slowly (Brooke)
    "Our duties did his welcome pay"---
        Thunder (Gleason)
        Blackout with dimmers and switches instantly: cauldron,
            right tower, left tower (Brooke)
    "Come in, without there"---
        Trumpet softly, Macbeth theme (Arnold)
    "What's your grace's will?"---
        Heat slowly right and left towers to 1/3 (both red am-
            ber) (Brooke). Right tower on Macbeth (Prior).
            Left tower on Lennox (Towle).
    "Fled to England"---
        WARN CURTAIN AND SCENE CHANGE
    "Come, bring me where they are"---
        Trumpet, Macbeth theme (Arnold)
        CURTAIN (Hill)

CHANGE TO ACT IV, SCENE II
    WAGONS
        Roll Wagon 1 back--half turn right (Pedder, Page, Mil-
            ton, Henderson)
        Roll Wagon 2 down--10 feet from portal line, wagon
            flippers bent out 4 feet (same as above)

    PORTAL FLIPPERS
        Right--lash to CD--120 degree angle (Davis)
        Left--lash to CA--120 degree angle (Muncey)

    FLATS
        AD-AE placed behind archway (Eichenberger, Ryan)

    PROPERTIES
        Tapestry stand placed (Robbins)
        Needle and yarns on tapestry stand (Ashen)
        Stool at tapestry stand (Petersen)
        Pillow (Petersen)
        Kneeling bench (Williams)

    LIGHTS
        Switchboard (Brooks)
            Kill:
            Leave: Left tower (#6)--daylight blue and frost
                   Right tower (#7)--straw and frost

CHANGE CONTINUED ON NEXT PAGE   IV-I, IV-II

FIGURE. 5. A portion of a combined cue-sheet and scene shifting plot for
the stage manager, used in connection with the mimeographed scene
shifting plot presented in Figure 4.

The flats for each setting are kept in a separate pack, the pack for the first scene being nearest the back wall and the last setting nearest the curtain line. When the first scene is over, the flats for that setting are stacked in the last packs, half going right and half left. The flats from the second packs are then brought down and put in place. This avoids the necessity for rearranging the packs between performances.

Where there is not sufficient room to use this method, you can have a "live" pack and a "dead" pack on each side of the stage, placing all scenery removed in the dead pack. This takes careful arrangement of the flats in advance of each performance.

On an extremely congested stage, it is sometimes wise to pack all live scenery on one side of the stage ready to be placed, and all dead scenery on the other side. Scenery which is removed from the stage, but is to be "kept alive" for a second use, should then be brought back to the live side. Except for such scenery as is to be kept alive, then, the scenery always will be shifted from left-stage to right-stage or vice versa, which will lessen traffic congestion. Properties are nearly always handled in this last manner, with all properties brought on at one side and taken off at the other. This is especially important when a permanent setting is being used and only the furniture changed each time, making use of the doors of the setting for the entrances and exits of the scene shifters. In this case it is best to have all properties to be kept alive moved out with the dead properties and carried around behind the setting to the live side. In making such changes in a permanent setting, it is sometimes wise to hinge one of the flats in each side wall so that it can be opened like a door and thus give a wider entrance than do the doors of the setting.

Another possibility is to have space provided off right for the furniture from the first scene, and also to place the third scene properties there, with the second scene properties placed left-stage. After the first scene, the properties are carried on at the left and off at the right. Following the second scene the shift is made in the opposite direction.

With more than two entrances to the setting, other plans can be used. The important thing is to plan the changes so as to prevent congestion at an entrance. During a change a doorway must be either an entrance or an exit—never both.

Space must be provided backstage for the effect machines and the property tables.

As indicated at the beginning of the chapter, the scene shifting plans may be made by the stage manager or by any other staff member. It may be divided among several workers.

CHAPTER IV

THE SET-UP

To the Superintendent of Moving and the Set-up:

It is your duty to plan and direct the moving of scenery from wherever it is built or stored to the theatre, and to set it up there. The moving and the setting-up are so closely related that the supervision of the processes cannot readily be separated. Much detailed calculation is required for the set-up in advance of the moving day if the scenery has to be transferred from the shop to a theatre located in a separate building. Somewhat less planning is required if the scenery only has to be moved from a room, such as a basement, in the same building. It is seldom possible for scenery to be built in close proximity to the stage of the theatre, but, if such is the case, still less system is needed.

For various reasons, the time allowed for the set-up is usually short and must be used thriftily. Too often a large crew comes to work at the set-up, and half of its members must stand around with nothing to do because the superintendent has failed to arrange the grouping of the tasks in such a manner that there is working room on the stage for all of them, or has failed to provide assistants to direct the work.

It is a good plan to divide the workers into groups, each under a group leader. These group leaders must be active and dependable people who will be diligent in keeping other people busy. You may divide your people into two classes, those who have been initiated into the work and those who are novices, and then the two classes into groups of about six each.

Put an experienced leader in charge of a major group composed of three men relatively well-experienced in backstage work, and two girls who at least know the names of tools. Assign them such work as assembling walls, setting up wagons, and doing other carpentering work. The girls are just as useful as the men for holding flats, locating tools and hardware, and doing the other light work that is always a part of the tasks involving heavy materials.

Under girl leaders you may form minor groups of three or four girls and a man or two with less experience in stage work than those in the major groups. Give them the lighter tasks of assembling the smaller units, setting up the parallels, hanging the doors, hanging and rigging the draperies, and the like. Unless some of the girls are adept at tool work, such as hinging, the men in the group are needed for this, because these otherwise easy tasks often include work of that kind. Even reasonably heavy work can be done by one of these minor groups, for the six members jointly can move almost any prop.

You may find groups that are larger or smaller than six in number more satisfactory for your particular situation, but few jobs in a set-up will require more than six people. When such is the case, however, two groups can be joined for particular tasks.

Strict independence need not be enforced between these groups, members of one group joining another one when needed. Hold each group leader responsible for keeping his five workers busy. When his next scheduled task must await the completion of a task by another group, the leader should cast about during the interval for other casual jobs for himself and his workers. As superintendent you should have a list of tasks which can be done at any time during the set-up.

The careful plotting of the succession of tasks is the first step toward attaining efficiency. For example, if a ground cloth is to be used, the scenery cannot be set up permanently until it is laid. In that case, the ground cloth is the first thing to be moved into the theatre with a crew to lay it. This crew can be composed largely of girls, who will then be more usefully employed than, for example, they would be in helping load the truck. Only one member of the group need know *how* to lay the cloth. If, on the other hand, no scenery remains in place throughout the production, the ground cloth should be laid last so as to avoid tearing it during the set-up.

Again, all material to be flied must be hung before anything can be permanently set up on the stage. The first truck load, then, should contain the drops, drapes, et cetera, and a group immediately put to work to fly them under the direction of the superintendent of flying, even though this leaves a smaller loading group. It is of no advantage to get the scenery moved into the theatre early if nothing can be done with it at once when it is there.

The order of tasks; the number of workers and trucks needed; the order of moving materials; the assignment of tasks to groups, with written instructions and plans; the measurement of the stage and the marking of it with chalk, should all be decided upon and done some days in advance of the day for the set-up.

As in the case of the stage manager during the performance, everything should be so definitely and carefully planned, written out, diagrammed, and assigned to assistants that you need not be present at any given place. By so transferring all specific tasks to others, you will be free for general supervision, correction, and consultation, and then you will be able to help where help is really needed.

If it is impossible to make measurements and markings on the stage floor or ground cloth in advance of the moving, you should go to the stage at the first possible moment—ahead of the trucks, or while the scenery is being carried in—and make these markings with the help of one or more assistants, or you may have assistants make them without your presence.

You should consult the construction carpenter to see what work in the way of attaching hinges, of building thicknesses, and the like, has been left until the set-up. All possible work of this kind should have been done in advance, but often such is not the case, and it must be included in your plans accordingly.

ARRANGEMENT OF SCENERY IN GYMNASIUM (Supervisor: Gleason)

Flats:
    Lotus-bud design--against the right front wall of the auditorium.
    Lotus-flower design--backwall of girls' gym.
    Plain flats--backwall of girls' gym.
    Flats with large drawings--backwall of girls' gym.
    Arch group (irregularly shaped pieces)--north wall of girls' gym near the ladders.
    Others--northeast corner of men's gym.

Flooring: Under north basket in men's gym, in these stacks:
    1--XX and XXI.
    2--3' x 6' parallel tops (small cracks, braced by 1" x 3" lumber.)
    3--12 foot pieces of flooring.
    4--3' pieces of flooring.
    5--Others.

Parallels: Under south basket of men's gym.

Steps: Under south basket of men's gym. EXCEPT the four foot high sections--one on each side of the stage for entrance to the stage from men's gym.

Columns: Southeast corner of men's gym.

Tools and 1" x 3" lumber: Southeast corner of girls' gym.

Properties (Throne, carrying couch, couch, tripods, symbols, statues, and small props): Southeast corner of men's

Anything else: Northeast corner of men's gym.

    Try to have these arranged as specified. If a statue is placed with the columns, etc., there is no harm done, for it can't be overlooked when needed, but flats must not be mixed, flooring and parallels and flats should not be mixed, and it is insurance against mistakes if the flooring is correctly distributed.
    When all this is finished, report to your crew leader. However, keep your ears and eyes open for people hunting for scenery. Help them find what they want.

FIGURE 6. Copy of instructions to the assistant superintendent of moving in charge of the stage.

Written instructions, readily available to all the workers, are as imperative at this time as in the scene shifting during a play. It is desirable to have one copy of them for yourself, one for the group leader, and one or more for posting at easily accessible places. With a limited amount of wall space on which to post them, a small book-masking-piece or two-fold serves well, for it can be set up at any point on the stage with the various instruction sheets pinned to it. Figures 6 to 10 are reproduction of different types of instruction sheets used for moving and setting up. Where called for, individual instructions to group leaders should be accompanied by diagrams.

Explain his work carefully to each group leader the day before moving.

To number flats, steps, platforms, and other scenic units aids greatly in their rapid handling. There are various systems that may be used. There should be distinct symbols for each type of scenic element. Every permanent piece of scenery in the shop may have a permanent arithmetical number for reference, with an extra number added in another color of paint when it is needed to expedite rapid changes during a performance. Symbols which may be used are Arabic numbers, 1, 2, 3, 4 . . . ; Roman numerals, I, II, III, IV . . . ; capital letters, A, B, C, D . . . ; small letters, a, b, c, d . . . ; or various colors and various combinations of them, or even letters and numbers inclosed in geometrical figures, such as squares, circles, triangles, et cetera. "Front," "left," "top," and even more specific directions may be painted on the back of a piece of scenery to explain its position in performance. A complete plan of the setting can be painted on the back of one of the flats of the setting, if it is needed.

These markings on pieces are not only useful in setting up, but also are helpful to the moving groups in placing them in the proper packs and scene-docks backstage. Placards posted conspicuously near these packs and docks will further aid in the stacking. The placards may bear such legends as, "I, II, III . . . ," "1, 2, 3, 4 . . . ,"

ALL FOR LOVE   PLAN OF SETTING UP

Charlotte Wilson--stage manager
Marie Ellert--shop supervisor of moving
Margaret Gleason--stage supervisor of moving
Marshall Brooke, Gene Callnon, Max Doan, Nanne Yost--
    electricians

CREWS

SPEAR: Silva, Smith, Robbins, Foster
AZZARA: Read, Beard, Smetherham, Chastain
SUTTER: Moller, Greene, Cleary
RYAN: Mosher, Moss, Tormey
YOUNG: Conard, Drollet, Hoffmeister
CARR: Williams, Miller, Gleason (after moving duties)
ELLERT: Fulton, Shurliff, Gaff

> The following is the approximate order in which the
> jobs should be started. The exact order will vary
> from this.

A. All crews will help on the first loads to gym except
   those who can begin tasks immediately (ground cloth,
   etc.) After these first loads, SUTTER, RYAN and ELLERT
   crews will move the scenery.
1. Hang borders and travellers (Probably finished Wednesday)
2. Remove basketball goal--AZZARA
3. Lay ground cloth--YOUNG AND CARR
4. Stack things in proper places--GLEASON directing
5. Assemble right sidewall and lean against side of gym--
   SPEAR
6. Assemble left sidewall and lean at side of gym--AZZARA
7. Set up platform frames--SPEAR
8. Assemble right portal--AZZARA
10.Assemble arch group--YOUNG
11.Place parallels at back--CARR
12.Place steps at back--CARR
13.Set up 12' x 6' parallels and place flooring--SUTTER
14.Place flats right and left front of gallery--RYAN
15.Place flat center of gallery--RYAN
16.Place parallels and steps for center flight--ELLERT
17.Assemble backwall and check hardward--AZZARA
18.Lay 12' wide section of flooring through center--SPEAR

FIGURE 7. Page 1 of the list of assignments used by the stage manager
(doubling as superintendent of set-up) on a very elaborate one-set play.
There were 42 tasks. The crew consisted of two groups for the complicated work, each composed of three men and two women; two groups for
easy but heavy work, each composed of four less experienced men; three
groups for light work, each composed of four girls; and one group for
the electrical work. The entire crew worked three hours in the afternoon.
The men and the women crew leaders worked three hours at night. The
remaining women spent two hours the next morning covering cracks,
eliminating rattles from the platforms, and touching up the painting.
Only the electricians worked at other times.

"A flats—All," "Large Props," "Hand Props," "Furniture." Even in performance these placards are sometimes useful.

The normal order of numbering the flats of a setting is the order in which they are set up. If the center flat is placed first, letter it C (for center) plus some symbol for the act or scene, and number R1, R2, R3 . . . (for right) and L1, L2, L3 . . . (for left) consecutively, R and L being with reference to the crew man facing the proscenium curtain. If the proscenium flats or returns are to be the first ones placed, they may be numbered R1 and L1, or the previously given method of marking them used in this case also, and the whole stage crew instructed that R7 and L6 are the returns.

Backings to mask off openings may be numbered BR3, BL2, et cetera, the last two symbols either referring to the entrance they mask—R1, R2, R3, RC (right center), C, LC, L3, L2, L1, or, what is preferable, to the flat whose opening they mask. A uniform practice with respect to this should be established and followed for all the plays of the producing group.

If the production is to be moved more than a few hundred feet, a truck saves energy, though it may not save any time. For a distance of over five hundred feet, you must have a truck. For a long distance, a large truck must be used that will hold flats securely when they rest on their sides, and which will carry drops. For a short distance—one to three blocks—a truck without sides, but with a flat bed at least seven feet long, will be quite as satisfactory. In this case, small objects should be carried by hand or in large boxes, and a few flats at a time laid across the bed of the truck, with workers walking beside the truck or riding on the back of it to make sure that the flats do not shift position or rub.

If the workshop is readily accessible to the street, five or six husky men are enough to load the truck. The major portion of the crew will be needed on the stage to set up during the progress of the moving.

In an elaborate production it is essential that an assistant, one who knows precisely what materials are to be moved, remain in the

SPEAR CREW: Silva, Smith, Robbins, Foster

In general, follow the plan as outlined below. When
some task cannot be done in order, do something else first,
or help another crew. Whenever you are doing something requiring more men, get them temporarily from other crews.
Spear is responsible for keeping the crew busy. Use
the girls wherever possible for holding, etc., and other
light work.
The numbers below are the numbers in relation to the
whole set-up work.

A. Report to Technical Director.
See that the flats are put on the first or second load
of scenery moved, and as soon as an appreciable number of them are over, start on your work, leaving the
other crews to finish moving.

1. With AZZARA crew hang the borders and travellers if they
were not finished Wednesday.

5. Assemble the right wall of the set on right half of the
stage floor. Lay flats WW, QQ-RR and the 6' x 12'
flat with a 4' x 8' opening, marked RIGHT, face down
on the floor, WW at the front and the 6' x 12' at the
back. Batten these together securely with 1" x 3"s
to make a solid wall. The 6' x 12' flat is to be approximately level with the top of the other flats.
Its bottom is to be exactly 4' up from the bottom of
the adjacent flat. The bottoms of the others must be
in a straight line.
See that there is lash hardware and rope on end flats.
Place hinges 8" upstage of the arch opening for a backing flat, so hinged that the backing could fold over
the opening.
When assembled and all hardware checked, get additional
help and raise and lean against right side of gym.

7. Get the platform frames and all stringers and unfinished
1" x 3"s from basement and erect as per attached
plan. Be sure to follow this plan exactly, as parts
of it are necessarily eccentric. Get assistance in
moving out the frames. You will need: 4 frames 4' x
6' (approximately), and 12 frames 4' x 9' (approximately). You will need 7, 12' 2" x 4" stringers;
3, 18'; and 3, 9'. You will need much rough 1" x 3"
for cross bracing, and as tie pieces across the ends
of stringers.
Be sure the whole structure is solid!

FIGURE 8. Page 1 of an individual crew instruction sheet for the set-up
plan shown in Figure 7. A copy was given to the group leader. Another
copy was pinned to a small two-fold placed on the stage near the footlights. Alongside it was a copy of the superintendent's set-up plot.

shop. He should have a list of these materials and check them as they are put on the truck. It is helpful to have another assistant to direct the disposal of scenery on the stage as it comes in. He must be given a complete list of the materials and their location on the stage, with a diagram of the arrangement on the stage. This stage supervisor is useful later for the information he can give the workers as to where on the backstage they will find the objects they are to use.

Girls make excellent supervisors, and can be so used most efficiently. It is inefficient to use a man merely to do checking work when he can be used on the heavy work.

A complete run-through of the settings should be made during the set-up. This can be best handled by doing at the same time all work on one setting, such as the battening of walls, the flying of walls, the assembling of wagon units and other large scenic or property units, trying out the whole arrangement at the end, and then storing all the material. In case packs have to be placed one on top of the other, set up the last scene first, and work backwards toward the first.

The final disposition of the scenery at the set-up should be what the stage manager wants at the opening of the dress rehearsal or the scenic rehearsal. You should get his ideas on the matter.

A brass plate imbedded in the floor just behind the front curtain to mark the center of the stage laterally, is a great help to scene shifting and setting up the scenery. It is called the pivot point. It should be a permanent part of the stage, but is frequently missing through oversight. If it has been neglected, there usually will be no objection to your marking the center point with brass headed tacks or with paint. As the center point is often involved in placing the back wall of a setting, it is also useful to mark another such pivotal point at some convenient depth, such as twelve or fifteen feet back of the curtain line, or just behind the area of the stage floor covered by the ground cloth.

In listing the tasks for the group leaders, make notes on your own

Superintendent in shop--Marie Ellert.
Superintendent on stage--Charlotte Wilson.
Nail Checker--Margaret Gleason. (See that every loose nail
    is removed from every flat, platform, etc., before it
    leaves the gym.)
Costumes--Mary Lynn, Dan Beard.
Properties--Evelyn Culver.
Electricians--Marshall Brooke, Max Doan, Nanne Yost, Gene
    Callnon.

CREWS

SPEAR: Silva, Smith, Robbins, Foster
  1. Remove right wall and lean against side of gym.
  2. Remove main backwall and take down archway group.
  3. Remove platforms and stack in basement. (Pile them all
     carefully and get Sutter or Ryan's crew to help
     yours in passing them in. BE SURE THEY ARE STACKED
     in good piles so we won't have to move them all the
     next time we want some of them.
     All flooring goes to the shop.
  4. Break up right wall of set.
  5. Get borders and other flied materials in order.

AZZARA: Read, Beard, Smetherham, Chastian.
  1. Remove left side wall of set and place against side of
     gym.
  2. Remove pin-hinges from the back three-fold.
  3. Remove backwall of the hall.
  4. Break up the portals.
  5. Help Spear break up the platforms. Take as your spec-
     ial task the removal of the two parallels on the
     sides. Remember they do not fold up, but must have
     the pins removed.
  6. Break up the left wall of set.
  7. Place the basketball goal.

SUTTER: Moller, Greene, Cleary.
  1. Load scenery. In this order:
     A. Columns and bases
     B. Properties
     C. Statues
     D. Steps and platforms
     E. Flats
     F. Flooring (This does not have to be exact order.)
  2. See that scenery is stacked correctly in the shop, or
     it will have to be restacked. The piles of flats
     must slant only a few inches, and must be tightly
     packed.

FIGURE 9. Page 1 of the instructions for moving scenery back after a performance, the production being the same as for Figures 7 and 8. A copy of this was posted. Another was cut up into sections and these were given to the group leaders.

copy of the instructions of those tasks which may be done earlier than the time assigned, and so be ready to reassign them to the same or to another group whose next task is being held up by some delay in the schedule.

The maker of the moving plot (either yourself, or an assistant who will do the detail work from your general plans), assistants in charge of the shop and stage, group leaders, and an assistant in charge of tools and supplies will be under you. Instructions for them follow.

In a simple production, you may be the stage manager also, and your whole staff be selected from the performance crew. Your stage assistant can easily take charge of the tools and supplies. The maker of the moving plot can serve in any of these capacities.

As in your own case, your assistants should be instructed never to do any work themselves until they have all their workers busy at tasks. Economy of effort and time demands that no one be idle except the executives. Many of the tasks which your workers will do are also part of the work under the performance stage manager. You will find instructions for them in Chapter VI. Only those which solely relate to the set-up have been included in this chapter.

You also will have supervision over the flymen, who form a division of the set-up staff, and over the electricians. While they will have separate directors, you will have to make provision for inter-relating their work with yours in setting up.

To the Maker of the Moving Plot (*Superintendent or an Assistant*):

One week in advance of moving, you will receive the general plans of the moving and the set-up from the superintendent of such work. You will make out precise and detailed plans for them. As needed under the circumstances, you will list:

1. Items for each truck load. (Copies to the superintendent, his assistants in the shop and on the stage, and one or more additional ones to be posted in the shop.)

2. Items for individuals to carry. (Copies to the same people as in 1. Possibly also special sheets to individuals by name, with copies of them to the superintendent.)

3. Items to be left in the shop, if the scenery not to be used is mixed with the articles to be used in this play, and is piled in the same packs with them. (Copies to the same people as in 1.)

4. Items to go in advance of the general moving. (Copies to the same people as in 1, and other individuals to whom they apply.)

5. Diagram of the stage, showing the exact disposition backstage during the set-up of articles by their class or symbol. (Copies to the superintendent, the stage assistant, and for posting.)

6. Order of tasks in the theatre, inter-relating these with the flying and electrical work, with the laying of the ground cloth and the flying of drops usually the first things to be done. (Copies to the superintendent, and for posting.)

7. Individual instructions to group leaders. (Copies to the group leaders, the superintendent, and for posting.)

8. Tool and supply list. (Copies to the superintendent, and the assistant in charge of tools and supplies.)

9. Such diagrams of work and stage floor plans as will be needed by the group leaders.

10. A similar set of lists and instructions for moving the scenery back to the shop after the end of the run. In doing this, it is best to assign the work to the same groups that made the set-up (in the reverse order), as they will know the forms of construction, how nails were driven, et cetera, and there is then less chance of damage being done. Also, if they know in advance that they will have to take the same things down, they may be a little more careful in putting them up than they otherwise might be. If the work is assigned to the same groups, little instruction need accompany the list of tasks. (See Figures 9 and 10.)

In moving back, the careful planning of truck loads is not so necessary, and many of the check-lists for moving over may be used again at this time without revision. New instructions should be

Alison's House--Moving Back

Everyone will help at anything they can after their own task is completed. No one is to leave until everything is in order. The faster each one works, the sooner we all can leave. Start 15 minutes after curtain is down.

Robbins: Props. All our props in back room of old shop.
Van Voorhis: Props, effects. Tie up chimes and get man to carry them. Put in attic of old shop.
Maaksted: Take down bed alcove. Help carry flats.
Hill: Take down bow window. Direct moving.
Thorne: Take bookcases apart and remove casters. With Kister carry bookcases to new shop.
Kister: Help Thorne carry bookshelves to new shop.
Muncey } Carry the five windows to new shop. Lean against
Hopkins } template. Help on furniture, etc.
Mills } Carry doors to old shop. Stack against old flats
Claton } on west wall. Tie all pieces of bed together securely and put in attic. Help on furniture, etc.
Conard } Fold curtains and store in chest in backroom of old
Perry } shop. Help on furniture and flats. Conard, get bolt of gauze from workbench in new shop and take back for credit on our bill.
Haas } Take down lights and put in booth. Pile all gelatine
Hunt } carefully. Hunt, get globes back to Mr. Jordan on Monday. Be sure all foots are taken out.
Culbert: Locate night watchman and get him to let you in music building with racks. Help on flats, etc.
Wilson: Take back tools except hammers, screwdrivers, etc. that will be needed in taking down the set. Bring over gingerale cases for odds and ends. Inspect building thoroughly for all hardware, etc. Put tools in cabinet.
Martin } Help on tearing down set, carrying flats, etc. See
Jensen } that fireplaces and backings go to new shop, and
Licty } finally that ladders go to new shop.
Gray } Carry furniture. All chairs, all tables except
Shannon } library table, and all other small things go in
Spear } balcony of old shop. Library table, dresser,
Dougherty } settee, are stacked in northeast corner of old
Lee } shop. Do not block the front wall with any
Yost } furniture, as flats go there. Help to carry
Rouse } the flats.

MEN ARE NOT TO CARRY FURNITURE EXCEPT PIECES THAT ARE TOO HEAVY FOR THE WOMEN.

FIGURE 10. Another form of instruction sheet for the final strike. This was a much simpler production.

provided for the shop assistant as to the disposition of the scenery there.

All these lists and instruction sheets must be in the hands of the superintendent of moving and set-up three days ahead of moving. Only in the most elaborate production will all the records specified be used. The superintendent will tell you which ones he wants. Examples of moving plans are given in Figures 6 to 10.

To the Shop and Stage Assistants:

You will receive check-lists for all items to be moved. You may be provided with one of several types of lists, according to your location, or with more than one type.

If you are in charge of the loading, you will remain in the shop, and will have in hand lists of what must go in each truck load. When a truck becomes overloaded or underloaded, you will use your judgment about what to omit or add. You will, of course, send any omitted articles on the next load. If you are moving a long distance, by careful packing you may be able to effect a saving in the number of loads. If, however, you are moving only a short distance, you then would consume more time in methodical packing than you would save in trips.

Be sure the packing is such that no possible damage can be done to the scenery. If you should have to move in the rain, repeatedly caution the workers not to touch the face of scenery when it is wet or allow the pieces to touch each other. Properly sized scene paint will not run, but it will rub when wet.

If individuals carry articles a short distance, they should have personal lists, but you will keep track of all articles being moved in order to see that nothing is omitted and that no one falls behind. You will give them assistance or a verbal prod depending on the cause for the delay.

The loading group may accompany and unload the truck at the theatre. Usually have them do so. But if they remain in the shop, you will have them collect and arrange the scenery for the next load.

You will check off each item as it is taken away from the shop. Mark the copy, however, in such a way that the same list may be used for checking when the scenery is moved back. When the last article has gone you will so report to the superintendent.

If you are in charge of the disposition of scenery on the stage, you must familiarize yourself with the pieces being moved so that you can direct the workers where to put them. You will have, however, a check-list for reference (see Figure 6) and a diagram of the stage showing their positions. Check every item as it is brought in. Any accidents enroute should be reported to you, and you should record and report them to the superintendent so that he can provide for the repair work. Have slips of paper with you for these memoranda.

You will occupy a position, such as at the door, if a single door is used, where you can easily check things.

In moving the material back to the shop, the character of your duties will be approximately reversed. The shop assistant must see that the scenery is well packed in the storage bins. The stage assistant should check all the flats, properties, platforms, et cetera, and see that all temporary nails have been removed before they are taken to the truck. An exposed nail may tear a flat or injure a worker.

To the Group Leaders:

Your tasks will be given you in writing by the superintendent. (See Figure 8.) Your group will consist of about six people. It is your duty to keep them busy. You will work just as fast as you can on your own tasks. If the failure of some other group to finish its job on time prevents your starting one of your own, report the matter to the superintendent, who will assign you something else to do in the meantime. If he can give you nothing, you will go to the other group leaders and have them put your group members to work on some of their tasks until you can start them on your next job. You yourself will never work until you have first put every member of your group to work. A clever superintendent, if he finds one of your workers shirking, will complain to you that you do not keep your group busy, as this is frequently more successful than for him to scold an individual group member, who will be able to excuse himself too easily by saying that you had given him nothing to do. Do not take such a scolding to heart, of course, though if it happens too often, it should be plain that it is your fault. Remember that it is only the executives who may be idle. If the leader becomes too preoccupied with his own tasks, the other workers will shirk. Show your group members how to do things, but do not let them entice you into doing it for them just because you know how to do it better than they. Do not let the men of your group waste their time doing things that the women can do just as well. But there is no need to be too bossy a task-master, or a slave-driver. If you see that they are tiring, give your workers a five or ten minute rest period before starting on a new job. If smoking is not prohibited, this interval can be used for cigarettes. It will give you an excuse to refuse permission to a worker to go outside to smoke at other times. If he finds other people smoking there, too, he will, without realizing it, fritter away fifteen or twenty minutes of time chatting. Never allow smoking on the stage, however, even though there may be no rule against it. There is too much inflammable material about to permit of it.

If you need additional help on any task, ask another leader to supply you with some of his workers, and be ready, in turn, to help him in the same way.

You will find most of the individual tasks discussed in the instructions for the grip crews in Chapter VI (pages 103–110), because, with the addition of some carpentry, much of your work is similar to that of the performance crew. Instructions on other tasks follow here:

GROUND CLOTH

Various methods are used for laying a ground cloth. It may be done by lashing it with a rope or sash cord to pins inserted in sockets in the floor and to the grommets in the ground cloth. The rope or cord should be left in the ground cloth in the periods between productions ready to be looped over the inserted pins and then pulled taut. The cloth must be laid wrinkleless. In the professional theatre, it is laid before and removed after each performance, but most amateur organizations leave it down throughout a run.

Sometimes the rope is omitted, and the pins put directly through the grommets. It may also be tacked to the floor. When this is done in the professional theatre, a spade is often used to pull the tacks.

THICKNESSES

"Thickness" is the stage term applied to a board or small flat attached to the back of a flat at an opening in order to supply the supposed thickness of a wall. This practice is the alternative to the cutout style, by which all walls are shown by the door and window openings to be only three-quarters of an inch thick.

If thickness is to be applied to a door or window opening, the customary and easiest way is to attach pieces of 1″ x 6″, 1″ x 8″, or 1″ x 12″ lumber to the back of the flat with nails (if it is to remain through the production, and will not get in the way in moving) or with loose-pin hinges (in which case the pin is removed from the hinge and the thickness moved independently of the flat). Door and window "boxes" are also thickness. They are explained in Chapter VI.

The pieces of lumber are so attached as to make the three faces of the door casing. The upper or horizontal piece of lumber must be fastened to the two upright ones in order to prevent the thickness collapsing when jarred. The door "shutter" that is fitted into the opening is attached to the back or near the back of the thickness. A door-stop strip may be put on the opposite side of the thickness.

When thickness is to be deeper than 12 inches, flats of the correct size should be built and used in lieu of the pieces of solid lumber. These may be either pin-hinged individually, or the whole structure, including a sill of three-ply wood-veneer or band-steel, may be so nailed or hinged as to constitute one unit, and may be held in place with two pin-hinges or by lash-lines.

If the thickness is to have other than straight lines, as in the case of an arch, arcs or other framed cutouts, called sweeps, are employed. They are used in conjunction with boards for the straight part of the lines.

Temporary thicknesses made of wall board or roofing paper are sometimes used. They must be handled carefully.

Pin-hinges

Pin-hinges are those having loose pins holding the two flanges together. The term is a misnomer, for all hinges have pins, but it is a shortening of the full term "loose-pin hinges."

When hinges are delivered to you with loose-pins, the pins are short heavy wires fitting exactly into the pin holes of the flanges. These usually fit tightly and, in consequence, are difficult to remove and insert quickly. So, for stage purposes, nails or short pieces of annealed wire that are bent over at the top are usually substituted for them after the initial fitting. Stage hardware dealers sell these wires ready cut.

Pin-hinges are used whenever objects must be temporarily held together tightly and strongly, but later must be separated readily. They may be used anywhere in place of regular tight-pin hinges. Their most frequent uses are for fastening door and window thicknesses where "boxes" are not used, and for holding together temporarily platforms, set-walls, and sometimes flats. Attach them like ordinary hinges.

Some organizations attach pin-hinges at a uniform point on the flats as part of the hardware equipment, so that they may be fastened together securely for use as a flat wall or as a book flat (two-fold), instead of the less permanent lashing.

Hinges 4″ x 2″ in size, each flange being 2″ x 2″, are the ones most frequently used, except for two-ways, when 1½″ x 3″ are best. They are called two-inch loose-pin back-flap hinges, and may be procured from dealers in stage hardware if not from your local hardware store.

Dutchman Hinging

"Dutchman" is the name given to the piece of wood inserted when hinging is done, in order to make it possible for three or more flats to fold together, when, without it, they would not so fold together.

If you have three flats, all of which must fold inward in order to allow the cracks to be covered with muslin strips (sometimes also called dutchmen), and thus to make an unbroken wall when set up, hinge a piece of 1″ x 2″ or 1″ x 3″ lumber between two of them on the same side as the other hinges. You may now fold the pair hinged directly together, and then on top of them fold the remaining flat, which is hinged to the dutchman. The dutchman will stand at right angles to the flats and equalize the thickness of the flat whose thickness, otherwise, would prevent the third flat of the three-fold lying flat on it. Let A, B, and C represent the flats, and X the 1″ x 2″ strip between B and C. Fold A on B. Then, X being equal to, or greater than, the thickness of the flat B, it will stand at right angles to the flats, and C will fold flat on A. Your flats are now packed B, A, C with X on one side at right angles to them. (See Figure 11.)

A variation of this is used for three-fold flats of the column or pylon type. Here one of the sides is made an inch or two shorter than the other. A strip of lumber of a corresponding thickness is nailed or screwed to the back of the flat used for the face, and the short side hinged to this rather than to the face itself, as is the other side. These will then fold up, the order being face, long side, short side.

If you have three flats or pieces of any kind—in this case usually

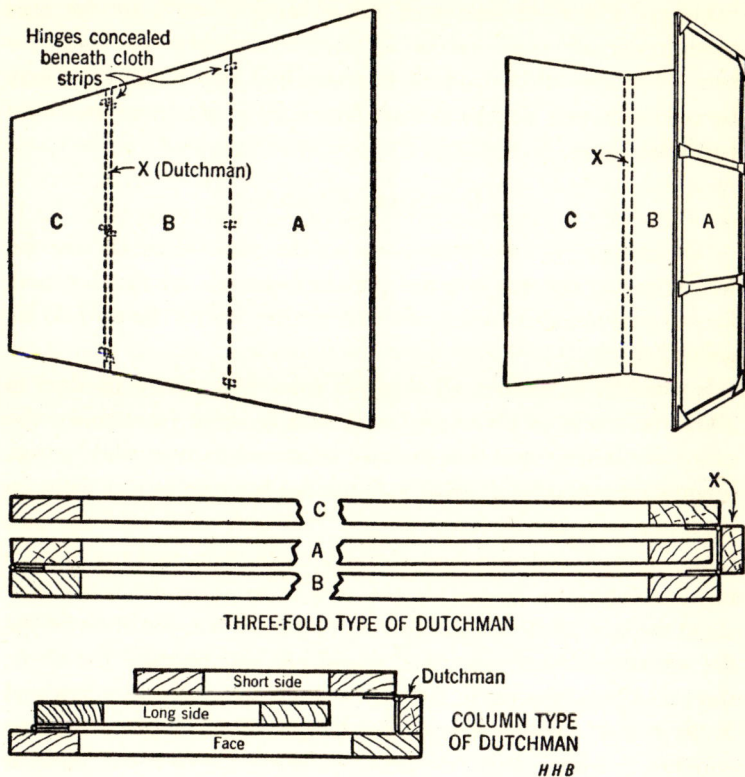

THREE-FOLD TYPE OF DUTCHMAN

COLUMN TYPE
OF DUTCHMAN

H H B

FIGURE 11. Two types of Dutchman—one for a three-fold, and one for a column. The cloth strip covering the cracks and hinges is sometimes called a cloth Dutchman. A wall type Dutchman is illustrated in Figure 12.

thicknesses—all meeting to form the three planes of the corner of a wall, again you will find it impossible to fold them together. If the flats are all of about equal size, one of them should usually be pin-hinged so that it can be removed from the group, or so arranged that it will fit some other temporary locking device, such as a hook and socket. The usual problem, however, is the face, end, and top of a wall, when two of the pieces are much smaller than the main one. In this case, all the pieces may be hinged, using another type of dutchman sometimes called a tumbler. Permanently hinge the two pieces that rest on the floor. Then fold them together. Along the top edge of the large flat, starting a half inch away from the small flat already hinged and which is now lying back on the larger one, and three-quarters of an inch (the thickness of the lumber in the top piece) from the top of the large flat, nail a piece of 1″ x 2″ batten lumber (the dutchman) to the large flat. Hinge the top flat to this board. The flats will now all fold together, and yet there will be perfect joints at all the edges. Calling the face of the wall A, the end B, and the top C, with X for the dutchman, you will then have, when folded, A, with B and X in the same plane, and C on the top. This provides for the face of the wall to lap both the top and the end, and for the top to lap the end. Slight adaptations will have to be made if any other lapping is wanted. (See Figure 12.)

Concealing Cracks

No matter how narrow the cracks between flats in the walls facing the audience, they are apt to allow light to pass through and show. Paper tape or some such material may be fastened on the back of the flats, thus sealing these cracks. The simplest covering, however, is burlap-webbing such as is used in building furniture. This can be attached with tacks at wide intervals, and has sufficient strength to be jerked off without tearing when it is to be removed, and so can be used again and again. The webbing on the back of the flats will fold into them if they are hinged, or it may be fastened on only one side, lapping the edge, so that the flats may be taken apart.

In order to conceal the lines of like cracks on the face of flats, paper tape may be pasted on the front side and then painted to match the setting. This tape, of course, can only be used on such cracks as are not broken in changing the setting. Sometimes these coverings also are called dutchmen.

Professionals use lips on flats. These are made of narrow pieces of profile board mitered into the front of a flat at an angle, and projecting just enough to cover the crack between the flat and the ad-

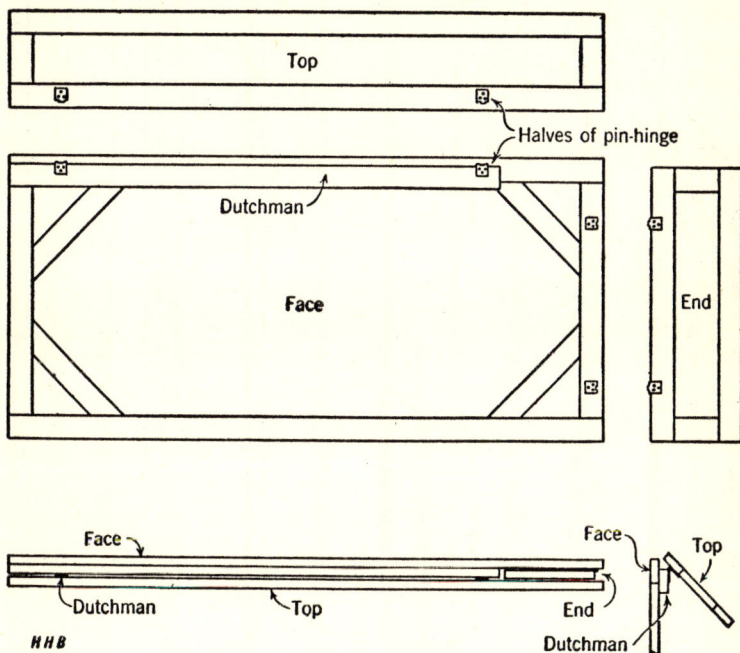

FIGURE 12. A wall type Dutchman.

jacent one and thus prevent a spill of light. There is no reason why amateurs cannot use them. They should be part of the original construction of the flat, but can be added later. Tin lips are also used, but are likely to become bent and also to tear other flats.

BRACING

When one setting is used for the entire performance, or when some parts of the setting are not to be moved, the flats may be nailed or screwed fast in their positions. This is likely to damage them to some extent, so other methods should be used when possible.

Foot irons, metal strips attached to a piece of scenery and fastened

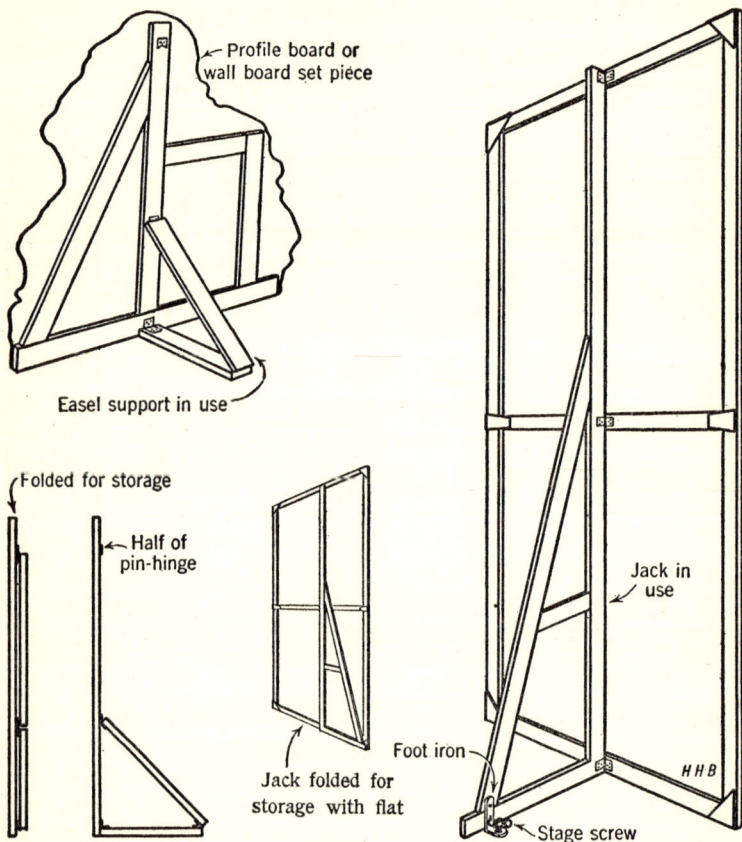

Profile board or wall board set piece

Easel support in use

Folded for storage

Half of pin-hinge

Jack folded for storage with flat

Jack in use

Foot iron

Stage screw

H H B

FIGURE 13. An easel support for a set piece and a flat supported by a jack.

to the floor with a stage-screw or a weight, may be used. This is the usual means of supporting profile set pieces that have small bases.

Set pieces sometimes may be braced by easel supports hinged to their backs.

Triangular braces, or jacks (see Figure 13), may be used on small pieces or on full sized flats. These may be made of either metal or wood. They may be secured to the floor by stage-screws or by weights. Occasionally they will stand of their own weight. They may be of any size up to two-thirds of the height of the flat on which they are used. A jack for a large flat is made of a 1″ x 3″ upright with a shorter piece running backwards at the bottom at right angles. A diagonal cross piece is mitered from the end of the bottom piece to a point two-thirds of the way up the long piece, and a foot-iron or other like device put on the back of the jack. This may be hinged or pin-hinged to a stile or the toggle rails (cross pieces) of the flat and folded against it when it is moved. The jack will hold the flat exactly upright. It also may be built in such shape as to hold the flat at any other angle desired.

Another method of triangular bracing is to hinge a short board to the bottom rail of the flat so it will rest on the floor, hinge another board to this as an easel support, and pin-hinge this at the point on the flat that will give the angle desired. (See Figure 13.) Half of another pin-hinge is then put on the flat at a height which will allow the two boards to be held tightly against it when not in use. This is not a strong brace, and so cannot be used on large flats.

Stage braces are the standard holding devices for large pieces of scenery. They are made of two sticks held together by clamps which allow the combined length to be altered. On one end is a foot-iron, on the other is a hook which will fit into a brace cleat, screw eye or stage-screw. The hook end of the brace is put through the eye, a stage-screw is inserted in the floor through the foot-iron at the other end, and the brace is then adjusted to the length needed in order to hold the flat in the desired position.

A long flat wall which shows a tendency to buckle may be strengthened and straightened by nailing a batten ("stiffener") across the flats, or by laying the batten in "S," or "keeper," hooks placed along the toggle rails. (See Figure 14.) In order to use S-hooks, the toggle-rails must be in a line, but special "independent toggle-rails" may be screwed on at the standard height wanted.

(See Chapter VII.) S-hooks and the stiffener may also be placed along the top of flats which do not have to be moved.

To the Assistant Superintendent in charge of tools and supplies:
You will pack the tools, hardware, supplies, et cetera, to be taken to the stage for use in setting up and in repair work.

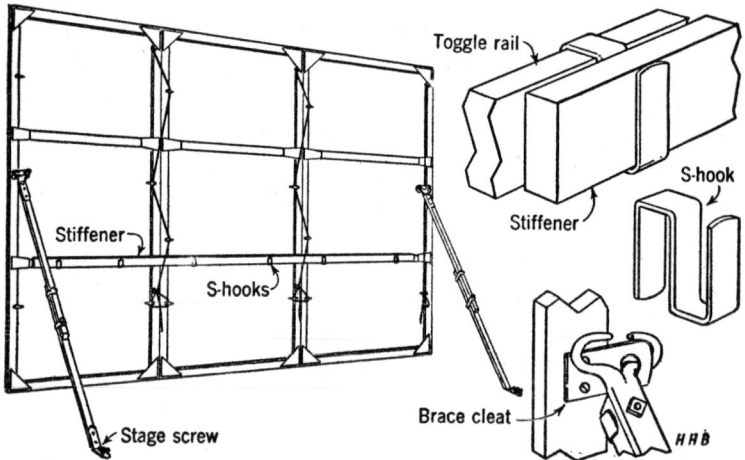

FIGURE 14. A stiffener and stage braces used on a flat wall.

Three days before moving, you will make up lists of the materials needed and see that they are on hand. If there are not sufficient tools, you will arrange to borrow them. You are most likely to need additional hammers and automatic (ratchet) screwdrivers. For the final "strike" (taking down the set) you may need crowbars.

The day before moving, pack the tools in small boxes—regular tool boxes or, in their absence, small unpartitioned wooden ginger-ale cases.

You will leave some of the tools in the shop if they will be needed there for any purpose during the set-up.

You will see that the boxes of tools are put on the first truck, or that they are taken to the theatre in advance of the scenery.

Give a copy of your inventory to the superintendent.

Individual circumstances will determine the exact items to be taken. Following are the tools, articles, and materials, all or part of which may be needed:

TOOLS

Claw hammers
Machinists' hammers
Tack hammers
Cross cut saws
Rip saws
Keyhole saws
Coping saws
Hack saws
Brace and bits
Screwdrivers
Automatic screwdrivers
Plyers
Nail cutters
Wrenches
Monkey wrenches
Crowbars

Planes
Vises
Files
Rasps
Miter boxes
Awls
Grommet dies
Clamps
Knives
Razor-blade knives
Draw knives
Clinching irons
Try squares
T-squares
Tape measures
Rulers and yardsticks

HARDWARE

Common nails
Box nails
Finishing nails
Clout nails
Brads
Staples
Tacks
Brass headed tacks
Thumbtacks
Screws
Screw eyes
Screw hooks
Bolts
Wing nuts
Corrugated fasteners
Nail boxes or cans (5 lb. coffee or hotel sized vegetable cans are good)
Hinges

Strap hinges
Shackle hinges
Loose-pin hinges
Pins or lengths of annealed wire
Angle irons
Flat corner braces
Door knobs
Locks
Grommets
Pins for ground cloth
Casters
Skids
Picture hooks
Pulleys
Needles
Pins
Safety pins

STAGE HARDWARE

Lash eyes
Lash cleats
Tie-off cleats
Stop cleats
Brace cleats
Hanging irons
Foot-irons

Stage-screws
Corner blocks
Keystones
S-hooks
Special hardware, such as patented picture hooks

SUPPLIES

Lumber (1″ × 2″, 1″ × 3″, 1″ × 4″ or 5/4″ × 4″, 1″ × 6″, etc., moulding)
Three-ply wood-veneer
Wall board
Pressed wood board
Cardboard
Wrapping paper
Webbing
Muslin
Hot glue
Prepared glue
Paste

Plastic wood
Manila rope
Sash cord
Heavy wrapping cord
Twine
Thread
Wire
Shellac
Wood alcohol
Turpentine
Dryer

MISCELLANEOUS

Rung ladders
Step ladders
Y-ladders
Independent toggle-rails
Jacks
Stage-braces
Sandbags
Brooms
Dust brushes

Dustpans
Paints
Paint cans
Brushes
Sponges
Rags
Paint cloth
First aid supplies

You will select a convenient place on the stage to deposit the tools, but one where they will not be in the way. Throughout the course of the work of setting up, you will gather up the tools one by one as they are laid aside by the workers and return them to this spot. With a large crew using them, you will find that your tools will be much scattered within a half hour or less, after which no one can find anything he wants unless they are re-assembled progressively.

Keep a close check on the materials being used so that you can replenish the supplies before they are exhausted. This is particularly important with respect to lumber. You are responsible if work is delayed while waiting for additional supplies.

Assemble all tools at the end of the work period; assemble them again just before the rehearsals or performances. Make a complete check of your inventory each time. Make a thorough search for missing tools—they can find their way into the most improbable places! Look on top of objects, under objects, between flats in the packs, on top of thicknesses, in properties, et cetera. If not found, report the loss to the superintendent.

Just before the final performance, sort out the tools which will be useful in striking the set, and pack the others so that they will be ready to go back to the shop on the first load.

During the strike see that any materials that were temporarily in use are returned to your boxes and piles—webbing, independent toggle-rails, S-hooks, stage-screws and stage-braces, battens, et cetera.

Verify the tools by the list as they are sent back to the shop, and, after the clean-up, check those that are missing, and then *search until you find every one of them!*

If it is not part of the janitor service of the theatre, you will sweep the stage after vacating it. Look carefully at that time for small tools and hardware. If the sweeping is done next day by a janitor, go to the theatre and ask him for any stage hardware and tools he may have found.

After the scenery has been returned to the shop, check the tools and put them in their proper places.

CHAPTER V

FLYING

To the Superintendent of Flying and the Flymen:

In advance of the set-up day, you will obtain a list of everything to be flied—drops, drapes, backwalls, sets, cycloramas, legs, furniture, ceilings, lights, et cetera, and will make out a plan for the work to be done with them. You will find which fly lines on the stage are free, and which ones can be freed for your use. You may have to hang additional sets of lines from extra pulleys or sheaves, and you may have to plan to use one set of lines for more than one article, changing them during an intermission. You may have to transfer scenery already hanging from one set of lines to another to free the lines you want for your equipment. You will do what parts of this work you can before the moving day. You will draw up exact plans of the scenery to be flied, showing the line number for each piece.

TERMINOLOGY

Because of the confusion in the use of the terms "curtains" and "draperies," it is well to establish some single meaning for each word in your written plans. A convenient distinction, based on stage usage, is the term "drop" for any flat painted surface hung from the flies, "curtain" for any unpainted cloth hung in folds and for the "act drop" or "front curtain" even though it is painted, "drapes" for unpainted cloth which makes up "curtains" or which is large enough to be so used, and "draperies" for the cloth used at window and door openings.

Set-up Day

On the set-up day, you will give instructions in writing to the various workers under you, having them work rapidly in order to get all the desired pieces in the flies and thus clear the stage floor for the other workers. Usually it is possible to have two or more groups working under you at the same time. You will arrange to have all your scenery to be flied moved into the theatre first, and then hang it while the other scenery is being moved in. You will arrange for this with the superintendent in charge of moving and set-up, under whom you will be working. In a simple production he may direct the flying as a part of the general set-up and dispense with a special superintendent for it.

You will check the work as it progresses to make sure that the pieces are put on the right lines and are correctly hung. Make sure, especially, that the ropes are strong and that the knots in them will hold. A bow-line knot is commonly used for straight lifts, and a clove-hitch for horizontal or bias pulls. Slip-knots may be used temporarily. "Bridles" or "stirrups" may be used where the fly lines are not placed far enough to the side of the stage to support a long batten. You will see that all tie-offs are marked and that all drops and curtains are "in trim," a process described below.

Drop Hanging

A drop is hung directly on a set of lines by its own batten, or this is attached to a permanently hung pipe batten. It may be attached by patent batten-clamps sold by stage hardware dealers, which require no holes through the drop. Holes may be bored in the batten with brace and bit and the lines tied through these, or slits may be cut in the canvas just below the batten and the ropes tied through them.

Establishing a Permanent Trim

"Trim" is the term for the perfect position of a drop as to level and height. In directing the trimming of a drop, the line nearest the man at the pin-rail is called the "short" line, the farthest one from him the "long" line, and the middle one the "center" line. When there are more than three, they usually are numbered serially starting from the man flying the curtain, the short line being "number one," or, as an alternative, the two center lines are called "short center" and "long center" respectively. Once the trimming is done, tie the ropes off on the pin-rail. To tie this knot, pass the ropes around the lower end of the belaying pin, make a loop in the free end of the rope and hook this over the top end of the pin after giving it a half twist so that the part of the rope bearing the strain passes over, and thereby locks, the free end into position. The safest way is to make two or three successive knots of this kind. Tie another rope or wire around this trim tie-off to prevent anyone's thoughtlessly untying it. Now the drop may be raised to the flies for storage, and the lines tied off on another pin or on top of the trim tie-off. At any time thereafter, the drop may be lowered to its exact position by letting out the temporary tie-off in the lines. With a counterweight system, the position of the rope or cable when the drop is in trim, may be shown by a band of paint on it or by other like means. Never rely on anything tied *around* a rope being secure, for it will slip. Counterweighting with sandbags is discussed later in this section.

Advanced Trimming for Two Heights

If a drop or curtain is to be used at two definite heights, such as a curtain resting on the floor and as a border, for example, it is tied off permanently at its lowest position, and then some other device is used for quickly making the higher position exact. The three ropes may be tied together in a knot and the knot slipped under a hook. This knot sometimes readjusts itself or slips, however, and corrections are difficult to make.

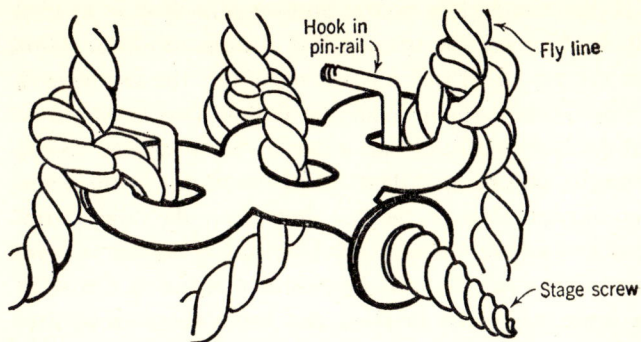

DETAIL OF KNOTS

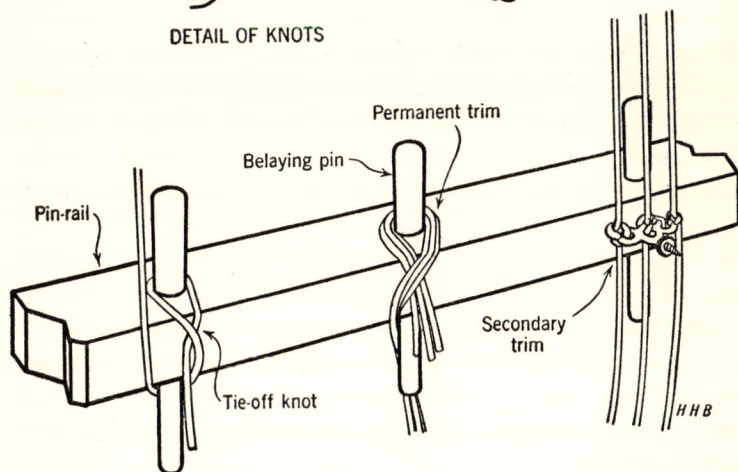

FIGURE 15. A tie-off knot and the special method described in this book for establishing a secondary trim. Each line of a set of lines is tied through a separate finger-hole of a stage-screw, which is then caught under a pair of hooks screwed into the pin-rail or wall.

Professionals use "trim blocks" to establish a definite trim on a drop and maintain it at any height. This block consists of two pieces of metal which can be bolted together. There are depressions for the lines in each half. These slots are lined with jagged teeth backed by a spring device. The teeth are set at such an angle that they permit an individual rope to be pulled downward, but not upward. The trim block is put on the lines and a sandbag is hooked to it to balance the drop. The ropes are then pulled downward one at a time until the drop is in trim. Later adjustments of the trim can be made easily so long as they can be made by pulling one or two ropes downward. In damp weather, ropes stretch. The "long line," having a greater length, will become slack. With this device, a slight jerk on the long line will take up the slack and restore the drop to trim.

A makeshift method, but one which is usually satisfactory and accurate, of establishing two different trims is to tie each rope individually through a different finger-hole of a stage-screw, tying the knots on the screw side, with this side pointing outward from the wall or pin-rail. This stage-screw may be caught under two hooks in the wall or pin-rail, one for each outside hole of the stage-screw. (See Figure 15.) The stage-screw must be put in the lines and this second trim perfected before the lower tie-off is made. If needed, more than one such extra trim may be made for a drop.

Hanging Drape Curtains

A curtain of drapes to be hung straight across the stage at any given distance from the footlights is usually made with fullness at the top hem, is usually strengthened with a webbing strip at the top, and has grommets every eighteen inches. If the drape is to be attached to a batten, tie 24″ to 30″ soft sash cord lengths into the grommet holes, and then around the batten. Double the cord and put the loop through the grommet. Then slip the two ends through this loop. This makes it easy to remove these cords, or "points," from the drapes later. If additional fullness is to be put in the drape while hanging it, in order to equalize the fullness, tie the two ends of the drape, then the middle, then the middle of the resulting sections, and so on. Where two pieces of drapes meet, always overlap them eight inches.

If the drape is to be attached to a set of travellers, use shorter lengths of smaller cord. Drapes equipped for travellers are provided with snaps to hook into rings on the traveller "runners." Grommet drops may be tied to these rings, however, and drapes with snap hooks may have cords tied through the snaps to be fastened to battens.

For various types of rigging, see later sections in the chapter.

DRAPE BORDER

Instead of in folds, a drape border may be hung straight. In this case, the center is tied, and the cords on each side are then tied until all of the desired portion is attached. All remaining parts of the cloth are tied at the ends of the batten, or the extra cloth is turned back on itself and tied behind the rest of the border.

DRAPE CYCLORAMA

A drape cyclorama is either tied to a batten having arms attached to it, or to a semi-circular pipe-batten made especially for the purpose. An arm-batten is made by hinging two short lengths of batten to one regular batten by 5″ to 8″ shackle hinges or strap hinges in such a way that the short lengths may fold against the main batten or extend out from it at a little more than a right angle and be attached there to the long and short lines of another set of lines.

Selden and Sellman's *Stage Scenery and Lighting* and Barber's *Scene Technician's Handbook* suggest a way to hang such an arm cyclorama so that, before flying it, it need not be lowered to the floor in order to unhook the lines to the arms. The long and short lines of the set immediately in front of that supporting the main batten are used to support the arms. When the batten is raised, these lines allow the arms to tip down and hang suspended from the main batten and thus to be raised with it. When it is again lowered, the arms tip up into correct trim. The same method may be used for ceilings. To prevent the resulting diagonal line of the arm-support lines from interfering with other flied scenery, they may be held close to the main batten for most of their distance by running them

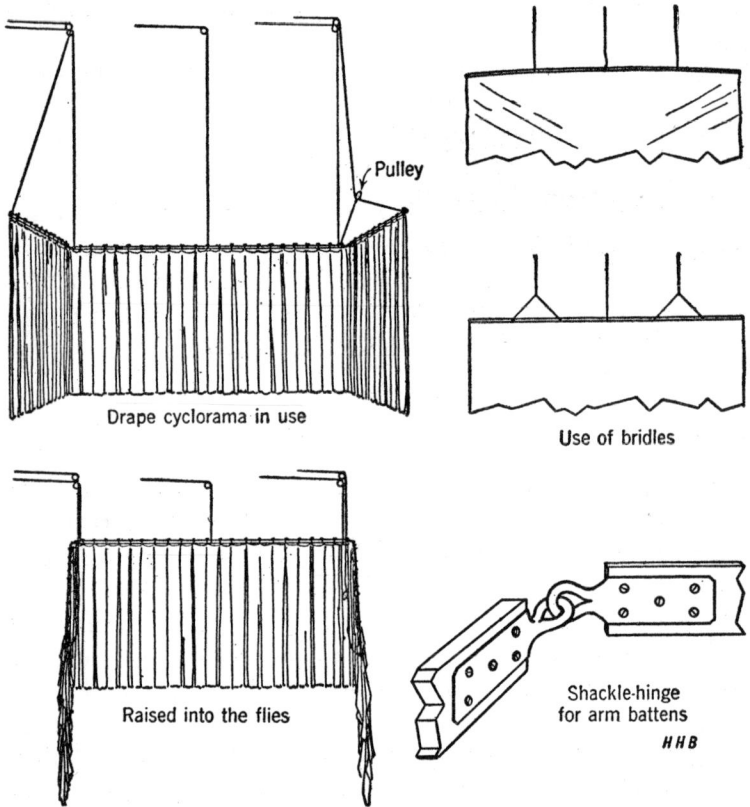

Pulley

Drape cyclorama in use

Use of bridles

Raised into the flies

Shackle-hinge
for arm battens
H H B

FIGURE 16. The method of rigging a drape cyclorama on an arm batten in such a way that, in order to fly it, it will not need to be lowered to the floor and the arms untied. One side is shown rigged with a pulley to hold the extra line close to the supporting line. This arrangement prevents the line interfering with other flied scenery. The shackle hinge used for the arm battens is shown on the left. Bridles to support a sagging drop are shown in the upper right-hand corner.

through small pulleys attached to the batten or to the lines supporting the batten. (See Figure 16.)

PERMANENTLY DRAPED CURTAINS

Curtains which are to hang permanently in folds may be sewed, pinned or tied into their position. A more satisfactory and surer way is to determine the points in the cloth to be tied together in order to give the proper folds, to have rings sewed to these places on patches of cloth, and then to tie the rings together.

RIGGING PULL DRAPES

The same methods of rigging are used for front curtains, for full drape curtains, and for draperies at windows and doors, when they open by being pulled to the sides. For convenience here, window draperies are discussed first. (See Figure 17.)

A very smooth round piece of wood, or of shellacked or greased metal, is used for the curtain-pole. Smooth rings (metal or wood) are strung on the pole. Attach two permanent screw eyes to the wall at the end of the pole where the cords hang down, and one screw eye at the other end. If conditions do not permit this, securely wire an extra curtain ring at each end of the pole. If you call these eyes X and Y at the end of the pole from which the cords hang, and Z at the other, and the curtain rings, starting at the cord end, 1, 2, 3, 4, 5, 6 on one curtain, and 7, 8, 9, 10, 11, 12 on the other, you then have on the curtain pole:

$$X, Y, 1, 2, 3, 4, 5, 6—7, 8, 9, 10, 11, 12, Z$$

You will need a cord of sufficient length to reach from the height at which you wish the cords to hang, upward to the curtain-rod, across it, back across it, and then down to the first point. Determine the height at which you want the pull-cord to hang when the drapes are completely open or closed. Measure downward from

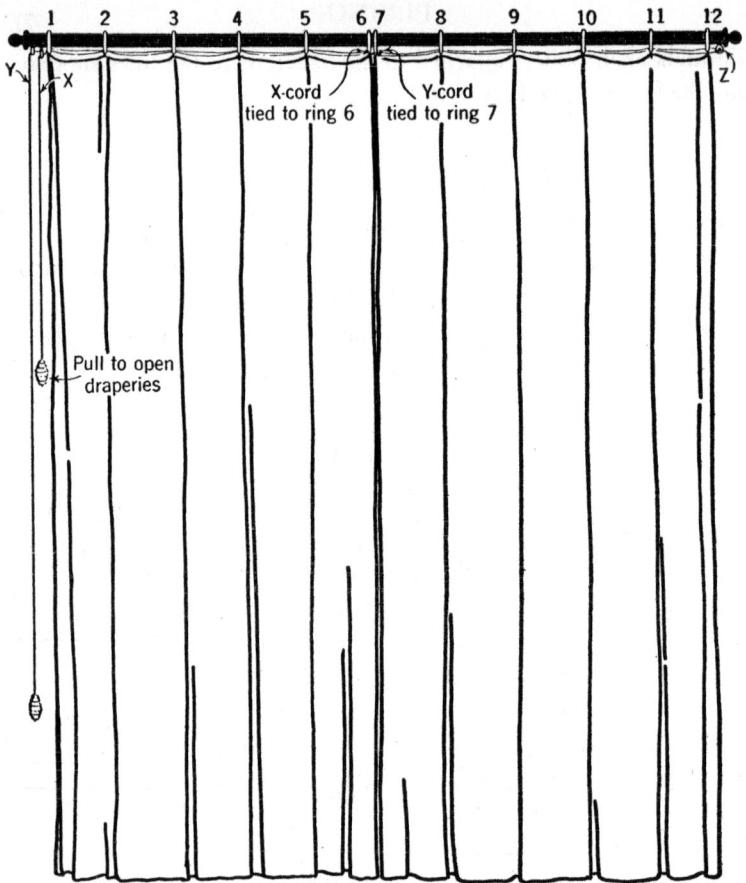

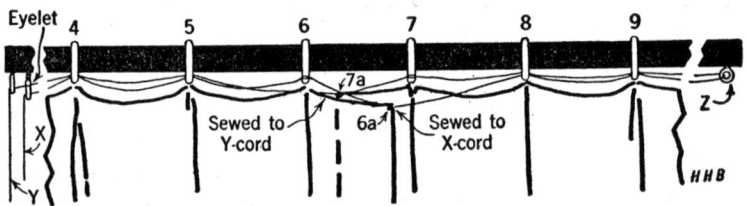

FIGURE 17. Two methods of rigging draperies to be drawn apart. The one at the bottom permits the draperies to overlap.

this height one-half the length of the portion of the curtain pole actually in use. This will give you the low point at which the other pull-cord will hang, and the point to which the other pull-cord (the high one) is brought down in order to reverse the curtains.

Hold one end of the cord at the high point just determined and, with the curtains closed, run it through X, 1, 2, 3, 4, 5, 6. Tie it to ring 6, pass it through 7, 8, 9, 10, 11, 12, Z, and back through 12, 11, 10, 9, 8, 7. With the curtains still closed, tie it to ring 7. Pass it through 6, 5, 4, 3, 2, 1 and Y. The end of the cord should then extend down to the previously determined low point. Now when you pull the X cord down to the low point, it will have opened the curtains. In the process the Y cord will have ascended to the high point. Pulling the Y cord will reverse all this. Pull one cord and then the other until you and the rest of the crew are tired playing with them! If the cords do not pull easily, put lard, axel grease or soap on the curtain rod.

The cords may be run on the outside of the curtain rings 1, 2, 3, 4, 5 and 8, 9, 10, 11, 12 instead of through them, except for the danger that they will be in sight or that they will catch. There must be no knots in the cord other than those given. At these knots, however, it is possible to attach a new cord to continue through the rest of the rigging, if you have only short lengths of cord.

Rigging a Home-made Traveller

A home-made set of travellers, although not a very satisfactory one because it is hard to operate and is noisy, may be made by using wood, iron, or wire rings on a wire or iron batten. In this case, the lap provided by all good travellers to make a good meeting may be secured by leaving the inside twelve inches of each curtain unattached to a ring, but carefully sewed to the rope which pulls the curtains. (See Figure 17.) Using the same numbers as above, and calling the loose corners 6a and 7a, the rigging would now be:

X, 1, 2, 3, 4, 5, 6 (knot), 6a (sewed), pass in front of 7 and 8, through 9, 10, 11, 12, Z, 12, 11, 10, 9, 8, 7 (knot), 7a (sewed), pass behind 6 and 5, pass through 4, 3, 2, 1, Y.

Pulleys are usually substituted for the screw eyes X, Y, and Z. The rope is threaded through a pulley and then is spliced so as to make it continuous. This pulley is screwed to the floor, or the pulley is mounted on a block, raised a foot off the floor, and tied at both ends to the floor, thus allowing for corrections due to the stretching of the ropes. This keeps the rope from twisting and from hanging down across the top, and makes it unnecessary to pass the rope through the curtain rings at all.

Drapes to be used in this manner are frequently fitted with snap-hooks instead of rings or grommets, and these hooks snapped to the rings that are permanently installed on the batten. With draperies, however, the rings are directly attached.

Rigging a French Drape, or Tab Curtain

Drapes or draperies may be so rigged as to be pulled upward and outward in what is known as a "French drape" (see Figure 18), by sewing rings across each half of the curtain in a diagonal line from the offstage edges of the curtain at the highest point of the opening desired, to a point near the floor where the two halves meet. A rope then is tied to the bottom ring of each half and, in order to insure their meeting, a weight attached to the corner below it. Even with the weights attached, it is frequently necessary for the crewmen to draw the curtain together by hand. In order to prevent their tearing out or being apparent when the cloth pulls, the rings should be attached to patches of material sewed to the curtain. The distance from the top center of the curtain to the lowest rings should be equal to, or greater than, the distance from the top point to the points at which it is desired that the lowest rings shall hang when the curtain is open. This must be the case with each ring from the point directly above it.

Much fullness must be allowed in the curtain if the outside edges touching the floor are to remain there when the curtain is opened. In order to obtain graceful folds, at least twelve rings should be

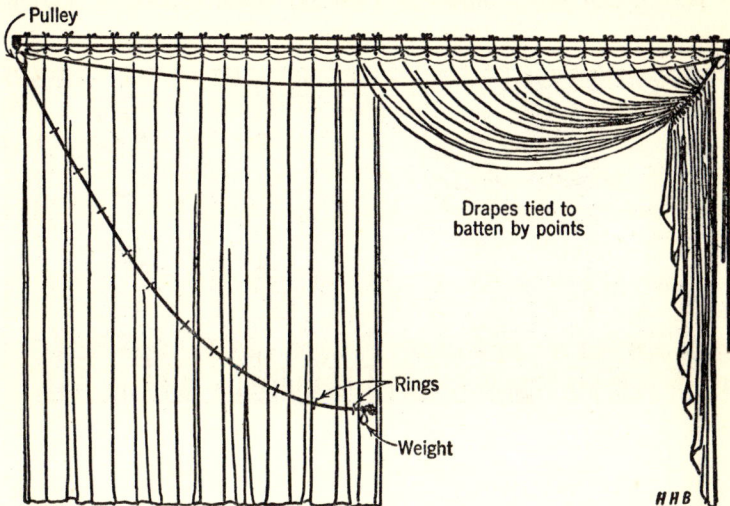

FIGURE 18. The rigging to pull a curtain upward and have it open as a French drape or tab curtain.

used on each half. A more graceful opening can also be secured by attaching the rings to the curtain in an arc.

This is sometimes referred to as a "tab curtain," which is a shortening of "tableau curtain."

RIGGING A FRENCH CURTAIN

A "French curtain" (see Figure 19) may be used anywhere, but it is rarely seen except for cloth window-shades and act drops. In an act drop it is more frequently represented, for its decorative appearance, than actually used—that is, the front curtain may be, or may look like, a French curtain, but is raised and lowered as a drop. The drapes are generally sewed so that there will be vertical gathers in the curtain, even when it fills the opening. If used as a means of flying a curtain when there is a low gridiron, it is hung straight.

The curtain, when obviously used as a French curtain, is com-

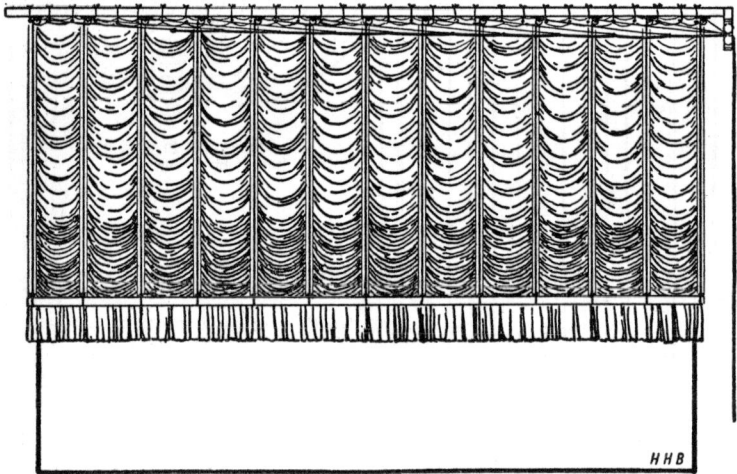

FIGURE 19. The mechanics of a French curtain. The small ropes are shown in the drawing, but are really concealed by the casings. They can be sewed to the bottom of the casings, but are shown here attached to a small batten. A flounce hangs from the batten. A double pulley is used at the head block to reduce the wear on the small ropes entering the pulley at an angle.

posed of alternate strips of gathered cloth and narrow strips of straight cloth, the latter often bearing an embroidered or painted pattern. These strips of straight cloth make the front edge of a casing in which ropes or wires run up to overhead pulleys. These ropes or wires are attached to a batten at the bottom or sewed to the bottom of the straight cloth strips. When they are pulled (over a multiple pulley down to the stage floor) the bottom of the curtain collapses against its top in an ever-increasing pile of folds. It gives an effect similar to a Venetian blind. The small ropes often are attached to a single large rope, by means of which all the ropes may be pulled simultaneously.

Sometimes rings are attached to the back of these casings, and the rope run through them instead of through the casings. This is the practice where the rigging is to be concealed. If rings are used, and the curtain is to be lifted in sight of the audience, they should be placed at least every eight or ten inches, in order to keep the folds small and graceful.

For sumptuous French curtains, the gathered material and the casing material must both be soft, thin materials or velvet, so that the folds will be especially graceful.

The celebrated curtain used in a George White production a few years ago, and the "contour" curtains installed permanently in the two Radio City theatres, are adaptations of the French curtain. They are rigged so that each line may be operated independently and thus an endless variety of folds and openings can be produced.

Leg Drops or Drapes

Leg drops or leg drapes are ones which do not extend all the way across the stage. They are usually strips six to eight feet in width and are hung in pairs, one on each side of the stage, in the approximate location of old-fashioned wings. In this location, they are used for masking the backstage and for giving the approximate effect of a cyclorama of drapes. They provide more entrances than a cyclorama, and do not have the right-angle arm battens that prevent a cyclorama being lifted into the flies without being first lowered and the arms swung back against the main batten.

A leg drop may be tied to the end of a regular batten, or it may be hung from a single line (spot-line) either directly or with a bridle. A single line will allow it to pivot. This is advantageous in that it allows the angle at which it is set to be adjusted to give any desired angle from one parallel to the footlights to one at full right angle. When at right angle to the footlights, a series of legs serve as a close approximation of a cyclorama. It is dangerous to fly a leg which swings around, however, for it may get crosswise in the flies and foul on other lines and battens. To prevent this, a snap hook is sometimes provided at one end. When the leg is to be flied, it is lowered to the stage, the snap hook attached to the line above the tie, and thus the leg is greatly reduced in width. A patented system now marketed supplies leg drapes of a cyclorama set on full length battens which may be firmly fastened in any position, but which may be moved at will as though they were on single lines. It also allows them to be slid on and off the stage freely.

A leg drop is tacked or tacked and pasted to its short batten. A leg drape is either tied to its batten or it has a short board inserted in its top seam to keep it stiff. In attaching a leg to a long batten, it needs to be tied at only its two ends.

If you are short of lines, leg drops or drapes may be hung from the same battens as the borders with which they are used. They are usually hung behind the borders.

Planning Legs and Borders

An easy way to determine the number and position of leg drops needed in the theatre with any setting is illustrated in Figure 20.

Set the tormentor in place or represent it in chalk on the floor. Draw a chalk line X-X' to represent the onstage edge of the row of leg drops, hung perpendicularly to the footlights or at any other angle you may wish. Draw another line Y-Y' at their offstage edge. This is the length of their battens from the first line.

Tie a cord to a seat in the first row of seats out-front, either an end seat or the one farthest to the side that will be occupied. Call this point A. Pass the cord over the spot on the opposite side of the stage which marks the onstage edge of the tormentor B. Determine the spot C where the cord crosses the line Y-Y', representing the offstage edge of the leg drops. This determines the stage depth of the first leg drop. Draw its position on the floor with chalk, the ends being C and D. Now pass the cord over the onstage edge of this first leg drop D, and proceed in the same way as in determining

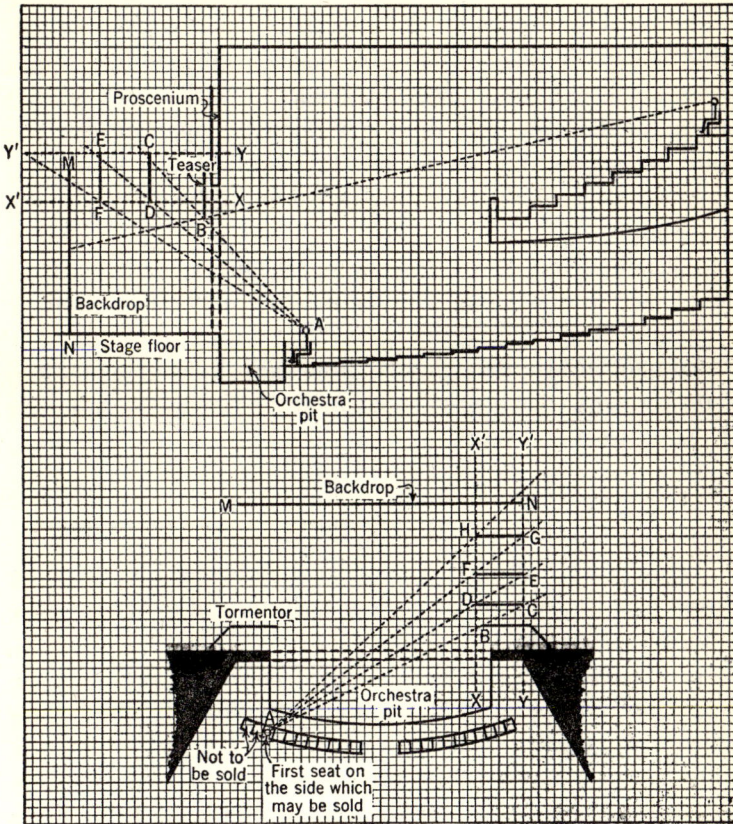

FIGURE 20. Graphical method of determining the necessary number of legs and borders for a set of drapes, as explained on page 84.

the first one until the backdrop M-N of the set is reached. Some alteration may have to be made in order to fit the sets of lines available, and some extra space may have to be allowed for a drop or leg drop that may be pushed slightly out of position. This should be done in the course of the process. This also can be plotted on graph paper, as it is in Figure 20.

Obviously it is impossible to use the cord method for determining borders, so you must either do it on graph paper or by trial and error. You will always be safe if you provide more than just enough borders. You will usually need one border for each cross-stage pair of legs, as the sight-lines in most theatres are approximately the same for legs and borders. Where the borders do not have to be adjusted for height, they may be attached to the same batten as the leg drops.

In planning borders, you must always take into account the masking of the top of a setting and the masking of the lights and all hanging scenery.

You must include the sight-lines from the balcony in your graph of the borders so that you will not cut off the view of the back wall of the set from that point.

Sky Cyclorama

Inferior practice allows a sky cyclorama to be tied directly to the curved pipe batten from which it is to hang, and sometimes even to another pipe batten at the bottom.

For a better result, lace the top and bottom of the sky cyclorama to the pipe battens with Manila rope or sash cord. The bottom batten may hang, if it is heavy enough, or if it is heavily weighted with sandbags; it may be clamped to the floor; or there may be a permanent pipe batten or a series of screw eyes or hooks to which the cyclorama may be laced at the bottom. The lacing allows the cyclorama to be stretched taut and every wrinkle disposed of.

Usually the pipe batten is hung by two sets of lines, one a complete set along the back, and the other the long and short lines of another set for the ends of the curved arms. It is possible to use a single set of lines with bridle ties, but it is then more difficult to get a taut surface.

Cycloramas sometimes run on double travellers (top and bottom), or on travellers with the bottom laced, or on double travellers that are also provided with lacing.

FLYING WITH A LOW GRIDIRON

If you have a low ceiling or a low gridiron on the stage, which will not permit drapes and drops to be flied out of sight if hung straight, trick methods must be used.

1. *Primary methods:* Several different methods of rigging drapes may partly meet the condition. Also, drops and drapes may be lowered to the stage, rolled up, and either tied off to the batten or carried offstage. Drapes may be looped over the batten supporting them and drawn upwards out of sight again.

It is sometimes possible to arrange your stage with a platform or other elevation in front of a drape or drop and to lower the drape or drop behind this with only the center line untied and raised out of sight. Use a snap hook on this center line, and replace the weight of the drop on the line by a sandbag. The center line should be marked or isolated in advance at the pin-rail so it can be located and pulled quickly without the other lines.

2. *Simple tripping of drops:* Attach the set of lines immediately behind the set used to support the drop to the bottom batten of the drop. Lift the drop as high as possible by means of its supporting lines, and then pull the second set of lines. This will cause the drop to double up, and it will then require just one-half of its height in hanging space. (See Figure 21.) Very large cloth sky cycloramas, which could not otherwise be flied out of the way, are often tripped in this manner.

3. *Two-sided drop:* With a two-sided drop, rig it like a drop to be tripped, pull the set of lines immediately behind and let the front

set down, thus reversing the drop. It will have to be painted, of course, with the top of one design at the bottom of the other. It is usually possible to pull the long and the short lines around the end of the drop in order to keep them out of sight without having to remove them. The other lines, if removed, should be fitted with snap hooks (the batten with rings for them) in order to preserve a good trim. The patented batten clamps can also be used.

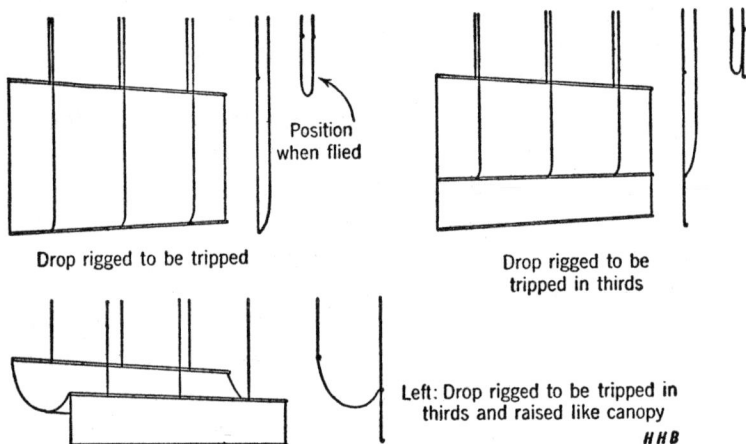

FIGURE 21. Three methods of tripping a drop.

4. *Tripping in thirds:* When simple tripping will not lift the drop high enough, a batten may be attached to the drop, preferably at the time of its construction, a third of the way up from the bottom. This must be securely pasted and tacked in order to prevent tearing, and must be handled very carefully. After a little use the point where the batten is attached will show distinctly, so it is used only when unavoidable.

Ropes are attached to the added batten or to the rings fastened to it. When the ropes are pulled, the drop will collapse to one third its height. (See Figure 21.)

5. *Tripping drapes:* The same method of tripping may be used

for drapes, except that the battens should not be tacked to the cloth, but sewed to it with cord, leaving cords six inches in length, more or less, between the drape and the batten. If the drape is only tripped double, the batten rests on the floor. When tripped in thirds, this batten should be permanently tied off at a height which will allow it to hang behind the drape in such a way that the points at which the batten is attached are neither pulled up or down, because this would reveal them. If the curtain material is not strong, patches should be sewed to the back of it at the points of attachment, or a strip of webbing "tacked" along it and the cords sewed to this.

If desired, the place of attachment may be so carefully determined that, when raised, the bottom edge of the drape becomes an extra drape border. The point at which it will hang may be marked by an ordinary knot in the lines or by the special knot making use of a stage-screw, as explained earlier in the chapter.

A drape curtain tripped in thirds makes a surprisingly good looking one as it rises and falls, particularly if the two sets of lines supporting it are some distance apart, thereby giving it the effect of a canopy.

6. *A roll drop:* An old-fashioned roller-curtain is also a possibility, but is difficult and expensive to make. The bottom batten of the drop is replaced by a wooden cylinder six to eight inches in diameter. Around one end of the cylinder is wrapped a length of rope that would reach upward to the gridiron. The loose end of the rope is then run over a pulley in the gridiron and back down to the pin-rail. When the rope is pulled it unwinds from the cylinder, thus revolving the cylinder and causing the drop to roll upon it.

FLYING A BACKWALL

In order to fly a backwall, lay the flats which are to make the wall together, face-down, on the floor. Line up the bottom edges. You may or may not lash the flats. Nail, or preferably screw, at least two long strips of batten lumber, $1'' \times 3''$, $1'' \times 4''$, or $5/4'' \times 4''$, securely to their backs, with such other cross-pieces as are needed to make the wall rigid. Usually the top batten is fastened six inches from the top of the flats and the flying lines are tied to it or attached with ceiling rings. The supporting lines never should be attached in such a way that all the weight is supported by the top battens of the flats themselves.

Flats should be clamped while being battened, with the clamps removed before flying. Cloth strips should be tacked on the back where flats join so as to prevent a spill of light through a crack.

The back wall may now have doors, windows, et cetera, set into it, pictures and curtains hung on it, and even furniture attached to it. All these objects must be securely fastened to it so that they cannot fall off.

When in use, the side walls are put in place, and the back wall dropped down and lashed to them. The back wall should be flied a few inches behind its set-up position. Such a flied back wall takes up little more room in the flies than does a drop.

Flying Complete Settings

For extremely quick changes, a complete setting may be raised into the flies. The exact method will depend upon circumstances:

1. A setting may be attached to an arm-batten with the three walls hinged and battened together. They are raised on one full set of lines and the long and short lines of another set.

2. A batten may be nailed, screwed, or tied across the front edge of the setting as well as across the back, and two full sets of lines used. This is a better method than the previous one.

3. The three walls may be attached to a strong ceiling-piece, and raised with it. The furniture may be attached to the ceiling with fine wires and raised with it, or a special floor may be attached to the setting to carry the furniture.

4. A solid floor may be built, the scenery set on this, and raised with it. Neither this nor the method last mentioned is suitable for

most amateur organizations because of the expense involved and the strong gridiron needed.

5. For a shallow setting, the side walls may be hinged to the back-wall, and swung to and from their places at the floor level. A rope should be attached to each downstage corner and tossed over the batten or run through a pulley. When the setting is collapsed ready to be lifted, this rope is tied tightly on the backwall to provide support for these free corners and to prevent the setting opening in mid-air.

These devices are ordinarily employed to drop one setting inside of another that is left standing, or that is changed during the scene that is played in the smaller one.

FLYING CEILINGS

Roll Ceiling: A roll ceiling consists of a large piece of linen (muslin is not strong enough) with battens tacked and pasted at the front and back edges, and a group of boards just long enough to hold the cloth taut when placed between the front and back battens. Each of these boards, called stretchers, has a metal plate attached at each end. An extension of the plate that is pierced by a hole permits it to be bolted to the batten. When the stretchers are bolted into place and the side edges of the linen are tacked to the outside stretchers, the ceiling becomes one large flat.

To assemble the ceiling, lay the cloth painted side down. The bolt-ends and the wing-nuts in the battens used to hold the pieces of the frame together will then point upwards. Place the stretchers across the ceiling and bolt them in place. Turn the sides of the canvas up over the outside stretchers, pull the cloth taut, and tack the sides temporarily every six inches. Such tacks *must not* be driven clear down. If they are, the cloth will be torn in taking the ceiling apart after the production. Tie or snap a set of lines to the ceiling rings along the back, and another at the front, and then lift the ceiling into position.

In storage, you may suspend the ceiling by one set of lines. In use, tie off the front set of lines permanently. Lift the ceiling by the back set. As you lower the ceiling into position, it will swing into nearly its correct place. Just as it is about to be dropped on the setting, pull slightly the other set of tied-off lines in order to allow all four edges to come down together.

Book Ceiling: A book ceiling is composed of two very large flats hinged to fold face together, with the joint concealed by a painted cloth strip (a cloth dutchman). It cannot be taken apart for moving.

To fly a book ceiling, attach the center rings of your book ceiling to a set of lines and lift it clear of the floor. Then tie sets of lines to the front and back edges. Always lift it by the center lines in order to prevent opening the book too wide and thus breaking the joint. In use, the front and back sets of lines are permanently tied-off, and the center set used to lift the book. As the ceiling is lowered into position the tied-off sets are pulled slightly in the same manner as the roll ceiling.

General Caution: If any part of the canvas appears to come down on the top of flats in such a manner that a hole may be punched in it, put in a temporary cross-piece of lumber to sustain its weight at that point. However, if the ceiling is strong and the pressure even, the back batten can be placed upstage of the back wall. The weight is supported by the cloth, and this helps to pull the ceiling taut.

It is seldom desirable to have the front edge of the ceiling extend forward even with the front of the setting as it then shuts off valuable lighting angles.

In case your ceiling is not deep enough for your setting, rest it on the back wall and lower your teaser until it conceals the front edge of the ceiling, use two ceilings, or use flats added to the ceiling.

Because the center rope of each set of lines will interfere, either type of ceiling will prevent the dropping of any scenery between the lines supporting it, even when flied. If scenic material must be dropped while the ceiling is flied ready for use, it will be necessary to drop the ceiling to the floor each time it is used in order to snap or unsnap the lines which tip the ceiling. Tie weights, usually sand-bags, to these free lines. A method of flying that avoids this loss of time is explained in the section on flying a drape cyclorama earlier in the chapter.

FLYING FURNITURE AND PROPERTIES

Where there is more free space in the flies than backstage, furni-ture and other properties may be flied during scene changes.

1. Objects to be flied may be permanently attached to a pipe or wood batten with invisible wires and thus let down into exact posi-tion.

2. Each line of a set of lines may be used for a different object.

3. Battens may have hooks fastened on them, may be lowered in a scene change, and then furniture and other properties suspended from the hooks. Snap hooks are the safest attachments. Rings or screw eyes should be attached to the objects to be flied.

It is possible to have one set of props removed and another at-tached to the same batten during a scene shift.

SUSPENDED PROPERTIES OR FIXTURES

Sometimes objects, such as lighting fixtures, are suspended visibly in the air during a performance. Suspend these by spot lines, or by snatch lines from battens. Where the support must be invisible, use fine wires or fishline. If needed, holes may be cut in the ceiling for such lines. The hole should be cut through wood; that is, the hole should be bored through a permanent or temporary cross-piece that is a part of the ceiling. If it is put through cloth alone, the line may tear the cloth. In a book ceiling, the hole is usually put in at the joint. Both stage cable and a rope may be run through the hole or, with light-weight electrical fixtures, the cable alone may be run through the hole and support the weight of the fixture.

COUNTERWEIGHTING

If a suspended drop or object is heavy, counterweight it so that one man can easily fly it. If you are not fortunate in possessing a theatre equipped with a counterweight system, tie sandbags *into* the lines, knotting the lines themselves around the sandbag rope. This makes the weights, should they become loosened, slide down the line instead of falling, as would be the case if they were tied *onto* the rope. There also is less chance of their loosening. Stage hardware firms have special clamps for attaching sandbags to lines. A combination trimblock and counterweight is explained earlier in the chapter.

A multiple pulley device can be substituted for counterweighting, but it has no important advantage for the stage, and is much more complicated to rig and operate. Its only advantage would be when a line had at one time a heavy weight attached to it and at another time none, as, for example, the lifting of an actor from the stage in *Peter Pan.*

To the Performance Flymen:

You will receive a cue-sheet detailing your work with the exact cues for it. When a cue comes at the end of a scene, ordinarily you will wait for the stage manager to signal "Strike!" before lifting or lowering a curtain. If you are in a position in the fly gallery to see the front curtain, you may be told to take your cue from the curtain. Be particularly careful if curtain calls are being taken, not to lift the drop before the final curtain call.

If you raise or lower a curtain during a scene, do it evenly and at a pre-determined speed. See that it is counterweighted so that this can be done.

In raising a curtain always be careful to see that furniture or other properties are not fouling it; and before lowering it, see that no person or object is beneath it.

You will usually have several sets of lines tied off in a trim. Inform yourself about this, and do not disturb the bottom trim unless you have to. See the section on Trim earlier in the chapter.

To the Curtain Man:

You will operate all curtains that are handled from the floor of the stage and that begin or end a scene, or that are pulled during the action. There may be only one curtain or there may be many, as an asbestos curtain which rises fifteen to five minutes before the performance, a front curtain which is used only at the beginning and the end of the performance, an act drop which is behind the front curtain and is used between scenes, individual curtains for some scenes, and special curtains, such as those composed of gauze, operated from the floor.

You will be given a cue-sheet, and will usually be warned and then given the cues by the stage manager or prompter. You will take up the front curtain and act drop on instructions from the stage manager. While your cue-sheet will give you the curtain cues, often you will take the exact cue from the prompter, as there may be a psychological moment at which the curtain must be lowered in order to get an emotional effect. You will always ascertain from your cue-sheet in advance of this hand cue from the prompter whether the curtain is to be medium, fast, slow, or a combination of such speeds. For example, it may move quickly until it becomes visible to the audience, then move slowly, and then move moderately fast for the last six feet of the fall. This depends upon the play and the theatre. A slow falling curtain should be accelerated the last four feet, unless, however, the chief point of interest, for example, is Salome lying on the floor with the head of John the Baptist on a platter, when the acceleration should begin later. Likewise, a slowly rising curtain at the opening of a scene is speeded up after it has revealed most of the setting. The same methods are used for curtains drawn to the sides of the stage on travellers. At all stages of handling the curtains you must move them smoothly and evenly without any jerks. *Be sure you pull the curtains in the right direction!*

CHAPTER VI

THE STAGE MANAGER AND ASSISTANTS

To the Stage Manager:

You are responsible for everything in connection with the performance of a play except the interpretations of the actors. Your various assistants will check certain matters in the course of their work, but you must recheck the same things to whatever extent you can. You should personally check all the more important conditions and not entirely rely upon your assistants for their correctness.

You may have to perform some of the tasks here assigned to assistants, such as those of the director of scene shifting, checker of scene shifting, call boy, timer, signal board operator, and curtain man. In a simple production in the professional theatre, the stage manager does all such work. He also does much of the advance planning and directing that is here assigned to others. You should mark in red on your cue-sheet (see Figures 1 to 5) all such tasks which you are to handle during the performance.

In addition to such tasks, there are certain other jobs which you should not delegate. Accordingly, you should reach the theatre at least an hour in advance of performance in order to:

1. Check the set that is standing in order to see that it has not been damaged, that the lashing is correct, that all the walls are secure, and that all the doors will swing without moving the setting. If the set has to be assembled each night, you will check it after it is assembled.

2. Check all scenery in the scene docks.

3. Check with the electrician to make sure that all lights will burn, that they will still light the correct places, that they will not show

through the setting, that the gelatines are in good condition and that those which are to be changed during the performance are ready and in good condition, that dimmers are correctly hooked up and will operate, and that all electricians have their cue-sheets.

4. Check with the property master in order to make sure that all properties are in hand and placed, and that none is damaged. Be especially careful to check all the properties located out of sight on the stage, as well as those that are located offstage. Be sure that the property master and his assistants have their cue-sheets.

5. Check with the costume master in order to see that all costumes are in hand and in good condition, especially those for changes.

6. Check with the effect master in order to see that all effects are ready and working, and that he has his cue-sheet.

7. Check with the flymen in order to see that all curtains are working, that none is fouled, and that the flymen have their cue-sheets.

8. Check the stage markings, if they are of chalk, in order to make sure that they are visible.

9. Check the arrangements for the quick changes of costumes.

10. Check all the special mechanical devices in use.

11. Check the presence of the actors, or obtain a report on them from the call boy, half an hour before the curtain.

12. Check the presence of the technical staff, and make sure that they all have their cue-sheets.

13. Check the presence of the call boys, signal board operator and prompter, and see that they have their cue-sheets.

14. Check with the make-up master to make sure that all make-ups are progressing properly a quarter-hour before the curtain.

15. Check the presence of the musicians and see that they have their cue-sheets.

16. Check the presence of "beginners" during the overture.

For each scene after the first, you will have a check-list showing all the people who must report to you before the curtain may be raised. This will include all those mentioned in the preliminary check-list, except those who have reported as present, and it may include actors who have to make costume changes or other persons engaged in special tasks. Insist upon all such people reporting to you—get them into the habit of doing so at the dress rehearsals. Nothing is more ridiculous than for the stage manager to call to the cast, "Are all the actors on the stage?" or "Is everybody ready?" It shows the same degree of intelligence as does the public speaker who bellows, "All those who can't hear me, please raise their hands!"

Check off the names as the people report to you. Do what other checking of the scene-shift you can, but always be at or near a known location so that the crew will know where to find you. Your check list will normally include:

1. Director of scene shifting, or checker, or both.
2. Electrician.
3. Property master.
4. Call Boy.
5. Anyone having cues in the first three minutes of the scene, as the effect master, the backstage musicians, and the actors having changes to make (as reported by the call boy).

You will give the signal for the raising of each curtain, and also may "take the curtain down." If the curtain rises without music, you will give the signal for it at the exact scheduled second, which may be no more than three minutes after the time stated in the program. When there is an orchestra, the curtain may be delayed more than the three minutes in order to accommodate a long overture. The overture, in this case, however, must start at or before the announced time for the curtain. If it is the custom in your theatre, you first may give a signal to the switchboard operator to start dimming the house-lights, and then the signal for the curtain at the completion of the dimming. Or you may give a noise cue, such as chimes, three knocks (European custom) or three gongs, in which case footlights go up on the first cue, house-lights out on the second, and the curtain up on the third gong. You may precede the signal for the curtain with one to the lobby. You will repeat the knock or gong cue each time the curtain rises. Knocks or gongs may be used at the opening of each act, but not more than one such sound should be used for the opening of subsequent scenes within an act.

If you take your cue from the orchestra, you will signal it when to start. On quick changes you often signal it when to stop, but naturally you will not do so for the overture. If there is applause, you will wait until the peak of it is passed, or until the leader has taken a bow, and then start the curtain signals. Do not raise the curtain until the audience is quiet. The house-lights are often brought down to half-light during the overture.

If you are to give the signal for the lowering of the curtain, you will have the cue for this marked in red on your combination cue-sheet, and you will learn the exact psychological moment for the curtain effect wanted. This cue is best given, however, by the prompter.

You will be told when and how to take curtain calls. You may take them at the end of acts, or only at the end of the play. You may raise the curtain for these calls, or they may be taken between the curtains. If the latter is the case, have the curtains held so that there is a passage for the actors at the center between the two parts, but so that the audience cannot see the setting; or pull them aside in a French drape and let the actors walk into the opening with part of the setting in sight behind them. Usually, you will take as many curtain calls as you can, but will space them so that each one after the first seems to be the appropriate response to an ovation. Never take any more calls than are justified by the applause, however, unless told to do so by the director. Stop them when the applause diminishes, even though you may not have taken all that have been rehearsed. The director will rehearse the curtain calls, and all extra ones are to be taken identically like the last one that was planned. Do not allow the actors to pull the director onstage for a curtain call unless he signifies his willingness to go. Even then he should never take a call with any actors on the stage in make-up, for he will look like a ghost among them.

Keep the house-lights off throughout the curtain calls, and bring them on as the applause lessens. If another call is demanded, dim out the lights again before taking it.

You will signal "Strike!" the minute you are ready to change scenery.

During the dress rehearsals you will make notes of all errors made, of any articles that are missing, and of any necessary changes in the plans or in connection with the scenery. Report them to the people responsible for making the changes.

Heavy units may be placed on rolling wagons with the flats that form the walls surrounding it nailed or screwed to the wagon. Even other nearby flats may be hinged to these. Such devices may sometimes be planned at the last minute without disturbing the general plan. Skids (large round metal disks attached to the bottom of articles in much the same way as casters), or actual casters, either ordinary or ball-bearing, may be added at the discretion of the stage-crew. It is usually necessary to insert wedges under rolling platforms to prevent their shifting position in performance.

In handling any such special devices, learn of their weak points and see that the entire crew knows of them. Be sure not to handle them at their weak points of construction. Do not push or pull a wagon by the flats attached to it, but nail ropes to the platform.

You will train your performance crew to do the scene shifting as rapidly as possible, and according to the written plans. The ideal duration of time for a scene change within an act is 30 to 45 seconds.

To the Director of Scene Shifting or Stage Carpenter (Assistant Stage Manager):

In a simple production the supervision of scene shifting is one of the tasks of the stage manager. In a more elaborate one, it is better to put it in charge of an assistant.

You will receive a complete scene shifting plot arranged in the order in which the tasks are to be done. During the scene-shifts at the dress rehearsals, you will make no corrections and give no suggestions to workers. As soon as the shift is made, you have reported to the stage manager, and he has pulled the curtain (in order to time the change), call the crew together and make the corrections, calling attention to everything that was slow, forgotten, done in the wrong order, or that must be slowed down or speeded up. Make corrections on the plots to correspond with the re-assignments of tasks, and with any other such necessary changes. Do not complain about the work of your people at this first rehearsal, for it is to be expected that some errors will occur, and your complaints will then not have the force they may need at later rehearsals. Your remarks should be entirely dispassionate and impersonal. You need not even mention individuals by name if you see that they have discovered their own errors or now realize them. You should call for a report of any difficulties that have arisen, and plan a way to avoid them. Be sure to check on the position of materials backstage in addition to that of the properties just placed onstage.

At the first dress rehearsal, if there is more than one of them, the director will allow you to use the stage, probably, for the purpose of making these corrections. At subsequent rehearsals you will follow the same practice of omitting corrections during the shift, merely noting them for later discussion. After the first rehearsal you will not be allowed to delay the rehearsal by corrections on the stage, so you will have to call the workers together elsewhere.

In performance, you will make corrections during the changes and will also note them and tell the worker about them after the performance.

You will check the setting as it is assembled and, when the last piece is placed, notify the stage manager and leave the stage. You will notify him accordingly even though there is a scene checker repeating the same work. The presence of the checker is no reflection on you, for each of you will approach it from a different point of view, and you should welcome the double-check as a measure of safety. It in no way lessens your responsibility. You are responsible personally for a stage that is not correctly set.

You may or may not help with the change. It should be possible at least for you to bring on an object when you first enter the set.

Your cue for the scene change will be the stage manager's "Strike!"

To the Assistant Stage Manager in charge of stage markings:

As the trial set-up is made and approved, you will mark with chalk the location of all key pieces, using a different color for each scene or different numerals for each scene. Indicate in your marks the corners of objects and the direction in which they extend from these marks. Make the marks heavy so that walking on them will not obliterate them. On the night of dress rehearsal, have a plan ready for the permanent markings, and have the materials for it in hand. On some stages, only chalk marks are permitted. They must be renewed every day. They can be made to last longer by dampening the floor and making them while the floor is still wet. On some stages, lines are painted on the floor or ground cloth with scene paint. Some theatres use brass headed tacks, employing a different number or a different grouping of them for the different scenes. In some places, cardboard shapes are glued or tacked to the floor. You will learn the method you are to use from the technical director or stage manager. You will make certain that, with the lights to be used, the markings are perfectly clear and distinctive. In a black-out change, instead of marks, luminous paint may be used, either on the floor or on tacks driven into the floor.

As each set is approved by the director at dress rehearsal, make permanent your markings for it. Co-operate with the lighting and properties departments by doing marks for them as well as for the scenery. Remove the temporary marks after the rehearsal.

Be on hand at subsequent dress rehearsals, in order to make the corrections. Keep out of the way of the crew so that they cannot fall back on you by asking what the marks mean, but be in a position to see the crew members when they are uncertain about the marks or when they make errors in connection with them. Make notes of these errors and explain or clarify the markings. Your refusal to help in the set-up is in order to compel the crew to learn the meaning of the marks and not to depend upon you for it. They will learn from their mistakes better than by your help at the time of the rehearsal.

If the markings are still confusing, even at the final dress rehearsal, and cannot be clarified, or if the technical director asks you to do so, be on hand at performances to supervise the placing of objects.

You are under the direction of the director of scene shifting or of the stage manager. The work often is done by one or the other of these officers as a part of their duties.

To the Grip Crews:

A "grip," or "stage carpenter," is a stagehand who handles articles classed as scenery as distinguished from properties. "Scenery" usually means any element of the setting which in actual life would be permanently affixed to its location—walls of houses, columns, doors, set walls, trees, bushes, et cetera. A more practical distinction between scenery and properties in the non-professional theatre, since it is not hampered by union rules, is to class as scenery all objects, except furniture, that require two or more workers to move. The work of the flyers has been separated herein from that of the grips, though this work is usually handled under the same superintendent and even by the same crew when the pin-rail is on the level of the stage floor.

The set-up grips and performance grips are usually the same persons, but in performance you will work under the stage manager or the director of scene shifting (his assistant), while in all preparation for it you will work under the set-up superintendent.

In the set-up, you will place all the permanent pieces of scenery. You will then set each scene in order to test it. Progressively as you complete them, you will store each set according to the plans, then set the first scene, and leave it standing, provided there are no contrary rules, as there are in unionized houses.

A crew of grips is usually made up of three men, two of them to handle the flats, and the third to do the lashing and direct the crew.

LASHING

A lash line of soft No. 7 or No. 8 sash cord should be put through the lash eye in the upper right-hand corner (from the rear) of each flat. It should be cut just long enough to miss the floor when allowed to hang. When not lashed to another flat, the line should be tied at the tie-off cleat so that it will not swing. This line is used to lash the flat to the adjacent one.

There are various kinds of lash cleats. Usually those which stick straight out at the side of the stile and are flush with it are the most satisfactory. Some kinds of lash cleats are made with hooks which are useful when there is no room for slipping the rope under the flat type, as where a door stile comes down too close to the outside stile, or where the door stile is the outside stile of the flat. If there is room for them, place these cleats on the inside narrow edge of the stile; if not, they may be put on the back, but the flat must then be handled very carefully in order to prevent the tearing or marking of other flats.

All this needed equipment should have been put on in the shop, but you may find that it was not.

In lashing the flats, toss the rope loosely over the highest left-hand lash cleat of the adjoining flat. Cast the rope so it will have slack, holding your hand well to the right. The moment it touches the canvas, or just a fraction of a second before it does so, pull it sharply. With practice, you will be able to do this every time you try. Then pass it alternately over the other lash cleats, pulling the rope as tightly as possible just before it reaches the tie-off cleats. Pass it under both of the tie-off cleats and then slip the free end over, back of, and under the taut rope—between the tie-off cleats and the lash cleat above. Pull this down in order to give increased tightness, and tie it with a slip knot. Such a knot can be untied with one hand.

In lashing flats around an angle of the setting, always lap the downstage flat over the upstage one so that if any light should show through the resulting crack it will not be visible to the audience.

Where you are making a straight wall with flats that are warped, clamps may help to hold them together evenly. S-hooks and battens, stop cleats, and hinges also may be used.

If two flats are lashed with their backs at a 90° angle, one flat may have a tendency to fall backwards and so to slip off the lashing hardware. In this case add "stop blocks," small pieces of wood nailed or screwed seven-eighths of an inch from the edge of the stile of the flat behind which the other flat falls. Removable stop-blocks may be made of pieces of scrap lumber with six-penny box-nails driven through them, and can be pressed into position by hand.

Moving Flats

Flats are not heavy—one man can easily carry all the material used in two or three flats—but their size and shape makes them unwieldy to handle. However, any woman can move, or "run," a twelve-foot flat alone, any man or any tall woman can handle a sixteen-foot flat, and a two-fold is not a great deal more difficult to handle than a single flat. The secret of successfully running them is the use of leverage. Place one hand just as high as possible on the edge of the flat and the other hand just as low as possible. By this means the flat can be moved about freely so long as it is carried erect. If it is necessary to tip the flat while running it, stand on one side of it and tip it downward toward you. Do not lift a corner off the floor if you can avoid it, and never lift the far corner!

The one exception to this rule, "never lift the far corner of a flat," is in stacking. In this case you can run your corner tight against the pack of flats, balance the weight so that the flat will tend to fall toward the pack, then raise the far corner an inch or two and pivot the flat toward the pack as it falls in that direction. Have someone ready to catch the other edge of the flat the first time or two you try this, for it is almost impossible for one man to keep a flat from falling once it becomes unbalanced.

To stack flats in a pack against a wall, stand the first flat at such an angle that it cannot tip forward. Stack all subsequent flats tightly against this one at the bottom. This is particularly important in stacking flats in storage, for if they are stacked loosely they will warp.

If the flat is to be laid on the floor, manipulate it so that it is standing where you will want the bottom rail when the flat is down, then "foot it" by placing your foot behind one corner and getting someone else to put theirs behind the opposite corner. Then let the flat fall. The pressure of the air will allow it to float gently down into position, but be prepared for a dust storm! Naturally, this will not work with flats having big openings. One person can foot a flat by jumping quickly to the center of it and placing the feet, spread apart as far as possible against the bottom on the side opposite to the direction in which it is to fall, but even a slight miscalculation will allow the flat to pivot as it falls.

It is safer to have a helper in setting a flat upright, because of the danger of its getting out of control when it approaches an upright position. First turn the flat on its side. Now foot it at the bottom corner and pull on the other bottom corner near your chin. Your helper should lift and toss the top of the flat as you pull on the bottom. He then runs in to grab the side of it nearest him as it assumes an upright position. Except for the difficulty of keeping the flat under control, one strong man can up-end a six-foot-wide sixteen-foot two-fold in this manner.

BACKINGS

Every opening of the setting must be masked so that the audience cannot see the backstage through it. Do not count on the fact that the backstage is dark, or that the door will mask its own opening.

Light from the footlights, or reflected light from the stage floor, will be sufficient to make people visible who are moving behind the opening, and the opening of a door attracts the attention of the audience to that spot. Only those members of the audience who are above the door opening will be unable to see over its top. Backings serve the further useful purpose of keeping actors and crewmen out of the entrance-way, or at least serve to make them conscious that, in case they stand in the entrance, they may expect the door to be opened on them at any minute.

A backing may be a single flat that is at least a third again as high as the opening, or it may be a hinged book or two-fold of the same extra height. Drapes, et cetera, also may be used for the purpose. The single flat is either lashed, hinged, or pin-hinged to the set, or held in place by a stage-brace or other similar device.

A hinged two-fold is the easiest backing to handle, since it stands alone when in use or when pulled out of the way in a change, and takes up less room in use. It consists of two small flats hinged together, with the hinges covered with a painted muslin strip, set up at a 90° to 150° angle, the inside edge touching the flat a short distance behind the opening. If used with a door, the first flat must be at least several inches wider than the door, and some device must be used to prevent the door swinging against it, such as a sandbag placed behind the door; or the masking must be far enough back so that it will not be struck by the door when opened.

The backing may be painted the same color as the set, or it may be painted differently. Standard masking pieces may be made up and used for any inconspicuous opening without repainting them from play to play.

The same type of backing may be used for a window opening, in which case it is usually painted blue or white. With a strong enough blue light, any light colored flat may be used. In a semi-permanent setting where the same opening is used for interior and exterior, a light color will do for both.

The larger the opening, the more care should there be taken with the masking. A piece of furniture, or a picture hung on the backing, will suggest another room.

In placing the backing, always see that it completely serves its purpose. Usually, when you can see the footlights past the backing, you may be sure someone in the audience can see you. For placing the masking with the curtains closed, a mark must be placed on the floor for it. Backings should be tested just before the curtain rises.

A makeshift backing for a door in a sidewall can consist of a piece of composition board tacked on the back of the door, extending eighteen inches above it, and painted a contrasting color.

INSETS

Insets are doors, windows, fireplaces, flats, et cetera, that are set into the openings of flats. They may be inserted in order to form architectural features, or in order to conceal the openings. They are of two kinds: box insets and flat insets or plugs.

Box insets, such as doors and windows, have strap hinges on the jambs, with the lower flange screwed on tightly, but with the other flange left loose. The box is set into the opening so that the frame rests lightly against the flat with the bottom resting on the floor or on the bottom batten of the opening, and the top flanges of the hinges are pulled downward until they bind tightly against the back of the upright boards, or "stiles," of the flat in which the box is inserted.

The two hinges are all that is needed to hold the door in the flat, but it may be necessary to use a stage-brace in order to make its position firmly upright and to prevent its shaking when the door is opened. Also a heavy door shutter will shift a flapped door frame off the square each time it is opened. It must be well braced. A door to be slammed should be braced free of the setting. Stage-braces are used, and the flap-hinges are not used.

Always be certain before inserting the box that the flange of the hinge is laid out flat on the jamb and not collapsed double. A box with a shutter or other solid covering of the opening will require two men to place—one to put it in and the other to tighten the hinges.

A plug is inserted to conceal an opening or part of it. It is usually put in from the back, and some stop device used to prevent it from falling forward through the opening. There are catches at the back to hold it in place. Be sure that the surface is flush with the surface of the flat. Tin rims are sometimes put around the opening to conceal the crack.

PARALLEL PLATFORMS

A "parallel" is a folding platform support. It consists of a group of wooden frames similiar to uncovered flats hinged together in such a way that they form a hollow square or rectangle to support a floor, but can be folded to be stored. It is the standard form of platform for use on the stage because of the small space it takes when stored. A short length of sash cord should be attached to one of the frames with the two ends of the cord free. When the parallel is folded, the rope is tied around the framework in such a way that there is no possibility of the parallel unfolding. It can then be leaned against a wall in any desired position with no danger of its falling down and damaging itself or other scenery.

STAIRS

"Two-steps," "three-steps," and other small groups of steps ("boy" steps) are usually built to stand alone. Longer runs of stairs, however, are usually made without support, consisting merely of the step stringers, or "sleepers," with the treads and risers attached. Hooks are then attached to the top of the stringers and these are slipped into slots in the platform to which the stairs lead. This is the case when the top step is to be at the same level as the platform. If the stairs are to end with the last step before the platform is reached, stop-cleats or other stage hardware are attached to the bottom of the sleeper at its top end, a short batten is nailed on the face of the platform in such a position that the top of the stringer will rest on it. The stop-cleats slip behind this batten and lock the steps into position.

When boy steps have a tendency to tip or slip away from the platform by which they stand, they can be attached to it temporarily with pin-hinges.

Some means of descent from platforms must be provided backstage. Regular stairs can be used when there is plenty of space. Ship ladders will take up less room. Be sure to build a hand rail. Rung ladders and step ladders should be a last resort.

At Performance

You will receive precise instructions for making the scene shifts, either in the form of a written explanation of the work to be performed by your group, or in the form of a scene shifting plot giving specific instructions to each crew member by name or title.

Reach the theatre at the time designated by the stage manager, report to him the minute you enter, and show him that you have your instructions.

You will be given definite cues to listen for, or will be given an oral or visual warning for a scene change. Go immediately and noiselessly to your position at the object to be placed, at the scenery to be removed, or at the entrance by which you will enter the stage. Instantly on cue, whether it be a lighting cue, a curtain cue, or the stage manager's "Strike!" begin your work. Complete it as quickly as possible, working rapidly, but not so much so as to make you bump into objects or have to handle scenery recklessly. If you have too much to do in the time allotted for a change, report the fact to the stage manager or the director of scene shifting. Be ready accordingly to help if you can when anyone else calls for assistance. Report this assistance to the director of scene shifting or the stage manager to be entered on the scene shifting plots.

As soon as you have finished your jobs, leave the stage and check over the tasks you have done to be sure that they were accurately and completely performed. Wait in the wings in case extra help may be needed. As soon as the curtain rises, leave the wings free for the use of the actors. You must not try to see the show from the wings. If you want to see it, ask permission at the first dress rehearsal to go out front during certain scenes. Thereafter you must be content only to hear it. It is very distracting to the actors to see faces in the wings, just as it is to hear whispering or talking backstage!

After a rehearsal or performance, no crewman should leave the theatre until he has been excused by his direct superior, who should have already secured a release through the line of officers up to the stage manager.

To the Effect Master and Staff:

Yours is a position requiring ingenuity. There is no limit to the variety of sound you may be expected to produce. Frequently you can provide yourself with the genuine implement for making the noise called for, but just as frequently you cannot. While there are standard methods for making certain sounds, others will necessitate much experimentation. In the professional theatre most of the effect machines are electrically controlled and are operated by the electrician from the switchboard. The others are taken care of by the property department. In the amateur theatre the effects usually are operated by hand, and by a special worker. References are given in the index for the standard effects that will be found described in books on stagecraft. Phonograph records now can be purchased for a great many sounds, including chimes, mobs, trains, storms, and nightingales.

Radio stations are good sources for sound machines. You may be able to borrow things with which to produce effects, or get ideas there for making them. You should realize, however, that effects created for the radio will not always give the same impression in the absence of a microphone.

All effects should be tried in the theatre in association with the voices of the actors, as they do not always sound the same or of the same intensity alone as when they are in competition with voices. Soft sounds can be amplified slightly by making them at the opening of the sound tube of a phonograph with the sound-arm removed.

A special cue-sheet for effects will be provided for your use, one similar to those here reproduced (see Figures 22 and 23), or you will prepare it as explained in Chapter III.

Assemble the machines as closely together backstage as is practicable, at a spot where they will not be interfered with by the crew or the actors, and where they will not be tempting as playthings! You should enforce an absolute rule of "Hands Off!" Between performances, store all those which are small or breakable in some locked room. Test them every night before the performance.

You may receive the sound cues from the stage manager or by a light from the switchboard. Usually, however, you will listen for them yourself. You may need an assistant in a location closer to the setting than yours, especially for stop cues on machine guns, thunder, and other noisy effects, or where he can look onstage if you must take an action cue. He may give signals either with his hands or with a flashlight.

When a number of cues fall closely together, you will need a reader to give you the cues and directions.

Always read the part of the play embracing your cues in order to learn the special effect expected of the sounds—whether they help form the emotional background, have a dramatic effect of their own, or heighten a dramatic moment in the scene, each condition varying the nature of the effect and the manner in which it is to be given.

Some special devices that have been developed for amateur performances, and that illustrate the required ingenuity, are the following:

Water running from a hose— Old gelatines rattled and crackled in a box; stiff wrapping paper crumpled.

THREE CORNERED MOON
EFFECTS

ACT I

Just before curtain.   **VICTROLA**

WARN: "But he mustn't bodder me."
CUE: "Stevens to psychoanalyze her."   DOOR SLAM

WARN: "You're so damn unnatural."
CUE: "Why not?" and a pause.   TELEPHONE

WARN: "Tied up for the day."
CUE: "I'm through!" Hangs up. Opens grip.   TELEPHONE

WARN: "Somebody ought to put a stop to it."
CUE: "I'll drop in to see you."   DOORBELL

WARN: "Aren't you taking a trunk?"
CUE: "Lafayette three-two-thousand."   DOOR SLAM

WARN: "I was always so happy in college."
CUE: "Spoil my one small pleasure in
      having had a zenith."   DOORBELL
CUE: "I don't want to compromise."   DOORBELL
CUE: "What, another one?"   DOOR SLAM

WARN: "I'd rather see you dead..."
CUE: "And different."   DOORBELL
CUE: "Give me that!"   DOOR SLAM

WARN: "What about gas?"
CUE: "Taxi? I'll be right out."   DOOR SLAM

WARN: "No cars, no college, no clothes."
CUE: "He's so practical, he drives me wild!"DOORBELL
CUE: "This is for passersby, you dumbbell." DOOR SLAM

WARN: "How about it, Elizabeth?"
CUE: "How much do you earn?"   DOORBELL

WARN: "What do you want?"
CUE: "Take cow vay,too."   DOOR SLAM

WARN: "You'll have to get rid of Jenny."
CUE: "Jenny, come out!" "I'm coming."   CRASH

FIGURE 22. A page from the effect cue-sheet for a simple production.

Drawbridge chains falling— A box of heavy bolts, nuts and iron washers poured into a partly filled box.

Carriage rumbling over cobblestones— An irregularly surfaced barrel rolled along the floor, containing a roll of muslin to give it weight and make its movements slightly erratic.

Rain— A keg two-thirds full of nails, rolled back and forth on a heavily padded floor.

Automobile door slam— Volume XXIII of the 11th Edition of the *Encyclopædia Britannica* dropped on the floor.

Automobile motor— A vacuum cleaner started and a non-soundproof door immediately closed between it and the stage, or with a heavy cloth immediately thrown over it; an electric kitchen beater started and allowed to run while being carried away from the stage to suggest the automobile driving away. A piece of cardboard lightly touched against the beater to simulate gear shifting.

The chiming of a new clock, and again, the same clock grown old and "tinny"— A set of dinner chimes struck with a padded mallet, and, for the old clock, struck with a fountain pen or the eraser end of a pencil with the eraser removed.

Church bells, playing a tune— A set of three-quarter inch angle-iron bars cut into lengths of 36, 39, 42, 45, 48, 51, 54, 57, 60, 63, 66, 69 and 72 inches to give an approximate tempered chromatic scale. If a perfectly tuned scale of bells is needed, all the bars except the first one can be cut a quarter inch too long and then filed until they are in exact pitch. Hermann Helmholtz, in *On the Sensations of Tones,* gives the relationship of the vibration rate of the untempered scale of eight notes as being that of 24, 27, 30, 32, 36, 40, 45, 48. This would, of course, be the inverse relationship of the lengths of the angle-iron bars necessary to produce the notes of this scale, because the shorter the length of the iron, the higher the rate of vibration.

To the Head Call Boy:

There is seldom a production elaborate enough to require a head call boy, a cue-sheet maker, and performance call boys, but should

CUE SHEET FOR WORKER 1
ACT I

As Della puts down tray to answer telephone, LOWER, FAINTER
TELEPHONE. CONTINUE UNTIL JO EXITS UNDER STAIRS.

Just after the second telephone ring of the second set,
BUZZER.

"Dinner at Mrs....", BUZZER LONGER.

Della enters with pile of boxes, DOORBELL.

Just after second telephone ring, DOORBELL A LITTLE LONGER.

"I'll bet Jo was using 'em" "All right...", BUZZER.

"Give me those", BUZZER LONGER.

"I've been here upwards of ten years...", DOORBELL.

"Pretends she's well...", TWO LONG AND DETERMINED PEALS OF
DOORBELL.

"Julie and Gwen in their play", DOORBELL TWICE (NOT IN-
SISTENT.)

ROYAL FAMILY   EFFECTS

CUE SHEET FOR WORKER 2
ACT I

(You are handling telephone only. It will overlap the
other effects. Each time that you ring it, continue
ringing it evenly on and off until it is answered.)

As curtain rises, Della and Jo are two steps from meeting
on the stairs. TELEPHONE CONTINUES UNTIL ANSWERED.

"Just what we need." (Count 1, 2, 3 quickly.) TELEPHONE
CONTINUES UNTIL ANSWERED.

Della enters with boxes. Doorbell rings. She puts down
the boxes. TELEPHONE CONTINUES UNTIL ANSWERED, BUT
SPACED MORE THAN ON FORMER CUES.

Della comes down stairs. This interrupts the quarrel
between Kitty and Dean. They stop until she is out.
As Kitty opens her mouth to speak again, TELEPHONE
CONTINUES UNTIL ANSWERED.

(This is all for you on this job. It will take about five
minutes.)

FIGURE 23. Above is part of the first page from the cue-sheet for the effect master in a production that called for a number of overlapping cues in the first act. Below is the cue-sheet for his assistant, who helped with properties for the rest of the play.

there be, you will have charge of all the other call boys and will check their work. You will probably sit onstage and check the performance call boys as they make their calls, or at a telephone by means of which you will keep in touch with the boys, who never come to the stage, but who will report to you as the actors they are attending start for the stage. In running a pageant there will be call boys at each entrance, each one reporting to the head call boy, who will be grouped with, or in communication by telephone with, the musicians, the electricians, the crew, et cetera.

In an ordinary production you will have charge of all the call boys, but probably will do part of the calling yourself, and will make out the call cue-sheets.

To the Assistant Call Boy making out the Cue-Sheet:

Before the dress rehearsal, prepare a list of all the actors who appear, or speak offstage, during the first three minutes of each act, and the dressing rooms which they are to occupy. They are "beginners." These people are to be specially notified in the general call for an act.

Follow this list of beginners in each act with a list of spoken cues which fall three to five minutes in advance of the entrance of every other actor in the act. In case a spoken cue will occur during the absence of the call boy on another call, use "Then" as the cue, its meaning being to call the first actor and then call the next one immediately afterwards. Also add a warning cue for the curtain three minutes in advance of its fall on each act or scene. This is a cue for a call to the stage-crew at whatever point it is assembled. The crew should be given a call even though all its members are onstage. Write in the instructions that the call boy is to read to them, as: "Curtain for Act I, special crew call only, no change," "Curtain for Act II, scene change from Interior to Garden," "Curtain for Act III, Scene 1. Quick change for lights, props and wall." Be sure to pick distinctive cues, as explained in Chapter III.

Copies of the cue-sheet should go to the head call boy, each performance call boy, and to the stage manager. The names of the characters in the play, instead of those of the actors, are ordinarily used. Samples of typical entries in such a cue-sheet follow:

Beginners, Act I: Nora, Porter, Maid, Helmer.
"Not been nibbling sweets?": Mrs. Linde.
"I have found other ways of earning money": Krogstad.
Then: Dr. Rank.
"What do I care about tiresome society?": Helmer.
Then: Nurse and children.
"As statesman . . . as orator . . . as general": Crew. Curtain for Act one, scene one. No scene change. Electricians and curtain man only.
"Today of all days! Your marriage day!": Crew. Curtain for Act one, scene two. Change from throne room to woods. Intermission.

Sometimes it is simpler to enter the calls in red in a copy of the play instead of making a call sheet. When the call boy has other back-stage responsibilities, the calls can be entered in the prompt book, and the call boy sent on calls by the prompter.

To the Performance Call Boys:

In a simple show, this task is performed by the stage manager or one of his assistants, but in an elaborate production there should be one or more special call boys.

Thirty-five minutes before the time of the curtain, call "Half-hour" in all dressing rooms, make-up rooms, and any other places where actors or technicians might be. At this time check the people present and report any absentees to the stage manager, with the exception of those actors who do not appear in the first act and those stage-hands whose presence is not required until the first scene change.

Twenty minutes before the time for the curtain, call "Quarter-hour" in all rooms. If the director should have any general instructions he wishes to give before the curtain rises, tell the actors at this time. Announce the exact time at which he wants the assembly, and how much time there is left before it. Make sure that any absentees at the time of the previous call are in the theatre. Again, with the same exception, report the names of any members of the cast who have not arrived.

If there should be a director's call, start the round of the dressing rooms at such a time that the actors in the last room notified will have two minutes to get on the stage. Call, "Everyone onstage for instructions."

If there is no such call to be made, at five minutes to curtain time call, "Orchestra. Beginners, please," (English usage) or "Orchestra. Places" (American). As you make the call, get a signal from each beginner that he will be ready.

Return immediately to the stage and, at three minutes before the curtain, check your lists of beginners. If any are missing, report it to the stage manager and then go in search of them. When the beginners are all in the wings, so report to the stage manager.

If an actor has a first entrance late in the play, ascertain the time at which he expects to reach the theatre, and check his presence at that time. Report to the Stage Manager his arrival or failure to arrive on scheduled time. Keep calling his dressing room until he arrives.

You will be given a call sheet containing this list of beginners for each act and a list of later calls for each act. As the line cue for any such call is spoken, you will call the actor from his dressing room. At dress rehearsal, if you should find that a cue for a call has been spoken while you were away or very shortly after your return from calling an actor, omit the cue and call the actor listed for such call immediately after the previous call. This is the meaning of "Then" in your cue-sheet. Report this change to the stage manager so that he may correct it on his copy of your cue-sheet. You are responsible for seeing that the actors are in the wings by the time of their entrance cue. However, do not be over-zealous and call actors before the cue on your call-sheet. If they find that you are in the habit of getting them on the stage long before their cue, they will be slow in coming to the stage thereafter, and it may result in their missing an entrance. The call should bring them on the stage with about two minutes to wait.

Some companies place the call boys under the direction of the prompter. Your calls then will be entered in the prompt book, and you will receive your instructions accordingly. Except when making a call, you will keep within signaling distance of the Prompter.

Your call-sheet also will contain cues for the backstage workers. You will usually find with the cue some instructions which you are to read to them.

To the Operator of Signal Board:

When the theatre is equipped with a signal board, or one is built for a play, you will give the cues for curtains, effects, lights, et cetera. Some of the duties of the call boys also may be transferred to you. The cue-sheet will be prepared for you, or you will make it out yourself from the complete cue-sheet, including all further items given you by the director or technical director.

If there is a bell system, you will follow the custom of the house with respect to the number of rings for each different signal. The same will be the case for light signals. There must be distinctive signals to the backstage crew for both warning cue and cue, and to the actor for half-hour, quarter-hour, orchestra or beginners, and the individual call to an actor.

If you signal a backstage worker with a light, a very efficient warning system for it is to turn on the light as a warning cue, and turn it off again as the cue. Your signals must tally exactly with the cues, and you should rehearse with the workers in advance of the first dress rehearsal in order to make sure that they will pick up the signal instantly. If they consistently fail to do this, and you can determine the time it takes them to pick it up, then give them an advance signal that will bring their response exactly on the cue.

In performance, you may work from either a cue-sheet, a marked manuscript of the play, or a cue-sheet and unmarked manuscript.

If you make out your own cue-sheet, be sure to select distinctive speeches for the warning cues, so that there will be no danger of your missing them.

The stage manager or the switchboard operator often runs the signal board.

To the Assistant Stage Manager in charge of checking:

In case the production is a very elaborate one, a checker may be provided to double-check the too-busy stage manager or director of scene shifting. You will provide yourself with a copy of his scene shifting plot and charts, and a list of the objects on the stage, and will check them starting from a different point than does he. Your checking does not take the place of his—it merely rechecks the same thing. If it should be found that one of you has checked the stage completely and it is supposedly ready, you can agree to run up the curtain rather than to wait for the other to finish the checking. Check during the course of placing the scenery—do not wait until everything is ready and then start the checking.

If all articles are not in place when you start the checking, make a record on your sheet of the missing pieces and them come back to them after you have checked the remainder.

Often you will be required to check all offstage cues during the action: lights, effects, music, et cetera, and to check the preparations for the next scene-shift. In case you do the latter, you will see that the flats, properties, and other scenery are in the places designated for them, and that other scenery does not block access to them; also that room is provided for the scenery that comes off the stage.

To the Reader for the Scene Shifting Rehearsal:

With elaborate or complicated scene changes, it may be found wise to call a special scenic rehearsal without the presence of the actors, or one with them present but going through only those scenes involving scenic changes. For this a reader will be needed to read the play or parts of it. This reading may be done by the prompter or by one of the directors or supervisors.

You will receive instructions from the technical director or the stage manager as to what parts of the play to read. Normally you will skip sections of the play where there are no cues, and will read only the pages preceding cues for action or scene-shift. Never start reading at the cue, for one of the major purposes of such a rehearsal is to train the staff to accurately anticipate and then catch their cues. Stand or sit on the stage and read the lines as nearly like the actors as possible, in order to accustom the crew to the way the warning cues and cues will sound in performance. Read straight through the warning cue and the cue, not betraying them in any way as they are passed. Make any necessary pauses that are appropriate to the action and give the action as best you can, describing it as you demonstrate if it will not be clear otherwise.

When you skip a section of the dialogue, announce it loudly and clearly, including the approximate time the omitted section will take in performance, in order to give the crew the time relationship between cues.

If the actors are present to read the lines, have them begin a scene, and, when you find where you want to make a deletion, stop them and then start them again on the next section that contains cues. Let them run past the cue and then announce the amount of time the deletion will take in performance. Then give the actors the speech starting the next section of dialogue.

Whether a reader or the actors are doing the reading, both the last page prior to a scene change and the first half page of dialogue following a change should be read.

To the Timer:

You will prepare a chart listing in order down the page, "Curtain up," "Curtain down," "Playing time," and "Intermission time" for every scene of the play. Across the top of the page, rule off a column for each dress rehearsal and performance, and one for the "Ideal Time."

You will take this to the director a few days in advance of the first dress rehearsal and ask him for the information with which to fill in the "Ideal Time" column. If he has not worked this out, you and he can together calculate it after the first dress rehearsal, for you can then give him the time each scene took at that rehearsal, and he will know whether it is the proper time for the action or whether it should be made slower or faster. The technical director will give you the time for the intermissions.

You will have a watch, setting it precisely with the watch or clock by which the production is conducted. You will enter in the proper column the time the curtain rises and falls on each scene. After the performance, put down the playing time and the intermission time in number of minutes. Where a quick change is made, enter it in seconds. After each performance show the playing time figures to the director, and the intermission time to the stage manager and technical director.

After the final dress rehearsal, on the basis of all the rehearsals, calculate the exact time the curtain will fall on the opening night. Subtract five minutes to allow for the speeding up which nearly always occurs at the first performance, and give the time to the box office manager for the information of customers who will inquire as to when to have their automobiles call for them, and so forth. After the first performance make any needed correction in this time.

When intermissions are scheduled for a certain number of minutes, notify the stage manager two minutes before the curtain should rise, and again at the exact second for it. This is information for him, not an order, for you have no such authority.

After the final performance, give copies of your timing sheet to the director and technical director.

The prompter often keeps this sheet. In this case, the time records may be entered in spaces that you mark for them in the prompt book at the beginning and end of scenes, and the calculations made from this for the director and technical director.

CHAPTER VII

PROPERTY DEPARTMENT

To the Property Master:

Read the play for enjoyment, and again for mood, atmosphere, historical period, and decorative style. Read it a third time, making a list at that time of all the properties called for in the descriptions of the settings. As you read the dialogue and stage business, check the properties as they are actually to be used or as reference is made to them in the dialogue. Note everything said about them. Sometimes you will find articles called for by the author's description of a setting, but which are never used in the action. With the consent of the technical director these might be omitted or replaced. Remember, however, that the author had some reason for putting them there, so get all such articles that you can. When an article is intended merely to suggest a certain period or locale, and you cannot find a suitable example of the one specified, it may be possible to substitute something entirely different which will produce the same effect. Old-fashioned rope portières would be a more satisfactory substitute for wax flowers under glass, for example, than a vase of fresh flowers.

Add to this list all articles required by the dialogue or the author's stage business which were not included in his description of the setting. When you have compiled your list, check it for omissions with the general scenic reference compilation. Also check it with the designer for additions, and with the director or the prompter for any further additions ordered by the director in setting the stage business. Notify the director of all properties mentioned in the text of the play that you do not think it possible or advisable to supply. He may tell you of others that he thinks are needless.

For a period play you may need to do library research on the properties. First consult the designer in order to see if he already has the historical material you want. If not, either assign the research work to an assistant or do it yourself. Make sketches or tracings of drawings and copy written explanations that will aid you.

Decide what articles you can use from your stock of properties. Assign repair and alteration work on them if such are needed. Assign to your assistants articles that are to be bought, borrowed, or rented. It is usually more economical in the end to buy or make cheap imitations than to borrow expensive genuine objects which might be damaged. Require periodic reports of their progress from these assistants.

List and assign articles that are to be made. You will be responsible for providing everything the performance property master will have to handle. You may, however, receive the co-operation of other departments for the actual construction of the properties—large construction work and furniture by the head carpenter, electrical properties by the electrician, draperies by the costume master, dyeing by the costume master, painting by the head painter, and the like. The property department usually is responsible for all sound effects except those operated from the switchboard. An explanation of the handling of effects by an independent worker directly under the stage manager is given in Chapter VI.

As properties are collected or made, store them together in a safe place ready to be delivered to the performance property master at the first property rehearsal. Check off the articles on your list as they are collected or finished, so that your list will show progressively those that are still to come and the sources for them.

If the director asks it of you, supply properties, or temporary substitutes for them, at the earlier rehearsals. Place them in charge of the performance property master, the prompter, assistant director, or a member of the cast, who will then be responsible for them.

You will plan and provide all the special devices or implements for changing properties during the performance.

Moving Draperies

When portières, draperies at windows, or wall hangings, must be placed or removed during the play, and the pole on which they are hung is too high to be reached from the floor, nail together two pieces of 1″ x 2″ lumber to make a "T." To the ends of the cross bar attach wire loops or strips of tin bent into a semi-circle in such a way as to make a cradle in which the curtain pole may be lifted to and from its position.

It is sometimes possible to attach sticks directly to each end of the curtain pole with nails or heavy twine, and to lift the draperies by them. The sticks will hang behind the cloth when the draperies are hung.

Where a pelmet is used on curtains to be removed or changed, a rectangular frame like a flat can be built and designed to fit into the panel design of the opening, or a slot provided for it in the window design. The entire group of draperies can then be removed in one operation.

Draperies on curtain poles also may be suspended from a batten by fine wires, and raised and lowered like a drop.

For the rigging of various types of pull curtains, see Chapter V.

Pictures and Other Hanging Objects

With a setting that is never moved, you may hang a picture or other object on a nail driven into any stile or toggle-rail. If the flat is standing, get someone to press or lean against the wood on the other side so that you will have a firm surface against which to hammer. If there is no wood at the point where you want to put a nail, place an independent toggle-rail on the back of the flat. This is a board cut to go between the stiles of the flat. A keystone is attached to it with clout nails at each end, the keystone butt extending two inches beyond the end of the board. Two screw holes are bored in these keystone flaps. This toggle-rail then may be attached to the stiles temporarily with four screws, and may be removed easily afterward. You may now nail to it.

In providing hooks for hanging pictures on scenery which is to be moved, care must be taken that there are no projections from the surface of the flat which might tear other flats resting against it. Stage hardware dealers have a patent hook for the purpose. It is a thin strip of metal having a screw hole in each end, and is so bent in the center as to make a socket in which a similar piece of metal may be slipped; and another strip of metal to be screwed to the object, so bent, hair-pin like, as to allow the free end to slip into the socket on the flat. Should the flat be used at other times with the hanging object removed, the metal strip can be painted with the set, and then will be invisible. There is hardware for the hanging of curtain poles that is made on the same principle.

Another safe way to hang pictures is to attach a ring to the flat and put a hook on the back of the picture frame. The ring may be nailed fast or fastened with wire or fishline to a more convenient cross-piece. Be sure the hook is not sharp enough to cut the canvas. Light objects may be hung from the top of the flat with fishline or thin wire.

In order to reduce weight, avoid breakage, and obviate reflected glare in the eyes of some spectator, it is preferable to use framed pictures that do not have a glass.

Mirrors must be carefully placed and tested from every angle of vision in the auditorium in order to make sure that there is no glare from them, and that there is no reflected view of the backstage, of the footlights, or of another part of the audience. If they cannot be hung so as to prevent such a view, soap them or substitute panels painted with aluminum radiator paint.

In some cases, objects may be fixed to the scenery, moved with it, and not removed from it during the production. Care must be taken that the twisting of the flat while moving it will not dislodge the objects attached to it.

Hanging wall cabinets and shelves may be suspended in similar ways.

To the Assistant in charge of borrowing and renting:

From the lists of the property master, you will compile one giving the articles to be borrowed or rented. Do not include any articles on your list that would be too fragile to be handled safely, and never accept the loan of any object that it would be impossible, or very expensive, to replace if broken—unless you have a stage crew composed of antique dealers!

In the presence of the individual with whom you arrange to rent or borrow an article, put down the owner's name, his address, his telephone number, the rental charge, the value of the object (if obtained from a commercial house), the date you are to get it, the method of its delivery, and the date and method of its return. This you do in order to make the person realize that he is incurring a definite and important obligation and will be expected to keep it. Live up to your part of the bargain, and try to make him feel that he must live up to his part of it. If anything is damaged, tell the technical director and see that it is made good. *Do not return it in a damaged condition!* When you return an article, insist that the person receiving it inspect it for damage. Consider yourself a liaison officer, whose duty it is to help preserve and enhance the good name of your organization.

The customary weekly rental paid by professional companies for the use of furniture is ten percent of its sale price. Amateur organizations often can secure it for less than this, and many times the loan of it without charge.

If it is the custom of the organization to give complimentary tickets, which is not necessary, have an agreement with the technical director on just how many tickets are to be given to each individual, and deliver them when you go for the properties. If you send someone for them, send the tickets and a note by mail several days in advance. Make it clear that the tickets are in appreciation of the co-operation given, rather than in payment for the use of the articles.

Always personally thank everyone from whom you borrow properties, both for yourself and on behalf of the technical director and director. You may do this when you return the object, or by telephone, or by mail. In the case of particularly generous co-operation, ask the technical director, in addition, to write a note to the individual or call him by phone, or take the technical director a typewritten letter of thanks to sign, and then send it. Written notes are always more impressive and better appreciated than verbal messages. They are particularly valuable in localities where there are other less careful theatrical organizations in making commercial houses familiar with your organization's name and its record of properly handling borrowed furniture.

Well in advance of the date of the performance, learn just what articles you will be able to borrow or rent, so that those that you cannot so obtain can be made. Turn in periodic reports on your progress. At the proper time, turn in a list of acknowledgments of favors for the printed program. This is just as much one of your duties as the collection of the articles. It may be the practice of the organization to acknowledge all loans, or just those for which no rental is paid.

All borrowed or rented articles should be returned, if possible, the day following their final use. By the third day afterward, give a report on the articles returned to the technical director.

To the Assistant in charge of buying:

After an effort has been made to rent or borrow properties, you will be given a list of the things it is necessary to buy. You will already have a list of those that it is obviously necessary to buy.

With this combined list, and a maximum price set by the technical director for each item, or a budget figure set by the business manager for the total, you will visit second hand stores, junk shops, Salvation Army stores, et cetera, in search of satisfactory used articles. You should know to what use each article is to be put so that you will know whether or not you may buy damaged ones. Failing to find what you want, you will pick up articles here and there that may be successfully altered for the purpose.

Only after this search for bargains, will you go to the regular stores.

Then, if possible, go first to a wholesaler. You may find damaged articles there that are usable. Finally go to the retailers, seeking damaged articles at low prices. If you are assigned to this job for a series of productions, watch for bargain sales. Then you can stock up on standard articles that are to be used regularly.

Buy unbreakable objects where possible—wooden instead of china dishes, celluloid instead of glass articles, for example. Ornamental wooden candles are sold at the "Five and Ten" stores.

In buying furniture, you usually will be expected to locate all the usable pieces and, before buying, take one of your superiors, probably the technical director, to inspect and approve them for permanent possession.

Always obtain receipts for money paid, and always arrange to return an article if it is not acceptable to the technical director. Return it immediately in order to obviate the suspicion of having used it. Always ask for a discount. When the purpose for which you are buying an article is made known, you will usually get it.

To the Assistant making the Property Cue-Sheet:

The moving of large properties will be covered specifically in the general scene shifting plot, for they call for special plans. You will make out charts and lists for the use of the performance property master. You also will check the scene shifting plot for additions to the properties embraced in it.

As is also explained in a prior chapter, there are rigid rules in the professional theatre on the distinction between "scenery" and "properties," over which there have been many controversies, sometimes leading to strikes. A useful distinction in the amateur theatre, based on the type of work they call for, is the inclusion in properties of all furniture, all small articles not attached to the scenery, and all other articles that can be handled by one person. However, heavy furniture may be handled for you by the grips.

You will make up a list of every article for the stage in each scene, and where it is to be placed. Record them in order from left to right or right to left as you encircle the stage, inserting architectural features and the like that will assist in locating the properties, as:

(*Down left*)
Chair
  shawl
Stand table
  blue vase
  paper knife
  silver box
    cigarettes
(*Entrance*)
Picture
(*Fireplace*)
  brass candlesticks
    lighted
  clock
    set 8:45
Picture on easel
(*Upper left corner*)
Whatnot
  20 objects
  Brass Buddha on top shelf
(*Window*)
  lace curtains
  blue drapes
    closed

. . . .

(*Center of room*)
  Davenport
    three pillows
  Green chair
  Table
  Orange chair

. . . .

From this list you will make out another showing the articles that each clearer, or property assistant, is to remove or place. The assignments should be planned to save steps. The first thing to be done is to remove all articles attached to the setting or leaning against it. You should assign a clearer to collect small properties in a numbered basket, giving a list of them, where the basket should be found, and where it is to be deposited backstage. Prepare a similar list of the small objects to go on the stage.

You now will prepare a list of the hand-properties (those to be carried on or off the stage by an actor) with the exact place for each one onstage, or backstage on the property table, the warning cue and actual cue for its use, the name of the character using it, and the entrance through which he carried it on or off the stage. You will include *all* the hand properties—even such personal properties as watches, wallets, handkerchiefs, money, hats, coats, and the like.

You will assign a hand-property man to take the property to the actor, or to take it from him when he brings it off. Explanations and exceptions in practice are noted in the instructions to the hand-property master, but you must not make exceptions in preparing the cue-sheet.

This preliminary work finished, prepare the following:

1. A general property cue-sheet, interweaving all these lists and recording everything in its chronological order. Usually the most efficient way is to start at the left of a page with the line or action cue, use a column indented about five spaces on the typewriter for the name of the clearer, and then list under or after his name the articles to be moved, with their location and disposition. If you do not know the names of all the clearers, leave underlined spaces followed by a number to represent the name, so that it can be filled in later. Make copies for the property master and his assistants at the performance, one for the stage manager, and one or two extra ones to post backstage.

2. Individual cue-sheets for the clearers made from this complete cue-sheet. Make copies for the individual and for the property master or stage manager. (See Figure 3.)

3. A complete diagram of all offstage property tables, and of the

disposition of properties otherwise. Make copies for the property master, the performance property master, the stage manager, and one or two extra ones for posting.

4. A tag to be tied to each property basket giving its contents, the placing of the contents on the stage, and the placing of the basket offstage. If possible, this tag should be tied or wired to the handle of the basket so that it can be read with the basket over the arm. Make lists of these tags and the information on them and distribute the lists as heretofore indicated.

5. Diagrammatic charts of each setting (from the various lists you have made) from which the performance property master may check the work. Make copies and distribute them as heretofore indicated. Figure 24 shows one form for this chart.

Figures 1 to 5 show forms of these cue-sheets assembled with the directions for moving the scenery.

To the Performance Property Master:

You will have general supervision of all property work during a performance, and will have a general cue-sheet containing all the cues for all the workers under you. You are under the direction of the stage manager.

You may do some of the moving of properties yourself, or you may only supervise it. The more complicated and the faster the changes, the less you should do, though you may carry articles as you enter the stage to check the work.

From a careful study of the designs and of the play, you will learn the exact placing of the properties in relation to their use, and will instruct the clearers with regard to this. Once the director and designer approve the placing of the furniture and other major articles, you may indicate their exact position on the floor with brass-headed tacks, paint, chalk, or bits of cloth sewed to rugs and carpets.

Plan the exact arrangement of your property tables with regard to

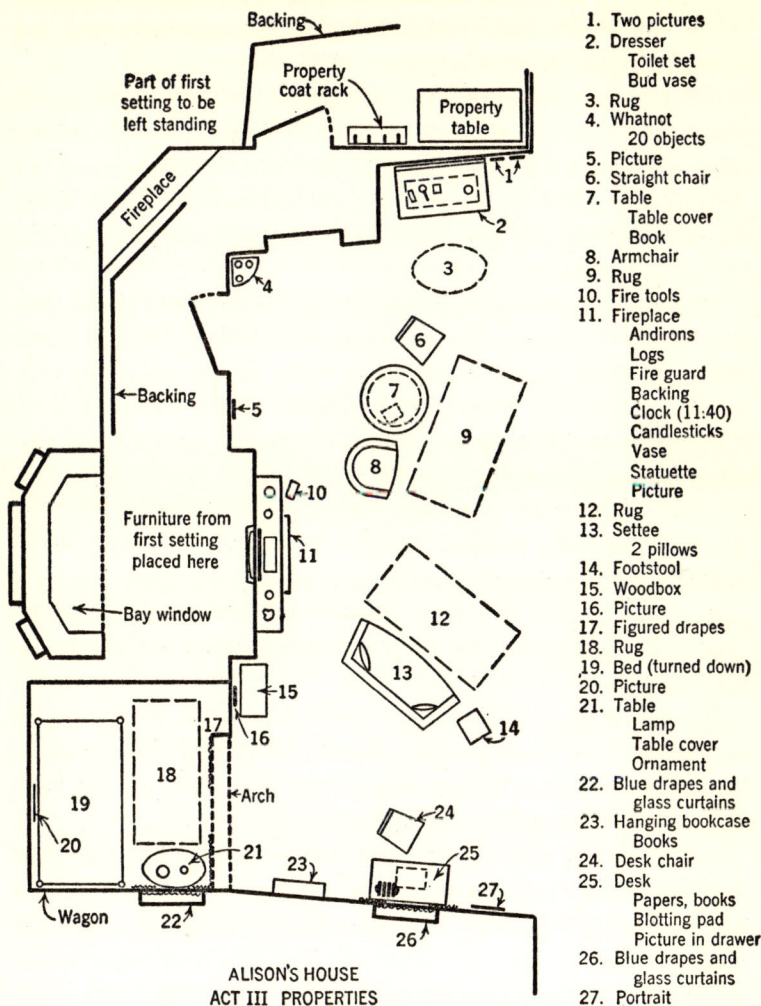

Backing

Part of first
setting to be
left standing

Fireplace

Property
coat rack

Property
table

1. Two pictures
2. Dresser
   Toilet set
   Bud vase
3. Rug
4. Whatnot
   20 objects
5. Picture
6. Straight chair
7. Table
   Table cover
   Book
8. Armchair
9. Rug
10. Fire tools
11. Fireplace
   Andirons
   Logs
   Fire guard
   Backing
   Clock (11:40)
   Candlesticks
   Vase
   Statuette
   Picture
12. Rug
13. Settee
   2 pillows
14. Footstool
15. Woodbox
16. Picture
17. Figured drapes
18. Rug
19. Bed (turned down)
20. Picture
21. Table
   Lamp
   Table cover
   Ornament
22. Blue drapes and
   glass curtains
23. Hanging bookcase
   Books
24. Desk chair
25. Desk
   Papers, books
   Blotting pad
   Picture in drawer
26. Blue drapes and
   glass curtains
27. Portrait

←Backing

Furniture from
first setting
placed here

←Bay window

←Arch

⌐Wagon

ALISON'S HOUSE
ACT III PROPERTIES

FIGURE 24. A check-list for the property master in the form of a diagram
of the setting.

use, and draw or paint the plan on a large sheet of wrapping paper. Oil cloth or muslin is better, if you can afford it, for there is then no chance of crackling sounds such as paper makes. Thumb-tack this on the property table, and insist on having each article put in its proper place. If the name of the article is printed on the spot it is to cover, you can read at a glance what items are missing.

If it is not convenient for your crew to handle them, you may get the stage manager to assign to the grips the handling of large pieces of furniture or other heavy properties. It is a wise practice, where possible, to have the property department handle only articles that may be moved by one person. These arrangements *must* be completed before the scene shifting plot is made.

Note that an ash tray into which a lighted cigarette is dropped in performance should contain a little water, so that the audience will not be distracted or alarmed by the smoke from a smouldering cigarette. Any liquid to be drunk by the actor, even the cold tea as a substitute for whiskey or wine, must be made fresh every day. Food should be replaced before it spoils!

See that the tags have been properly fastened on the property baskets, giving contents, the placing of the contents, and the backstage location of the basket afterwards.

You will reach the theatre each night long enough in advance of the curtain to check and arrange all properties, and find any mislaid ones. You will sweep the stage and dust the furniture, or have these done, before each performance and dress rehearsal.

In performance, you will perform all tasks specifically assigned to you, will supervise all work, and will check the properties in each setting as it is placed. When everything is placed properly, notify the stage manager.

You will put in safekeeping each night all valuable articles that might disappear or be easily broken. Cover all furniture to protect it from dust and scratches.

Immediately after the final performance you will gather and pack all the properties according to a previously made plan. You are responsible for them until they are turned over to the movers or to the assistant property master who borrowed them.

To the Clearers, or Performance Property Assistants:

You will work directly under the performance property master. You will be given individual cue-sheets showing each warning cue ("get ready"), each cue, and your tasks that immediately follow the cue. This usually will be for a change of setting. If so, you will take any article you are to place to the point at which you will enter the stage. You will wait there for the stage manager to signal "Strike!" so that you may be sure that the curtain calls are ended and the curtain is down. You then will "hurry slowly" in placing your articles and removing those assigned you. *Do only what you are instructed to do!* If you do someone else's work one night without reporting it, you may find that you are left to do it every night thereafter. It is not backbiting to report scene shifting errors. It is merely the best way to obtain an efficiently running machine. Such errors usually are the result of misunderstanding, not of intention or even of carelessness.

If you receive your instructions orally from the performance property master, write them down and carry these notes in order to check your memory.

Your cue-sheet should have your tasks listed in the order in which they are to be performed. If so, always follow this order. If not, or if you find that something has to be done otherwise in order to be more efficient, note the change on your instruction sheet and report it to the performance property master so that he may make the alteration on his cue-sheet, on the other cue-sheets used on the stage, and on the duplicate copy of your instruction sheet. You should learn your tasks and their order so thoroughly that you will not have to take time out to refer to the instructions during the change, but always check yourself by them immediately after you leave the stage.

When you have completed all your tasks in a given change, report to the property master and get off the set.

If you are to help with hand properties offstage during scenes, you will receive other instructions about them.

One of you will sweep the stage and dust the furniture before each dress rehearsal and performance.

To the Hand-Property Master and Assistants:

The term hand-property may be used to refer to all properties small enough to be handled by an actor, all properties actually handled by an actor, or only to those carried on or off the stage by an actor. Since only the last category requires special handling backstage, the term is used here in this limited sense. In most productions, the work is part of that of the regular property crew, but is a distinct division of their labor, and, for this reason, is described here as an independent task.

You will receive a list of the hand-properties to be carried on or off the stage by actors, with a warning cue for each of them.

If it is something to be carried on, you will meet the actor at the entrance he will use, and hand him the article. If the object is one he is furnishing, such as a watch, a handkerchief, or a hat, and which he will keep in his dressing room, you still will meet him at the entrance to make sure he has it with him. Amateur actors frequently forget such "pocket properties."

If the article is to be carried off the stage, you will wait for the actor and take it from him, unless it will go in his pocket and he will be the first to use it again. Even if this is the case, you will meet him every night to make sure that he didn't leave it onstage, and so will need a substitute article.

After the act or the performance, you will round up all the articles for which you are responsible and put them away safely with the other properties. Do not allow the actors to carry them out of the theatre in their pockets, for they might leave them at home.

CHAPTER VIII

ELECTRICAL DEPARTMENT

To the Head Electrician:

An executive is necessary for supervising all phases of the stage lighting. He is seldom a separate member of the staff. More often the technical director, the electrical planner, or the performance electrician serves in that capacity.

You will have charge of all the electrical equipment and of the lighting of the production, co-operating with the property master and the carpenter, however, in the building of any equipment to be operated by electricity. You also will help the effect master in producing and operating such equipment. You will deal with the scenic designer, the technical director, the chief technical assistant, and others, in planning the lights, acting as a go-between for them and the operators working under you. You will see that the scenery plans will permit the use of the lighting equipment and make possible the effects that you contemplate having. You also will co-ordinate the work of your department with that of the painter, property master, costume master, and make-up master in order to make sure that you can give them the proper lights and that it will be practicable to effectively light the scenery and costumes that they are preparing.

You will attend the dress rehearsals and there check the lighting, particularly in its relation to the mood called for by the play, and the effect of the lights on the other colors on the stage. Both the technical director and the director will be too busy with other matters to observe other than the more obvious defects in the stage lighting.

When the lighting plans reach their final form, you will have the construction and supply electrician indicate to you the needed equipment. Always allow for breakage of lamps and gelatines during the rehearsals and performance. You will see that all the needed supplies of them are ordered.

Do not yourself, or allow your assistants, to be misled by the current notion, both professional and amateur, that lighting cannot be minutely planned in advance of the set-up. It is impossible, of course, for one who does not know lighting and color to do so, or one who has not taken the trouble to study the play and the rehearsals for the lighting requirements. Anyone, however, who knows the fundamentals of stage lighting, and who does the work listed for the electrical planner, can plot a lighting set-up that will need only slight changes in the size and the direction of beams, in the tints of gelatines, in the intensities of the general lighting, and in the spot lighting on cues. A lighting rehearsal of not more than half an hour to a setting or to each act, with the director determining the correct intensities, and with changes of color and the direction and size of beams being scrutinized and noted for correction after the rehearsal, should be sufficient to give correct lighting at the first dress rehearsal of the most complicated play. A few more corrections may have to be made at that time in connection with the position of actors and the color of their costumes.

If there is to be any difficult electrical construction, the general features of the lighting should be planned far in advance, and, in any case, all the plans should be ready one week in advance of the performance so that gelatines and equipment can be ordered. This is especially necessary if the supplies must be obtained from out-of-town.

The work under your direction has been divided here into a great many tasks. In a simple production, all the work can be done by one man or by two men working together. Any combination of the tasks is possible.

To the Assistant Electrician in charge of planning:
You will receive the design for the lighting from the lighting de-

signer, or you will design it in consultation with the head electrician.

You will read the play several times to get the correct mood of each scene and of each part of it. You will find it helpful to attend rehearsals in order to learn of the effects that the director wants, the exact positions of the actors in the crucial scenes, and the paths on the stage that the actors most frequently use.

You will consult with the head carpenter and head painter as to the scenic elements to be emphasized and those to be obscured, the colors to be used, the distribution of highlights and shadows in painting, and the positions at the tormentor, teaser, et cetera, from which light may be thrown. This work may be done by the head electrician and turned over to you in the form of memoranda.

You will make a series of rough sketches showing the ideal lighting for every moment of the play. You will then co-ordinate these from a practical point of view—the equipment available; the angles obtainable; the possibilities of changing the colors, the shapes, and the directions of beams during performance; and the possibilities of making such changes without unduly attracting the attention of the audience to them. Out of all this study you will evolve the final design for the lighting. If you do this planning long enough in advance of the production, you will have the opportunity to show the director how you can give his actors the best possible lighting and he may be willing to change the actors' business to some extent to facilitate your plans. For the same reason the designer and head carpenter may be willing to change their plans to some degree. You may find it necessary, also, to ask various people working with color to alter their original plans so that they will harmonize with yours. But if you do not do this until the last minute, you will have to accept the conditions already established because they are then unchangeable.

In very few amateur theatres can you expect to possess sufficient equipment to produce the lighting exactly as you would like to have it. With sufficient ingenuity this condition should not prevent your approximating any effect that you want. Either factory-made or home-built color boomerangs, for example, which change gelatines mechanically, will add greatly to the flexibility of the lighting equipment and multiply the usefulness of your spotlights.

You will present your plans for approval to the head electrician, technical director, and designer, and then will turn them over to the lighting cue-sheet maker to be tabulated for cues, and to the electrical draughtsman for making working drawings and plans, unless you also are this electrical draughtsman, as is often the case.

You will need to be present at the lighting rehearsals and the dress rehearsals in order to alter your plans if the need arises.

To the Electrical Draughtsman:

You will receive the plans for the lighting from the assistant electrician in charge of planning, and will make working drawings from them for the use of the electricians at the set-up and the performance.

Make a list of all the equipment and supplies needed for the production and give it to the assistant electrician in charge of construction and supplies at least one week before the production. He may have to order some of them from out-of-town. He should have been informed of any complicated construction long before this.

You will make plans for the exact placing of every piece of electrical equipment, showing its wiring, its beam, its focus, its lamp, its color, and its shield (see Figure 25). In a simple production, all these data can be put on one sheet. In a complicated set-up, more detailed information will be needed. The use of colored pencils and inks sometimes serves to make a plan more easily understood. There is danger of confusion in this. There should be either strict relation between the colors of the pencils or inks used and the colors of the gelatines or there should be no relation at all between them.

Indicate on the plan all the uses of each unit, or make no indication there of such uses and then make a separate chart of them. All these plans may be in either diagrammatic or memoranda form.

Have your plans accurate as to the order of the spotlights and other units on the tormentors, teaser, bridge, balcony, et cetera.

Your plans should be so definite and clear that a backstage lighting worker who had never served in that theatre in any capacity would be able readily to set-up, hook-up, and wire the production.

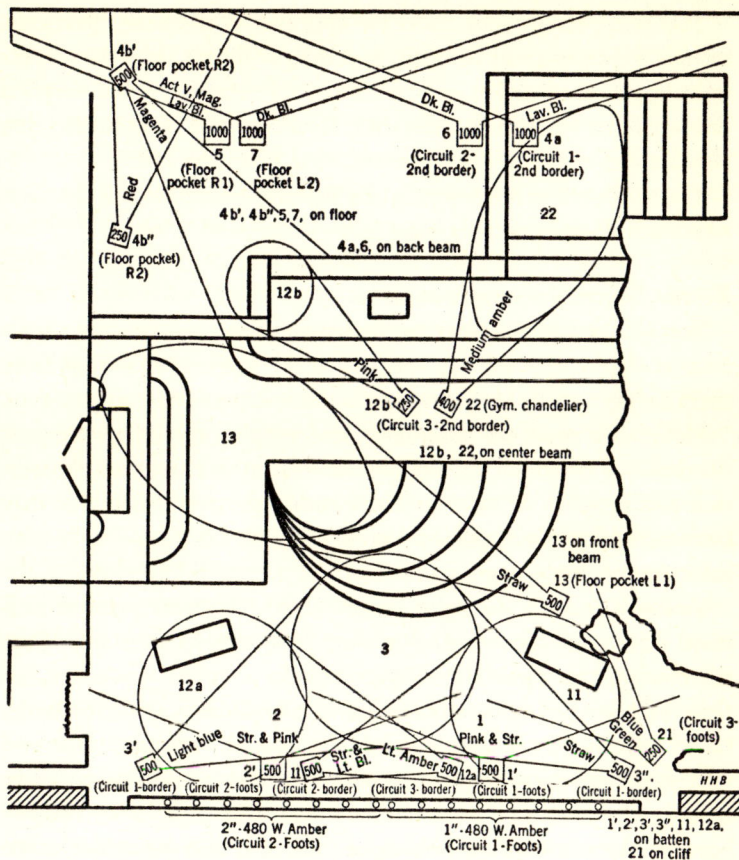

FIGURE 25. A lighting plot for a production of Grillparzer's *Sappho*. The switchboard chart and a cue-sheet for the same production are given in Figures 27 and 28.

Make a plan of the switchboard (see Figure 27), to be tacked or clamped to the board, for the use of the switchboard operator in performance. In case the switchboard already is permanently wired, this chart will show only the lighting unit that is controlled by each switch, as "#18, R. teaser spot on desk, Amber." If the switchboard and dimmer bank are of the adaptable types, to be hooked up for each production, plan the hook-up, give directions for doing it, and then make a chart of it as it will be when completed. In planning the hook-up of independent switches or independent dimmers, follow some logical plan, so that the switchboard operator can learn the set-up in a few minutes, and will not need to search frantically on the chart for the switch number of a light he wants quickly.

Consult the switchboard operator for his preference as to the order of lights. You must know the switchboard perfectly in order to plan its use effectively and in order not to propose impossible things for it.

Devise a system of numbers for labeling the switches and lights. Always plan it with reference to the logical order of switches or dimmers on the switchboard, and use the same numerals for the lighting units themselves as are designated for them on the switchboard. If two lights are connected to one switch or to one independent dimmer at different times, label the lights according to the number corresponding to the switch, plus a letter, as "13a, 106d, 42x."

In numbering the switchboard, start at either the right-hand or the left-hand side with the main switches and the master dimmers. If there are no such master switches, start at the side of the board where there are the most vertical correspondences.

If there are less than ten switches in a horizontal row, the master switches forming the first vertical row may be numbered 0, 10, 20, . . . The switches in the horizontal rows which they control may be numbered 1, 2, 3, . . . , 11, 12, 13, . . . , 21, 22, 23, . . . , carrying out the respective numerical sequences. The switchboard would then be diagrammed by numbers as:

Masters	Switches								
0	1	2	3	4	5	6	.	.	.
10	11	12	13	14	15	16	.	.	.
20	21	22	23	24	25	26	.	.	.
30	31	32	.	.	.				

MIDSUMMER NIGHT'S DREAM -- Information for Lighting

Houselights to half during overture.
Houselights out and stage lights on at cue in overture

ACT I (Played in one scene.) MORNING

At rise of curtain stage is fairly full. Chief characters are on the low platform. No one on ramps.

After page one, important characters enter and stand
right and left on the floor level.

"And confer with you of something nearly that concerns
yourself." (line 125) Duke and court leave. Two lovers
remain center stage.

"Tomorrow truly will I meet with thee." (line 178)
Helena enters on left lower ramp. She speaks from here and
then from low platform. Then leaves it and no more action
on the platform, except a long speech by her as she sits on
center of steps.

"To have his sight thither and back again." (line 250)
Helena exits, and mechanicals enter immediately. They come
down the lower two ramps, but do not speak until they are
on the stage floor. Whole scene is played on stage floor.
This scene should be bright.

Curtain cue: "At the duke's oak we meet." Fast curtain.

INTERMISSION AND SCENE CHANGE

ACTS II to IV (Played continuously.) Woods. NIGHT

Houselights to half on music.
Houselights out and stage lights up on music cue.
Curtain rises on second music cue.

Puck dances center stage, up left ramp to top. First
Fairy enters up the top left ramp. They meet at the top
and speak fifteen lines. Both then run to the low platform.

"But room, fairy, here comes Oberon." (line 58) Enter
Titania and train, who dance on floor level, then go up the
right ramps. Titania and Oberon meet at the peak for the
quarrel scene. They play at the peak. Then Oberon plays
half-way down the right ramp. The lower stage is not used
except for an exit cross until:

FIGURE 26. The first page of the information furnished by the director
for the use of the electrical planner in preparing a light cue-sheet. It gives
the location of important characters during the scenes and the cues for
lighting changes.

Some electricians prefer to dispense with the single digits, 1, 2, 3, . . . , and start the system with the numeral 10 for the first master switch. The single digits would then be used for other independent switches.

If there are more than ten switches in a row, 100, 200, 300, . . . , may be used for the master switches or dimmers. The board might then be diagrammed numerically:

Masters	Switches									
100	101	102	103	104	105	.	.	.	.	126	127
200	201	202	203	204	205	.	.	.	.	226	227
300	301	.	.	.	.						

Or a combination of numbers and letters can be used:

Masters	Switches									
A	A1	A2	A3	A4	A5	.	.	.	.	A26	A27
B	B1	B2	B3	B4	B5	.	.	.	.	B26	B27
C	C1	.	.	.	.						

Be careful not to overload dimmers with wattage, and to specify extra resistance where a dimmer is underloaded and will not, in consequence, dim to black-out. This extra resistance, or phantom load, can be in the form of concealed light globes or an electric toaster, fan, iron, or the like, wired into the circuit.

To the Assistant Electrician in charge of Cue-Sheets:

You will be given the plans for the lighting showing the point in the course of the play for each lighting effect (see Figure 26). You also may receive a copy of the general cue-sheet or an individual one for the general lighting effects. Except in the simplest lighting plans, where there are no changes other than those called for by the script, this cue-sheet will be a preliminary one, and you will have to expand it (see Figures 28 to 31).

Make up a trial cue-sheet including:

1. The cue at which every lighting effect must be produced, the cue on which to start making the change (if it is a change by means of dimmers), and a warning cue for beginning it. You will arrange

No.	Type	Watt	Area Lighted	Location of light	Color
1.	Flood & foots	500 500	Left side Left half	Batten L.C. Foots·	Straw & pink Amber
2.	Flood & foots	500 500	Right side Right half	Batten R.C. Foots	Pink & straw Amber
3.	Spots	2-500s	Center stage	Batten ends	Str. & L.blue
4a.	Flood (Change dimmer plug Act V.)	1000	Left sky day	Back beam	Lav. blue
4b.	Spots	500 250	Sunrise spots " "	Floor R. " "	Magenta Red
5.	Flood (in Act V:)	1000	Right sky day Sunrise glow	Floor R. " "	Lav. blue Magenta
6.	Flood	1000	L. sky night	Back beam	Dark blue
7.	Flood	1000	R. sky night	Floor R.	Dark blue
11.	Spot	500	Left bench	Batten R.C.	Str. & L. blue
12a.	Spot (Change dimmer plug from b. to a. Act I.)	500	Right bench	Batten L.C.	Light amber
12b.	Spot	250 240	Muse Phan. load	Center beam	Pink
13.	Spot	500	Second level	Front beam	Straw
21.	Spot	250	Moonlight fl.	Batten L.	Blue-green
22.	Spot	400	Back steps & platform IV	Center beam	Med. amber

FIGURE 27. A sample of a chart posted on the switchboard for ready use by the switchboard operator. The dimmers were independent ones that could be inserted into circuits by plugging them into dwelling-type fuse sockets of the typical school fuse-box. The numbers 4a and 4b indicate the switches for two distinct lighting units, an olivette and a pair of spotlights, that bear corresponding numbers. During the first four acts, dimmer 4 was plugged into 4a (the olivette). Just before Act V, the dimmer was plugged into 4b (the spotlights). While the dimmer was plugged into one unit, the other could be used at full intensity by inserting a fuse in its fuse socket, but it could not be dimmed. The same arrangement was used for 12a and 12b.

these in chronological order. Note that one effect frequently over-laps another, so that the warning cues, cues and the completions of effects will be intermingled. Make a note of the individual who is re-sponsible for each effect—switchboard operator, bridge operator, bal-cony operator, floor operator, et cetera—by name, if possible. The terms "hit," "kill," "bring up" or "heat," and "dim" are used re-spectively for "turn on," "turn off," "make brighter," and "make less bright."

2. A written plot of the lighting at the rise of each curtain.

3. All signals operated by an electrician, such as those in the lobby, in the dressing rooms, in the greenrooms, et cetera.

4. Specific and orderly directions for the lighting changes during intermissions, including house lights.

5. The cues for the switching off and on of the lights dimmed out (in order to prevent the dimmers getting hot).

6. Changes during the action or during the intermissions in the focus of any piece of equipment or in the direction and color of the beam it is to throw, with the name or position of the operator who will make the change.

7. Cues for the backstage lights and the work-lights.

8. Check-lists from which the switchboard operator can check his board in the first lull in his work after he has made an elaborate lighting change. Show all switches and dimmers in their established order and what their position must be.

9. All pre-set lighting arrangements.

10. Notes to indicate the last lighting change in a scene, or a con-siderable lapse of time prior to the next lighting cue. Such intervals will be rest periods for the switchboard operator.

11. Everything else that must be done by any operator.

Go over all of this carefully with the electrical planner and obtain his approval. Then go over it with the performance electrician and get his approval of the assignment of the various tasks to the workers. Have him assign those about which you are in doubt, and add any additional cues, changes, and the like, that are needed. From the elec-

ACT II

Change during five minute intermission:
                          DIM   1 and 2 to $\frac{1}{2}$ (Gen. flds.)
                          HEAT   11 to full (Left bench)

	CHECK LIST	
1.	Gen. flood	$\frac{1}{2}$
2.	Gen. flood	$\frac{1}{2}$
3.	Center	full
4a.	Day sky	full
5.	Day sky	full
6.	Night sky	1/3
7.	Night sky	2/3
11.	Left bench	full
12a.	Right bench	$\frac{1}{2}$
13.	Second level	2/3
21.	Moonlight	off
22.	Platform IV	on

First knock: nothing
Second knock: KILL Houselights
Third knock: Curtain: nothing

"Should envy's poisonous
   breath assail her.."   HEAT   1, 2 to full (Gen. floods)
                                     12a to full (Right bench)

"forsaken, solitary..."   DIM   13 to 1/3 (Second level)

"hast answered me."   DIM   12a to 1/3 (Right bench)

"stripped the bushes."   DIM   1, 2, 4a, 5, for four
                                     pages to 1/3 (Floods &
                                     day skies)

"the branch for thee."   HEAT   13 to full (Second level)

"Wilt thou go?"   DIM   13 to 1/3 (Second level)

"should waken wishes..."   HEAT   12a to full (R. bench)

CURTAIN WARN: "How an unrequitted love can torture."
CURTAIN: "Here I will lie and rest my weary head."
   20 second pause. No curtain calls. No house lights.

FIGURE 28. A portion of the cue-sheet for the switchboard operator, making use of the set-up given in Figure 27.

trical draughtsman and performance electrician or an assistant get the numbers of the switches, and place them next to the name of the light unit in your trial cue-sheet.

Now put this in final form, making out one cue-sheet for the performance electrician containing all this material (with a copy to the maker of the combined cue-sheet and scene shifting plot if it is to go in that, or to the stage manager if it is not, and a copy to be posted near the switchboard), and individual cue-sheets for each switchboard operator, and each bridge, balcony, and floor operator.[1]

Sometimes it is simpler or more efficient to prepare a marked copy of the play for the use of the head performance electrician or the switchboard operator. The cue-sheet for the switchboard operator may be in diagrammatic form. (See Figure 29.)

To the Assistant Electrician in charge of construction and supplies:

One week before the production, the planner or draughtsman will give you a list of the equipment needed for the production. You will check this with what is on hand and give the head electrician a list of the missing items to be ordered. Insist on having spare lamps of each size and style, and extra gelatines to replace those that break. You will do everything that is practicable in the setting up of lights in advance of the set-up day. You will be present at the set-up and dress rehearsals in order to supply unexpected lighting needs.

The head electrician may assign to you the construction of electrical equipment. It is possible to construct temporary equipment easily and cheaply.[2]

[1] Louis Hartman's *Theatre Lighting* contains an excellent example of a long and complicated lighting plot, giving various forms of it. There is a descriptive preliminary form such as might be used by the stage manager, a working plot which is the equivalent of a complete electrical cue-sheet, and individual cue-sheets for two balcony operators and the switchboard operators.

Full lighting plans for a production are given in the chapters contributed by Stanley R. McCandless and Louis Erhardt to H. L. Bricker's *Our Theatre Today.* The cue-sheets there are in diagrammatic form.

[2] See references in the Index to Textbooks at the end of the book under "Lighting —Home-made," particularly those to *Stage Lighting* by Theodore Fuchs and *Stage Scenery and Lighting* by Samuel Selden and Hunton D. Sellman.

Symbols
↑ Bring up
↓ Dim
K Kill
F Full

Notes
All dimming is to be imperceptible unless otherwise indicated.
Numerals in squares indicate dimmer markings.
A circle around a symbol indicates that the dimmer should be set at this reading already.
Numerals or symbols without arrows indicate switch is to be thrown with dimmer at that reading.

SCENES AND CUES	INSTRUMENT, SWITCH AND DIMMER NUMBERS													
	1	2	3	4	5	6	7	11	12	21	22	23	24	25
	Left Spots	Right Spots	I Shadow Spot II,III UpR.Cen.	L.Flood & Foots	R.Flood & Foots	I,III Sky Frost II Pink Flood	Sky Blue	Cen. Spot Blue	C. Spot Straw	Lamps&Portrait	Fireplace	Entr. Strips	Moon Flood	Desk Spot
OPEN I-1	6	4		5	1	5	5	6	8		F			
Maid lights candles					6↑ jerks									
"What have you there?"						3↓	3↓							
"Why so classical?"	9↑	8↑												
"Mother presses me so."	6↓	4↓			4↓									
"Damned if I can find him."			F											
Clock; door opens; curtsy.	0↓ fast	0↓ fast	0↓ fast	0↓ fast	0↓ fast			0↓ fast	0↓ fast					
OPEN I-2	3↑	3↑	K	3↑	4↑	5↑	7↑	⓪	⓪		Ⓕ			
"It isn't respectful."	F↑ fast			8↑ fast	9↑ fast			6↑ fast	8↑ fast		F			F
"those dreadful cocktails."						3↓	5↓							
"Peter, what's the matter?"	K (4↓)	K (0↓)		2↓ fast	2↓ fast			K	K	K				K
Peter lights candle.	4			4↑										
"to fix the lights"					4↑									
"I don't know, Miss."			F											
"I'll get a lamp."				2↓	2↓									
OPEN I-3	0↓	0	K	0↓	0↓	5↑	⑤	0	0		Ⓕ			
Rise of curtain.	6↑ fast	4↑ fast		5↑ fast	6↑ fast			6↑ fast	8↑ fast					
"great many fogs."	9↑	8↑		8↑	9↑			F↑	F↑					

INTERMISSION: Plug Dimmer #3 into Up Right Center Spots.
Plug Dimmer #6 into Pink Hanging Flood.

FIGURE 29. A page from a lighting cue-sheet in diagrammatic form.

Special shields, louvres, masks, and spill-shields may be easily made up of cardboard or tin. Laminated cardboard or pressed board should be used to obviate warping under heat. Tin must be used where cardboard would be so heated as to char or burn.

Color-medium frames for olivettes, or floods, are made of tin or thin wooden strips, having fine wire over them in three inch squares. Spot slides may be made of tin, or of two layers of cardboard folded together and held fast by paper-clips. Adjustable masks, or cutoffs, or mats, are made of tin, but cardboard is satisfactory for non-adjustable ones.

You will dip lamp globes that need coloring. You will either re-new the gelatines in olivette and spot frames or make new frames. Ordinary gelatines deteriorate very rapidly from the effect of heat, and for full intensity sometimes must be replaced during the run of a show. Examine them daily. Transolene and glass slides can also be used. Cellophane is coming into use as a substitute for gelatine be-cause of its greater toughness and its relative cheapness. It is, however, now obtainable only in a small range of tints. Many more colors may be produced by using two to ten sheets superimposed, though this reduces the intensity of the light somewhat more than does ordinary gelatine, and accelerates the rate of fading by creating heat pockets. If bought in quantity in order to obtain bulk prices, cellophane is much cheaper than gelatine. The "silk" and "satin" clear or colored cellophane is excellent for slight diffusion of light.

A gelatine chest will more than pay for itself in the saving of gela-tine in the course of a series of productions. This is composed of shallow drawers, each large enough to hold a sheet of unrolled gela-tine with an inch or more space to spare all around it. The drawers need be no more than one inch in depth. Gelatines then may be stored by individual colors, or by closely related ones, and only a few sheets will be disturbed in seeking a given one. The next best method is to store the gelatines by colors in telescoping two-piece mailing tubes three or more inches in diameter and twenty-four inches long. Both pieces of the tube should be properly labeled. For further identi-

DURING ACT II, SCENE I (Doan assisting)

"How goes the night, boy?"
HEAT #6	left tower	light amber
fairly fast		

"gives way to in repose."
HEAT TO ½ #7	right tower	light amber
HEAT to 1/3 #13	amber flood	medium amber

"Get thee to bed."
DIM OUT #7	right tower	light amber
DIM OUT #13	amber flood	medium amber

"My husband."
HEAT SLOWLY #7	right tower	light red

"royal master's murdered."
HEAT SLOWLY to		
1/3 #13	amber flood	medium amber

"meet i' the hall..."
DIM MODERATELY to		
1/3 #13	amber flood	medium amber
DIM OUT #7	right tower	light red
DIM OUT #6	left tower	light amber

CHANGE TO ACT II, SCENE IV

KILL #13	amber flood	medium amber
KILL # 7	right tower	light red
KILL #21	blue border	blue
LEAVE # 6 HEAT to 2/3	left tower	pale straw
HIT #24	natural flood	natural
HIT #23 HEAT to 2/3	throne spot	daylight

Then heat to full any dimmers now off.

FIGURE 30. A portion of the cue-sheet used by the switchboard operator in a production of *Macbeth*. A portable board made up of two rows of independent dimmers was operated most of the time by one man, but in this scene he was assisted by the floor operator (Doan). The first column gives the direction, and the switch or dimmer number; the second, the unit controlled by the switch; and the last, the color of the medium in the unit.

fication, a piece of the gelatine may be glued on the outside with a piece of white paper beneath it.

Made-up slides may be stored when not in use in grooved boxes provided with lids.

If many slides are used in one spotlight or olivette in a performance, special boxes should be provided for them. If more than five colors are used on a spotlight, duplicate slides should be provided for every change, and arranged in order, so that they can be used consecutively. The slides should be numbered, and you will check the box of slides each night to see that the gelatines are in good condition and are arranged in proper order.

Slides always should be marked to indicate their color, as the electrician may not have a white light with which to determine it when he is using them.

If flashlights are used backstage, keep a supply of batteries for them on hand.

There must always be extra fuses of all sizes on hand.

You will provide any extra resistance (phantom load) the electrical draughtsman calls for. As explained in the directions to him, this may be in the form of some noiseless electrical device.

All wiring should be done with insulated stage cable—No. 14 or larger. A saving may be effected by having all long cables—those from ten to sixty feet—equipped permanently with male and female stage connectors, which are never to be removed. Have additional three-foot cables equipped with female stage connectors and stage plugs, or female stage connectors and heavy-duty, male convenience plugs (screw-in plugs used in dwellings), according to how the theatre is wired. The use of these short lengths of cable in order to convert one type of connector into another will avoid constant changes of the plugs and connectors on the ends of cables. All equipment should be wired with male stage connectors.

Various types of special electrical effects may be needed for the production. Reference to plans for these in books on stagecraft are contained in the special index at the back of the book. Effect ma-

MACBETH--LIGHTING PLOT--RIGHT TOWER (Prior)

Before play: set for I-II   on Captain (pink-#1)

Act I--Scene I (Witch scene--very short)

Act I--Scene II (Camp scene--Duncan, captain, etc.)
     on captain (pink-#1)

Act I--Scene III (Witches and Macbeth, etc.)
     change to Tango (#2) on center stage to left stage

Act I--Scene IV (Throne room)
     change to daylight blue (#3) on left portal. (Dimmed
     to ½ at opening. Will heat to full on Duncan's en-
     trance, and dim to ½ after Macbeth's entrance.)

Act I--Scene V (Letter scene)
     change to peach (#4) on center stage, medium focus

Act I--Scene VI (Castle Gate scene)
     change to magenta (#5) on gateway and in front, wide
     focus

Act I--Scene VII (Macbeth, L. Macbeth, banquet offstage)
     change to blue-green (#6) cover the downstage

Act II--Scenes I to III (Murder of Duncan)
     change to light amber (#7) on left second entrance.
     (Out at opening. Heats on cue: "Gives way to in
     repose." FOLLOW TORCH. Dims out quickly on cue:
     "Get thee to bed.")
     change to light red (#8) and focus center stage for
     the Macbeths. (Heats slowly on cue: "My husband."
     Perhaps move it slightly to catch Macbeths, but no
     light on walls or steps.)
     spread inconspicuously as torches begin to enter.
     (Dims out on cue: "And meet i' the hall together.")

Act II--Scenes II and III are continuous with above

FIGURE 31. A portion of the individual cue-sheet used by one of the
tower electricians for the same production of *Macbeth*. The numbers in
parentheses were those for the color medium frames.

chines may be rented or purchased from stage lighting concerns. Following is a check-list of supplies you may need to order:

CHECK-LIST OF EQUIPMENT AND SUPPLIES

Strip lights
Olivettes
Hanging olivettes
Spotlights
Baby spotlights
Arc lights
Foot spotlights
Effect machines
Projectors
Standards
Yokes
Pipe clamps
Spotlight battens or cradles
Lenses
Long throw lenses
Independent dimmers
Switches
Cable
Plug boxes
Stage plugs
Stage connectors
Three-way connectors, etc.
Convenience plugs
Socket extensions
Dim-o-light sockets
Lamp globes
Gelatines
Color frames for spots and floods
Shields
Soft edge masks, etc.
Shutters
Spill shields
Funnels
Cut-offs

Louvres
Color boomerangs
Color wheels
Carbons
Lamp dip
Lamp dip remover
Roundels
Color caps
Orchestra lights
Music stands
Mechanical sound effects
Wire
Fuses
Couplings
Plyers
Hammers
Wrenches
Jackknives
Solder and iron
Screwdrivers
Wood screws
Machine screws and nuts
Stove bolts
Rivets
Tacks
Staples
Friction tape
Rubber tape
Asbestos gloves
Paper clips
Chalk
Lamp guards
Scissors
Razor blades (to cut gelatine)

To the Set-up Electrican and Assistants:

This position is seldom an independent task, usually being combined with one of the other electrical assignments.

You will familiarize yourself with the plans of the electrical draughtsman for the lighting well in advance of the day of the set-up. At the set-up you must be able to give specific instructions to your assistants about everything. You will plan in advance, and, in a complicated set-up, give the order of the task to them in written instructions. This must be arranged with the superintendent of set-up, so that your use of the stage floor may be correlated with his. You will see in advance that pipes, towers, bridges, light battens and everything else you need to mount your equipment are provided and installed.

A tower is a built-up frame of wood or pipe at the side of the stage, which may be mounted by a ladder, either attached or detached. It may be built as part of a false proscenium arch or it may be mounted on rollers. Occasionally a tower is still called a boomerang. A bridge is any contrivance by which an operator can be suspended above the stage in order to handle moving lights or to adjust them. The true bridge is, of course, shaped like a bridge, running from side to side and supported at the ends by uprights resting on the floor. Frequently, however, lighting bridges are either balconies built into the proscenium or are platforms supported by cables from the gridiron. A batten for lights usually is made of two long pipes connected by one to two foot lengths of pipe. The batten is supported by the top pipe and the lights are hung from both the long pipes and from the uprights. Two pipes are used in order to minimize their twisting and that of the attached equipment when lighting units are suspended at angles from the batten.

Be very sure that all overhead equipment is securely fastened and that all flied scenery will clear it.

Remember to have all cable connections knotted so that they will pull still tighter rather than apart when under strain. Tape the connections on battens, et cetera, when space does not permit the knotting.

For suspending a lighting fixture see Chapter V. If you are using wall lights, put an independent toggle-rail (see instructions in Chapter VII) on the back of the flat to which it is attached, bore a hole not more than three-quarters of an inch in diameter, and through this put some kind of a temporary holding device on the back of the fixture which will pass through the hole, carrying the wires of the fixture with it. There are attachment plugs that are small enough to pass through such a hole. The type of plug used for radio hook-up wires also can be used. If the fixture is not to be removed during the play, it can be attached by its regular screws to one or two independent toggle-rails, and the wires put through a smaller hole and then attached to a regular convenience plug or stage connector.

In a one-set show where the onstage light switch is used to turn the stage lights on and off, it is advisable to wire this to a remote control switch for the stage lights. If this is not possible, it can be wired to a light globe placed at the switchboard so that the switchboard operator can take his cue from this. It will mean a fraction of a second delay in turning off the lights, but not a long enough one to be perceptible, and the signal is more exact than one relayed by hand.

SWITCHBOARD

Label the switchboard according to the plans of the electrical draughtsman, explaining the use of each switch, so that the performance switchboard operator may work as readily and confidently as possible. You may insert paper slips in slots provided for them, mark on the face of the board with chalk, or paste paper slips on the board. With certain set-ups, tags may be attached to the wires, or the connectors at each end of a wire may be numbered with paint, or given a distinctive color, et cetera. Everything possible should be done to make the operation of the board both simple and accurate.

If a switchboard light is not installed, wire one in, so that the switchboard operator and reader may have the needed light. If this light shows on the stage, a shield must be made for it. If there are complete black-outs in performance, a dim-o-light socket may be provided so that the switchboard operator can reduce the light from it to a minimum. A blue-dipped lamp gives local light, but little spill. Lacking something better, flashlights may be used.

You must set the board so that anyone operating it for the first time at a dress rehearsal, or anyone who replaces the regular switchboard operator at any time during the performance, may operate it without difficulty.

Check the set-up to make sure that no dimmer is carrying more than its maximum load in wattage.

Sound Effects

Unless the electrically operated sound effects are wired into the switchboard, they will be operated by the effect master or the prompter, but they will be set up by an electrician.

You will learn at what place the performance effect master wants to operate his equipment, and will wire the electrical ones, either attaching them to a wall plug (stage or dwelling type), into an electric light socket, or to batteries provided for them. You also will provide him with a light for his own vision.

To the Head Performance Electrician:

You will have general supervision of all electrical work during a performance, and may or may not reserve one of the specific tasks to do yourself.

Before each rehearsal or performance you will have the switchboard operator turn on each one of his lights in succession as you call it by position. You will check each one for color, direction, and focus. You will also rehearse the bridge, tower, balcony and floor operators. You will check to make sure that extra gelatines, slides, cut-offs, et cetera, to be used are in their accustomed places. This will have to be done before the doors of the auditorium are opened to the audience, which is usually half an hour before the curtain. This same checking has been assigned to the stage manager, because it is rare that a separate individual acts as head performance electrician. If you have checked everything, you will so report to him and save him that trouble.

You then will check the lighting for the first scene. You will have a general lighting cue-sheet by which you can do the checking.

During the performance, you will follow the general lighting cue-sheet and will check on all the lighting work. When there is no backstage checking to be done, you will stand on the same side of the stage as is the switchboard in a position where you can see the stage, and will follow the lighting changes as they are made. As the lights are set for a new scene you will check them. This is especially important when it is impossible for the switchboard operator to see the stage effects being produced. When any particularly tricky "heating" or dimming of the lights has to take place with the switchboard operator unable to see the stage, you will check this to the exclusion of everything else, and signal him or his reader. If assistance is needed at the switchboard only once or twice during the performance, you can give that also.

You will report to the stage manager when the lights are made ready for the next scene. You are responsible to him during performance, and to the head electrician at other times. Your assistants may include switchoard operators and their readers, and bridge, tower, balcony, and floor operators.

To the Switchboard Operator and Assistants:

You will have the switchboard wired for you by the set-up crew, and you will be given a cue-sheet listing all lighting changes during the performance. If the lighting is so complicated that the cues overlap, you will need a reader. He will stand beside you at the board and read to you all the data from the cue-sheet as each cue is spoken.

You will acknowledge having heard him by repeating the important parts of what he has read in order to inform him that you have heard it correctly. If the cues come so fast that you cannot handle them alone, you may have assistants. He or they may operate individual switches, may pre-set the board for you, or may handle the master-switch and master-dimmer controls for you. The same reader may serve all of you, or you may have extra cue-sheets or extra readers for the assistants.

You will operate the board by means of the switch and dimmer numbers, or by the names and locations of lighting units, according to the set-up of the board and the way the cue-sheet is prepared. If you have a preference in the matter, indicate it to the cue-sheet maker at least a week before the first dress rehearsal.

You will arrange, if possible, to see the stage during the performance. When no clear view of it is possible, sometimes a mirror can be so hung as to give you a reflected view of it. If even that is impracticable, you will make sure that the head performance electrician, or someone else who knows the show, stands in a position where he can see the stage and signal you by means of previously arranged signs.

When your cue for an effect is action rather than lines and you cannot see it yourself, you will have this signal given you by the head performance electrician or by the prompter.

You must be orderly in the operation of the board. When any major change of the board is necessary (the dimming of a number of lights, or a change between scenes) you always will work in a definite order, taking your instructions directly from the reader or from the cue-sheet. You will snap switches on and off, dim the lights, et cetera, in the order given, and then, as soon as possible, check them from the check-list provided on the cue-sheet. The cue-sheet should be arranged in the most effective manner possible. See in advance that this is the case. Do not try to remember variations from it. If you find anything omitted, such as the snapping off of a switch when the light has been dimmed to black-out and will not be used again, write this in the cue-sheet the first time you do it (never as late as the last rehearsal) and do it only on cue. Otherwise you will have no cue for turning it on again and thus you may bring up the dimmer only to find the switch turned off.

If you have a pre-set board, pre-set as much of the lighting as possible in advance of the curtain and check this with the head performance electrician at the same time that you check all the lights and dimmers with him before the performance. Write in any presetting you may do that is not already called for on the cue-sheets. Report all changes you make to the head performance electrician so that he can make them on his and any other copies of the cue-sheets in use.

If the cue-sheet has so many changes and additions that it is not perfectly clear, turn it in to the head electrician for re-copying. If this is done between the last rehearsal and the performance, you *must* run through the entire new cue-sheet again with one of the directors before it is used. It is not sufficient simply to proof-read the new copy, for there may be errors in the typographical arrangement of the cue-sheet which would not be caught by ordinary proof-reading. The director should watch the old sheet containing the corrections as you run through the new cue-sheet. Remember that corrections do not imply that the cue-sheet maker was inaccurate originally—only that a director and technical director nearly always make revisions when they finally see the production in full rehearsal.

To the Reader for the Switchboard Operator:

You will be given a cue-sheet or a copy of the play marked for the switchboard operator, and will read the instructions to him whenever a cue is spoken. You will be used only when the lighting is so complicated that he cannot follow the cue-sheet and operate the board at the same time. Thus, your presence means that the work is complicated, and, in consequence, you must be extremely attentive.

Unless the cue-sheet shows that there are no cues during a scene, you will give attention exclusively to it, talking to no one. If you want to know "how the switchboard works," ask about it at some other time!

As you read a direction, have the switchboard operator repeat it to you in order to make sure that he understands it. He should do nothing with the lights that is not called for by the cue-sheet. If he has corrections to make, they must be entered on the cue-sheet. They must not be made during performance unless they have been proven to be correct in rehearsal. You will enter such corrections (even if only the addition of work-lights, or the snapping off of switches on dimmed-out lights, or any pre-setting done in advance of that recorded on the cue-sheet). You will also enter in the cue-sheet corrections made by any of the directors. Changes other than those for the operation of the switchboard must have the approval of the head electrician and the technical director.

Major changes of lights, such as the dimming of a number of them, or a change between scenes, or any pre-setting, should be double-checked. The operator will make these changes in the order you give them to him, and, at the first opportunity, you, or both of you, will go over them with a check-list. If this check-list is not provided on the cue-sheet, you will add one. Sometimes a suitably drafted diagram of the switchboard will be the most efficient means for checking. This diagram should show the position of all switches and of all dimmers.

If it is impossible to see the stage, and cues for it must be relayed by an individual, such as the head performance electrician, who can see it, you may help the operator by watching for such signals.

Be extremely careful to distinguish between warning cues and cues. The most common errors in the switchboard operation occur because of a confusion between them.

When there are only a few times at which the operator will need help on complicated switchboard operation, you may help him for those few cues and thus avoid having an assistant switchboard operator. When it is necessary to have more than one operator, you will note which one takes each cue, and include that information in your cue-sheet. It may be possible to make an individual cue-sheet for the assistant, which he will read for himself, or, when necessary, give him a separate cue-sheet and a separate reader.

To the Floor Operator:

You will make all the changes in lights on the stage floor other than those from the switchboard. This includes the placing of standing units; the re-direction of standing or hanging units; the changing of gelatines, masks, and slides; the operation of any "follow-spots" or other moving lights; the changing of any wiring; the operation of any purely electrical effects such as lightning or projections; the operation of any dimmer on a spot or olivette standard; the placing of any lamps onstage; the hanging of wall lights or center lighting fixtures in an interior setting, and the checking of wiring after a scene change to make certain that connections have not loosened.

You will have a cue-sheet of your own, or a general lighting cue-sheet with your own tasks especially marked. Should anything go wrong, you will report to the head performance electrician or stage manager. You also will report it to the switchboard operator if it concerns his work.

You will mark with chalk, paint, or brass headed tacks, according to the practice in vogue, the position and angle of all standing lights, and the like. When it is possible to do so, in order to check its correctness, you will have the switchboard operator turn on, in advance of its use, any light you have placed. Where there is no possibility of checking a change before its use, you must carefully examine the wiring. It may help you to paint the stage connectors with numbers or distinctive colors, but beware of the alterations made in these colors by colored lights!

In making a connection, always tie the connectors together with a knot so that an actor or grip will not pull the connectors apart if he trips over the cable. In making such a knot, lay the two cables on the floor, the ends crossing each other at right angles eight inches from the connectors, the left-hand cable on top. Reach under the cable from the right with your right hand, take the connector of the left-hand cable and draw it toward you under the right-hand one. Now fasten the two connectors together and pull both cables in order to tighten the knot.

If there is the possibility of a plug being pulled out of a floor or wall socket by accident, secure the connection by wiring (using insulated wire) or by other means of fastening the cable near the socket. A cable running across the floor may be fastened to it by staples.

To the Bridge, Tower, and Balcony Operators:

The use of a balcony, bridge, or tower operator usually implies a follow-spot, though you may be there merely to change the gelatines and masks, or the direction and focus of the light when it is out.

You will have a cue-sheet giving the warning cues and cues. On a warning cue, you will make sure that your light is pointed correctly and is free to move smoothly at the slightest pressure of your hands. The light may be turned on from the switchboard or by a switch or dimmer on the standard. If it is operated from the switchboard, and should fail to light at the cue, you will follow the actor with the unlighted spot, so that when it finally comes on, the beam will be where it should be. When you operate the light from a switch, dimmer, or a shutter such as an iris, it is possible to find your point of focus with a very dim light or a slightly open shutter in advance of the cue if you do it so carefully that it cannot be noticed. You will be careful to keep the spot off the scenery and other actors on which it does not belong.

You must know the exact movements of the actor you are to follow with the light so that you can anticipate them and be ready to manipulate the light accordingly.

If you are handling color media, they should be marked as to color and use, as it will be difficult to identify them during the performance in the absence of white light. You must change gelatines, et cetera, on cue—not from memory.

You probably will need heavy canvas or asbestos gloves.

If you are in the balcony, never place anything on the hand-rail that might fall off. No matter how safe it appears, someone coming to speak to you might accidentally brush it off. Be as inconspicuous as possible in your movements, in order not to distract the attention of the audience from the stage. Be sure that the spot does not spill light into the eyes of any member of the audience. If you are to use an arc spotlight, see that the carbons are in good condition and then get them hot in advance of the performance or before the beginning of the act in which the light is to be used, in order to minimize the buzzing noise that will be made. Watch it constantly in order to make sure that the adjustment of carbons is correct.

If you are on a bridge that is inclined to sway, you must take one position and keep it. You can arrange in advance to make yourself comfortable. Never carry to the bridge tools which might drop off. If you must have them there, fasten them either to the bridge or to your person.

To the Reader for Lighting Rehearsal:

When the lighting is complicated, a special lighting rehearsal frequently is called in advance of the first dress rehearsal, between dress rehearsals, or between dress rehearsal and performance. The actors usually are not asked to be present. If there are many light changes on spoken or action cues, a reader is required. One of the directors or electricians may do the reading, but they usually will need to give their entire attention to the lights. The prompter makes an excellent reader for such a rehearsal because of his knowledge of the play.

You will receive instructions from the technical director as to how much of the play he wants you to read. In a very complicated production, you will read the entire play aloud to the electricians. In less complicated ones, you will read particular scenes; or only the page immediately preceding and including the cues, and a sufficient number of the speeches following them to show when the effect is to be completed. Where you skip sections of a scene you will announce it so that the operators will know the length of the interval between cues. Pause before this announcement so that they will know it is not a part of the text. They will not be listening to you for the sense of the text, but merely for their cues, so they will not distinguish your comment from the reading of the script unless you first draw attention to it.

You will read the play from the stage, simulating the tone, voice, and style of the actors, and you will move about the stage taking the more important positions the actors will occupy, so that the lighting can be studied with relation to those positions. In other words, you will give an impersonation reading. It is especially important that you imitate the movements of those actors that are followed by a spotlight. If there are darkened scenes in which you cannot read the text, you will provide yourself with a flashlight for the purpose, but you will keep this light off the scenery as much as possible.

CHAPTER IX

COSTUME DEPARTMENT

To the Costume Master:

You will have general supervision over all the work of constructing, repairing, renting, and purchasing costumes, and of everything else related to them, including accessories and the make-up of the actors. You may do some of the work yourself, or you may assign part or all of it to assistants. You will co-ordinate your work with that of the other departments, keeping costume colors in harmony with the settings and lights, and relieving other departments of sewing that may arise in the course of their work.

Instructions on the designing, cutting, and sewing of garments and accessories are given fully by many books on stage costuming.

Either you or an assistant will make out a complete costume plot of the production, listing all items of both costumes and accessories to be worn by every actor in each of the scenes. If under-dressing or over-dressing is necessary for quick costume changes, you will provide instructions for it, and will see that the changes are rehearsed until they can be made in the time allotted for them. In the case of very quick changes, you should write minute instructions for every movement of the actor and the dressers. An example of such a set of instructions is given in Figure 32.

You will give copies of the costume plot to your assistants in charge of borrowing, renting, purchasing, and to the performance costume master, wardrobe master, stage manager, and to the maker of the combination cue-sheet and scene shifting plot.

An individual costume list and instruction sheet should be given to each actor if he has to supply his own costumes, and a copy of it

posted in his dressing room for the guidance of the valets and dressers. You should give the dressers written instructions on the changes
in which they are to assist.

To the Assistant Costume Master in charge of borrowing:

This task will be assigned to you in case a play is being done for
which it is desirable to borrow garments, such as one placed in the
present period, in a recent period, or in an earlier one for which people are apt to own masquerade costumes.

In the case of a modern play, first see whether the actor himself has
or can borrow suitable garments. Ordinarily this will be possible. At
least a week in advance of the dress rehearsals, you should see and
approve of, or have your superiors approve of, every costume to be
used in the play.

If you have to borrow costumes, appeal for them first to the cast
and those otherwise interested in the production, then to your friends,
and last to the stores. In doing this, avoid all comments about actors
and actresses that might be considered disparaging. Tactless explanations to people solicited, such as, "He has no suit that will do,"
may lower his prestige, and, if it reaches his ears, wound his pride.
People always have clothes which meet their own needs, or, if they
do not, are unable to afford them. In either case, it is not considerate
to mention the matter in such a way. Say, rather, if any comment of
the kind is necessary, that the actor's own clothes are not suited to
the character he is to play. Remember that it is less embarrassing to
you to try to borrow garments than for an actor to ask for them
himself. If the individual solicited refuses your request, neither of
you is embarrassed, while, in the other case, both he and the actor
might be.

In a costume play, you must thoroughly familiarize yourself with
the period in which the play is placed so that when you are offered
an unsuitable costume you can say definitely and confidently that
it belongs to a different period from that of the play, and so cannot
be used, "though you appreciate the offer," and so forth. You must

know the related periods. You may not be able to decline the loan of a costume gracefully if you only know that the costume is "not right," but cannot explain why. This also is a convenient way to decline a costume that is unsuitable otherwise. The owner of a costume seldom has exact knowledge of its period. If you talk glibly of farthingales and pickadils, or liripipes and lappets, of hymatia and chlamyses, the owner will take your word for anything!

All garments to be borrowed must be located well in advance of the dress rehearsals so that you will know what cannot be thus obtained, and then get them from a costumer or have them made.

At the time you obtain the promise of a garment, write down all the details of the transaction in the presence of the owner—his name, address, and telephone number, the date it is to be called for, the date it is to be returned, and how you are to get it—in order that he may realize that he is assuming a definite obligation. Should the plans for the use of the garment be changed, be certain to call him by telephone and explain the circumstances, or you will have lost that source for a costume in the future. Report in writing, and in detail, these matters to the costume master.

Great care must be exercised in the handling of borrowed costumes, for they must be returned in perfect condition. Examine them carefully after the production, and repair any damage that they may have sustained. In case the damage is serious, consult the technical director and see that it is made good by either the organization or the person responsible for it. Always have the costume cleaned before it is returned, unless you are told not to do so. If the material is old and fragile, ask, before you borrow it, about having it cleaned. Explain that because of the inevitable soil from the make-up of the actor it will have to be cleaned after the play. Do not borrow it if it cannot be cleaned. Do not make any promises about special care in handling a costume that you cannot be sure will be carried out.

The organization pays for cleaning the special costumes, but the actor pays for cleaning a present-day costume borrowed as an accommodation to him. There is some variation in this practice among theatre groups, but if you once start cleaning borrowed modern clothes, the rest of the cast will expect you to pay for cleaning their own clothes that they wear in the play.

See that costumes are returned immediately! If you do not return them personally, call the owner and thank him for the favor. Insist that he examine the costume carefully for damage so he will know that it was delivered in good condition and will not blame you for injuries which occur later. Report all repairs that had to be made. In short, be straightforward in the whole transaction.

To the Assistant Costume Master in charge of renting and buying:

From the technical director, costume master, or at a conference of the costume staff, you will receive the list of costumes that are to be secured.

Collect enough pictures of the exact types of costumes wanted, and information on their prevailing colors, to make the period entirely clear to a commercial costume house. Few salespeople in costume houses really know periods. Determine the exact colors desired, giving second and third choices, having reference always to the interplay of the colors of costumes in important scenes, their relation to the setting and the lights, and to the characters to be portrayed. If you are ordering costumes by letter, you will find that this frequently entails the making of a dozen or more complete color schemes. For instance, if you give two acceptable colors for the feminine lead's costume, and two for the male lead's to go with each of them, and similar conditional choices, you will find extended charts necessary. If at all possible, even though it involves extra expense, have someone from your organization see the stock of costumes and make the selections personally. Even though you go yourself, you can save much time for the costumer and yourself if you have a list of all possible colors each character might wear in a given scene, with an indication of the general relationship between them. In the final judgment, always have the whole set of costumes laid out so that they can be studied together. If you are making some costumes and renting others, take with you, when you visit the costumer, *large* samples of the material for those to be made.

Pay little attention to the color preferences of the actors and actresses, or the colors they say they "can't wear." This is almost entirely a matter of complexion and color of hair. The one can be altered by make-up and the other by a wig, bronzing powder, a rinse, or mascaro.

When you go to the costumer's, have the following measurements for the women:

Waist
Bust
Hips
Height (All measurements in the type of shoes they will wear.)
  Neckline to the floor
  Neckline to the waist
  Waist to the floor
Width of shoulders
Sleeve length
Shoe size
Hat size
Wig size

Measurements for the men:

Waist
Hips
Chest (Around, and also across front and across back.)
Width of shoulders
Length of arms from shoulder to sleeve cuff
Height from shoulder to floor
Length of in-seam of trousers
Shoe size
Wig size
Hat size

When a woman is to play a man's part, or vice versa, you must give the size of shoes in the sex of the character, not that of the actor.

The measurements taken for a wig are the circumference of the head at its largest point, which usually will be from the line of the hair on the forehead around a spot level with the bottom of the ears at the back, and the distance over the head from the front to the back of this rough circle. Note that a black wig, unless made of undyed real hair, is very trying on the appearance of the wearer, just as is living hair dyed black. It makes the person look older and his expression harder. Substitute very dark brown wigs when possible, and use a dark make-up. When a wig has to be worn by a girl with long hair, the less the amount of hair it contains the better.

Make arrangement in advance on the terms as well as the price to be paid for the use of the costumes. If you do not do so, expect to have them sent C.O.D. for the entire amount, including expressage. There should be an understanding as to who is to pay the expressage. It is usually paid by the renter. If the costumes are obtained from a local dealer, you may be expected to send for them.

When the costumes arrive, take an inventory of them and notify the technical director immediately if the costumer's invoice does not check with the costumes received, or if anything that was ordered was omitted from the shipment.

After you so check the costumes, check them again when you turn them over to the wardrobe master, or have him help you on the first inspection. Give the invoice bearing your O.K. to the technical director.

After the final performance, check the costumes again with the wardrobe master, and repack them for return shipment the next day. Include a new inventory that is signed by yourself. Give a copy of it to the technical director, and ask him if you are responsible for returning the costumes. If you are, do it immediately, as the costumer charges for costumes held overtime.

In most states, the costumer is required by law to clean costumes before each rental, the cost of it being included in the rental charge. If that is not the law where you are and the costumes arrive with signs of having been worn since they were cleaned, obtain cleaning fluid and dip them.

To the Performance Costume Master:

You yourself may take one of the tasks in addition to the general supervision and direction of the costume work at performances. You are responsible to the costume master for all phases of the costume work, but at performance you work under the orders of the stage manager.

You may have assistants, and, if needed, assistants for your dressers. The more elaborate the production, the less the work for which you should take personal responsibility.

On the night of the dress rehearsal, and each night of performance, ask the technical director, stage manager, or costume master, what costumes need pressing, cleaning, altering, or repairing before the next performance. Check this work in ample time to have it redone if necessary. All major alterations or repairs should be done for the valet by the members of the staff who make costumes, but you and he are responsible for its being done.

You may have as assistants, a wardrobe master, valets, and dressers. The make-up work may be under either your supervision or that of the make-up master.

Assign the dressing rooms to the actors. Make them as happy as possible in such arrangements, when possible putting friends together. Take into account the fact that certain actors may have long and complicated make-ups, and, in consequence, need longer use of a mirror than some others. More than the ordinary space is needed by an actor who has a costume change to make. On the other hand, if a certain actor does not have to begin dressing until after the curtain has gone up on the first act, he can be put into an otherwise full dressing room. In some theatres dressing rooms have become traditional as "star," "second," "third," and so on. Some organizations follow this scheme, but it is not a beneficial one in an amateur organization. It is rather ridiculous to permit a leading man, with only a straight make-up to put on, to monopolize a whole dressing room, while two or three character men take turns using the mirror in another one. Fortunately, few amateur actors expect such favoritism.

See that all dressing rooms are adequately supplied with coat-hangers—adequate in number for street clothes as well as costumes.

To the Wardrobe Master:

You are the assistant performance costume master in charge of issuing costumes. You will receive the costumes from the assistant costume masters in charge of construction, of borrowing, and of rental and purchasing, and a list of the costumes and accessories to be worn by each actor in each scene from the costume master. Often you will work as a member of the construction costume crew, getting out of stock such garments as are needed.

Assemble all costumes in wrapped bundles, in boxes, or on hangers, and make out a sheet for each complete unit, listing all its separate pieces. Tabulate these, making columns for checking them each time they are issued and returned. Thus, if the costumes are issued at the first dress rehearsal and taken up again only after the last performance, there need be only two columns, but if they are given out and taken up each night, you need two such columns for each dress rehearsal and performance. At the bottom of the sheet you will list the date of each rehearsal and performance at which costumes will change hands, with spaces for the initials of the actor when he receives the costume and your own when it is returned. Loss of a costume or any part of it must be made good by the person having custody of it at the time it disappears, unless it is found to be a theft for which he cannot be held responsible. Some organizations even then require payment for the loss.

If the costumes are kept in the dressing rooms between performances, you will see that such rooms are locked at night and opened again in time for the actors to dress in them. When the costumes are in your hands, see that they are locked up, and that no one is allowed to touch them except in the presence of the director, technical director, valet, or yourself. Always obtain a receipt for any part of a costume taken out.

You are directly responsible to the performance costume master.

To the Valet:

On the day of the first performance, you will gather a crew of workers, and collect the irons, clothes brushes, cleaning fluid, and other materials for making the costume repairs, and will go over all the costumes and costume accessories carefully, cleaning, mending, and ironing them. Be particularly attentive to holes in stockings and tights. After each performance you will inquire of the performance costume master, who will have been in touch with his superiors, whether this servicing, or any part of it, needs to be repeated before the next performance. Garments made of stiff silk, organdy, rayon, or other easily wrinkled cloth, will need daily attention. Note that the shabby appearance of costumes is nearly always due to limpness which can be remedied by fresh pressing. A very old costume often can be fully revived for stage purposes by skillful pressing, including the proper use of starch.

You will service all costumes, whether furnished by the producing organization or by the actor. You are responsible also for redressing wigs.

See that the janitor or someone else thoroughly cleans all dressing rooms between performances.

You are directly responsible to the performance costume master.

To the Dressers:

You will have thoroughly studied the costumes of the period by means of pictures in order to know how the costumes should be worn—where ornaments are attached, where a cape is fastened and how carried, the way in which trains were handled both when flowing and when caught up, the appropriate footwear, the type of jewelry, et cetera—so that you can answer the questions of the actors on all such points. Capes and other draperies held over the arm should be draped from the front backward. This permits freer gestures and makes it easier for the actor to catch the drapery should it start to fall.

Provide yourself with a liberal supply of safety pins, straight pins, hooks and eyes, snaps, needles and thread, white linen tape or bands (when wigs are worn), elastic tape (when garters may be needed), hairpins, et cetera, and make all the needed repairs, corrections, and adjustments in the costumes.

Wigs should be kept dressed by the valet, but a very light combing of the surface of a wig that has just a few hairs flying, will improve its appearance. Hairpins at the brows will keep a wig snug on the head, when, in order to look natural, it must lie flat. If the wig will not hold these hairpins properly, tie a band of linen tape or plain material around the head just above the wig line and pin the wig to that. This must always be done for a wig that gets rough usage, such as when a hat is worn over it and is taken off in the action by the actor, when a fall is to be made by the actor, or when the hair has to be touched by another actor. A wig that is too large may have a tuck sewed or pinned in the back or at the side. Wig-bands—strips of dampened cloth tied around the head over the wig to mold it firmly to the head—should be provided for each actor that wears a wig. The broad part of the band should be placed at the back with the knot on the forehead, in order to avoid an irregular line or a cowlick at the back. You must see that the actor removes the wig-band before he goes on the stage.

You will help the actors with quick changes. If they need it, you also will help the actors to plan under-dressing (part of his next costume worn under the first) or over-dressing (putting the next costume on over the first).

An example of the way in which very quick changes must be planned is shown in Figure 32. Even more difficult and faster ones can be made. These are done in the same manner, but require more dressers.

When you have the time for it during the dress rehearsals, go out front to appraise the wearing and the handling of costumes. You may be able to make suggestions to the actors on how to make more effective use of their costumes. Never criticise unless you can improve, and allow no one else to do so, lest it make some of the actors dissatisfied with their costumes.

Be sure that the actors are made as comfortable as possible in their costumes. You can insist on alterations being made when requests for them by the actor might seem to be merely "temperament" on his part.

You are directly responsible to the performance costume master.

To the Make-up Master:

Make-up is a division of the work of the costumer. When the actors make up themselves, the make-up designer in consultation with them should decide on the colors and elements for the characterization. The work here outlined supposes a special crew of people to make up all or a portion of the cast.

As make-up master you will exercise a directional and critical authority over all the work. You will assign the make-ups to the make-up assistants. You yourself may do some of the tasks here assigned to your assistants, such as designing or supervising the make-up room.

You are responsible to the costume master.

To the Make-up Designer:

This task is a much needed one in many amateur organizations, where the actors know only three types of make-ups: straight, ruddy old age, and sallow old age. They thereby forget many subtle make-up effects that would improve their characterizations.

Read the play several times and note the information in the script that gives clues to the make-up of each character—age, nationality, ancestry, occupation, physical condition, past experiences, emotions, the time he spends out-of-doors, and other unique characteristics. Find pictures of people who have faces of the same type as the actor playing the part, and who have the appearance of the character as you conceive it. Show these to the director and obtain his approval of them. Make notes on the mountings of the pictures of any matters to which you want to direct attention or of any necessary deviations from the pictures selected. Photographs, newspaper pictures

```
COSTUME CHANGES                    PETER STANDISH: Bob Clare
BERKELEY SQUARE                    Dresser: Warren Hill

              Act I, Scene 2
Underdressed:     shoes
                  stockings, black
                  breeches
                  waistcoat

Over these:       trousers(belted, no buttons buttoned)
                  shirt(open at neck, partly buttoned)
                  dressing robe

              Change for Act I, Scene 3
Undo robe and shirt as you go to quick change room.
Dresser remove robe and shirt together.
Clare unbuckle trousers and let them fall.  Sit and dresser
   pin on jabot.
Dresser remove trousers and put buckles on shoes while Clare
   adjusts wig.
Dresser pick up coat, which has been hung wrong side out
   over the back of a chair, and signal Stage Manager as
   Clare puts it on, adjusting it as he goes to entrance.

              Change for Act II
Complete change: white breeches, waistcoat, coat, white
   stockings, black shoes, jabot, white wig.

              Change for Act III, Scene 1
Underdressed:     sox
                  shirt
                  four-in-hand tied, but not tightened

Over these:       riding breeches
                  waistcoat and coat
                  jabot
                  boots
                  dark wig

              Change for Act III, Scene 2
Remove wig on way to dressing room.
Dresser remove coat, undo waistcoat which Clare removes,
   and remove jabot.
Dresser put on vest and suitcoat which have been hung wrong
   side out over the back of a chair.
Clare sit, tighten tie, button vest, comb hair, while dress-
   er remove boots and put on shoes.
Clare put on trousers and button them on way to entrance.
   (This will not be difficult to put on trousers after vest,
   since shirt is tucked in riding breeches.)
```

FIGURE 32. Example of instructions to actor and dresser for a series of costume changes. The time required for the quick-changes was from fifty-five to sixty-five seconds. They were rehearsed with forty-five seconds as the goal.

from both the news and rotogravure sections, magazine covers, advertisements, and original drawings may be used. It is well to have an abundant supply of good pictures of such kind on hand.

A week before the first make-up, discuss it with each actor, obtaining ideas from him to supplement your own. In consultation with him or the assistant who will make him up, decide on just what will be done, making out a form detailing what grease paint and lining colors he will use and precisely what he will do otherwise. Keep these forms and give them to the superintendent of the make-up rooms, who will distribute and collect them each time the make-ups are put on.

If the organization supplies make-up materials, make a list of all supplies needed and give it to the make-up supply master.

Watch the first make-ups and be ready at dress rehearsal to criticise them. Give any special directions needed about them to the superintendent of the make-up rooms.

During the rehearsal go out front and there study the make-ups from the front row of seats, from the middle of the house, and from the back row. Discuss the make-ups with the make-up master and the director between acts and after the performance.

To the Superintendent of Make-up Rooms:

You will receive a full set of form-sheets from the make-up designer giving instructions for each make-up. You will distribute these each time make-ups are put on, and will collect them afterwards. You will see to it that all comments or corrections are noted on the sheets.

In case they are furnished by the organization, you will receive the supplies for the make-up from the make-up supply master. This task and yours often are combined.

In cases where actors do not put on their own make-up, you will, after consultation with the designer of make-ups, secure make-up assistants for the purpose.

At dress rehearsal you will approve the make-ups as they are completed, and send the actor, or actor and assistant together, to the director or make-up master for approval. He will study the actor's make-up on the stage and make notes on the form-sheet of corrections or of approval. After once having the make-up of an actor approved on the stage, only send him for approval again if his make-up has been changed, or when you fear he has altered its strength, the effect of which can only be judged on the stage.

Be ready to help anyone in making up, but take no job upon yourself as a permanent task.

You will go out front during the rehearsals with the make-up designer, and there study the make-ups. You will make notes on the possible betterments in make-ups and discuss them with the make-up master or director between the acts or after the rehearsal. You will convey the changes agreed upon to the actors or assistants, either verbally, requiring them to add them to their form-sheets, or by means of a posted bulletin. Such corrections are not to be treated as mistakes on the part of assistants or the designer, for make-ups can only be finally judged on the stage under lights. The preliminary ones are only experimental.

No actor should be excused from dress rehearsal make-up. He may not need practice in it, but you will need to have all actors made up in order to judge of the comparative colors. It is sometimes possible to appear in a part without grease paint, but the actor's natural face is then studied from the auditorium in order to see if it gives the effect wanted.

If there is more than one dress rehearsal, it is a good practice to have make-ups put on at the next to the last one. Those which are satisfactory need not be put on again at the last dress rehearsal.

You are responsible to the make-up master and, through him, to the performance costume master and the stage manager.

To the Make-up Supply Master:

Obtain a list of materials from the make-up designer showing what each make-up will require. See that there is a sufficient supply of everything needed. Give a list of items to be ordered to the technical director at least four days before the first make-up day. A check-list is given below.

If any of the supplies used are not to be furnished by the organization, such as cold cream, make-up rags, Kleenex, and protective clothing, be sure that it is announced to the actors in advance.

Each night, after the make-ups have been put on, check the supplies that may have been exhausted—crêpe hair, spirit gum, mascara paste, body color, Kleenex, et cetera.

On the first make-up day, see that the supplies reach the theatre, take an inventory of them, and put them in order. Thereafter, you will be responsible for them, putting them in safe-keeping after each performance, and distributing them each night. You must see that the make-up room is in order before you leave each night unless that is part of the janitor service of the theatre.

After the final performance, you will take inventory again, and report depleted supplies to the technical director.

You are responsible, through the superintendent of make-up rooms, to the make-up master, the performance costume master, and the stage manager.

CHECK-LIST OF MAKE-UP SUPPLIES

Body colors
Bases
Highlight bases
Shadow bases
Liners
Pencils (lining)
Moist rouges
Dry rouges
Under rouges
Powders
Powder puffs
Material for coloring hair
Baby brushes
Lining brushes, stomps, etc.

Cosmetic
Cosmetic stoves
Cosmetic appliers
Matches
Mascaro
Mascaro brushes
Nose putty
Olive oil
Adhesive tape
Energine (or other non-inflammable adhesive remover)
Spirit gum
Alcohol
Crêpe hair (straightened, if needed)

Beards
Glue
Collodion
Cold cream
Hairpins, etc.

Kleenex, cheese cloth, towels, or
    other make-up rags
Clothes protection
White mascara in tubes
Lip sticks
Eyebrow pencils

To the Make-up Assistants or Actors:

At least one week in advance of the first make-up, discuss the matter with the actor you are to make up and with the make-up designer. With them, make out a form-sheet showing exactly what is to be done and what paints are to be used.

On the first make-up day, reproduce the make-up from this form. If you make any changes, note them on the form.

Take the actor to the superintendent of the make-up rooms for approval, giving him the form-sheet to study with the make-up. When he has approved it, he should send you to the make-up designer, technical director, or director, who will criticise the make-up on the stage under the lights. You will note their comments on your make-up form-sheet.

Once approved, you will reproduce the make-up exactly the same thereafter. You may, however, obtain permission to try something else at other dress rehearsals. Never vary without permission from that decided upon.

You may be expected to furnish part or all of your supplies. You almost certainly will be expected to furnish protective clothing for yourself and the actor that you make up, unless he is told to bring it himself. He should never be made up without protection for his costume.

Realize that make-up is a comparative matter. You must adapt your methods to those of the organization, because what may be good when all follow the same practice, will be impossible when the other make-ups are differently designed.

You must reach the theatre on time. It is very disturbing to an actor's peace of mind to have to worry about a delay in make-up. Remember that he will have to finish dressing after his make-up is completed.

You are under the direction of the superintendent of the make-up rooms. Make-up assistants who do not take part in the play as actors or crewmen will help straighten up the make-up room.

CHAPTER X

MUSIC DEPARTMENT

To the Musical Director and Arranger:

You will arrange with the director of the play for the music that is to be used, whether it is part of the play or consists of entr'acte numbers. The overture, the entr'acte pieces, and the exit march should be in harmony in mood, tempo, force, period, and general effect, with the play and the particular scenes which they follow and precede.

Learn from the stage manager if the shifting of scenery is apt to be noisy and, if so, select musical numbers that may be played loudly during these changes.

You will cut the music, expand it by repetition of passages, and make other adaptations. If you find it necessary, you may have this done for you. Except for that one task, the nature of your duties does not require musical training.

You must know the exact amount of time allotted for each intermission, and fit the music to it. Waits in the theatre are so important in their effect on the audience, that an unnecessarily long musical interlude breaks the mood of the play. It is still more unfortunate, however, to have the musical number shorter than the length of the intermission, and thus to have it end before the curtain is ready to be raised. In order to prevent this possibility, provide for a repeat near the end of the score. The leader will receive a signal during the number showing that the stage is ready. If he receives the signal before he comes to the repeat, he will conclude the piece. If he does not receive such a signal, he will have the orchestra play the repeat and continue with it until he gets the signal.

183

Always provide an extra number to be played in case of so long a delay that the leader will be forced to conclude his selection, including the repeat.

Give the score you have selected to the orchestra leader or the concert master.

You will supervise all the musical work, including the arrangements for the moving of instruments, the placing of chairs, stands, lights, and the like. You cannot ask the orchestra to play more than a few bars in total darkness. If the auditorium is not to be lighted brightly during musical numbers, orchestra lights must be provided.

To the Assistant Musical Director in charge of Cue-sheets:

You will make out a complete music cue-sheet and, from this, the orchestra cue-sheet and, if there are backstage musicians, the various onstage and offstage music cue-sheets (see Figure 33).

Always include warning (stand-by) cues and warning stop cues, as well as start cues and stop cues, so that the actual ones will not come unexpectedly. Also give instructions as to whether the music is to start softly and swell to full volume, or is to begin sharply; and whether it is to die away, come to a full stop on a cue, or be completed after the cue.

When an orchestra score accompanies much of the dialogue of a play, as the Mendelssohn music for *A Midsummer Night's Dream,* it is advisable to enter the cues for the orchestra leader in a copy of the text of the play. For Shakespeare's plays, the Yale interleaved edition may be obtained so that there is a blank page for notes opposite every page of text. For other plays, it is possible to prepare such a copy, or to paste the pages of the text into a large-size notebook and put the cue-sheet information alongside the pages of text.

Remember that the orchestra leader may come to the performance without having seen the play in rehearsal, and must have such explicit instructions that he will make no errors.

Make a cue-sheet for each backstage musical leader or solo musician. Record the time at which they should reach the theatre, or, if

MUCH ADO ABOUT NOTHING   for Mr. Burnam

8:12 (on signal) Overture "Orpheus"

Bugler go backstage left (actor's left) immediately. Give
   bugle call of ten notes or less on "Not till a hot Jan-
   uary."

        (Long scene concluding with Leonato and Antonio on-
           stage, "Go you and tell her of it." Curtain. No
           music.)

        (Short scene concluding with Don Juan, Borachio and
           Conrade. "We'll wait upon your lordship." Cur-
           tain. Music.)

Drigo's "Serenade" (Three pieces of the orchestra back-
        stage right. As the curtains open the orchestra in pit
        stops, but the backstage music continues.)
   Backstage stop on "You apprehend passing shrewdly."
   Backstage start again on "I would he had boarded me."
   Continue for a short time and then die away.
   Return to pit in next intermission.

        (Long scene concluding with Borachio and Don Juan,
           "I will go learn their day of marriage." Curtain.
           Music.)

Drigo's "Serenade" (Die away with curtain.)

        (No further music until intermission and house
           lights. There will be three long scenes with
           very short curtains before the intermission.)

"Torch Dance" followed by "Shepherd's Dance". Then
"March of the Marionettes" (Die away as Dogberry enters.)

        (Long scene, Dogberry and then drunk scene, "Come,
           we'll obey you." Curtain. Music.)

Drigo's "Serenade" (Die away with curtain.)

        (Short scene, Hero, Beatrice, Ursula, and Margaret
           "Help me to dress, good coz, good Margaret, good
           Ursula." Curtain. Very short music.)

FIGURE 33. The first page from a music cue-sheet used by the orchestra
leader. Separate instructions were given to the musicians from the pit
orchestra who played backstage.

they are part of the orchestra, the time at which they should go back-stage. If the dress rehearsals and the performances begin at different hours, indicate that clearly. If there is to be applause following the backstage music, the musicians should furnish it, aided by the actors and crewmen, who will take their signal from the musicians.

An onstage musician is an actor, and, in consequence, will re-hearse with the cast and should know his cues at the dress rehearsal. Since, however, he may not have a copy of the play, you will furnish him with all such instructions from the text and any additional ones that the director may want to give him. Give him the point in the play at which he is to appear, the length of time he is to be onstage, instructions as to his costume and make-up, the warning cue for his entrance, where he will enter, his entrance cue, his actions on the stage, all his lines or business, his music cues, his exit cues, and the place of his exit.

To the Orchestra Leader:

You will receive your music from the musical director. You will rehearse the musical selections and have them ready for the director's approval some time in advance of the first dress rehearsal.

Learn the theatre's practice with respect to musical numbers dur-ing scene changes. Sometimes the orchestra is allowed to conclude a selection and the curtain raised immediately afterwards. Sometimes, when a change may not have been completed in the allotted time, provision for a repeat is made in the music. If you do not receive your signal before the repeat is reached, you will have the orchestra play it, and continue to do so until you receive the signal to stop. When there is a long delay you will conclude the selection and then play the extra number provided for such emergencies, or any other piece for which you have the score.

On quick changes, music ordinarily is used only as a filler. The orchestra plays until signalled to stop, or until the curtains open, then the music fades away.

If the backstage is likely to be noisy during rapid changes, have your musicians play loudly enough to drown out the noise, even at the expense of good rendition. The audience gives critical attention to the music only during long intermissions.

During quick changes, the orchestra will sometimes be expected to play short numbers without lights. This must, of course, be rehearsed. You can conduct with a lighted baton, or a flashlight covered with colored gelatine so that it is just barely visible.

You may, at your pleasure, acknowledge applause for the overture and the numbers between acts, but should not do so for those played at the time of quick changes during an act.

Continue to play exit marches until the auditorium is empty.

You will receive a cue-sheet from the music cue-sheet maker, or a copy of the play showing your cues. You should study this in advance of the first appearance of your orchestra with the actors, asking questions freely in order to have everything clearly understood. If you are expected to pick up cues quickly, you must attend one or more dress rehearsals whether your orchestra does so or not. If the music must be related to the stage action, the full orchestra must be rehearsed with the actors. It is not imperative that this be done at a dress rehearsal. Instead, the actors may come to an orchestra rehearsal.

Where the relation of the music and the stage action is important, it is helpful for the orchestra leader to delegate his pianist, or some other musician, to supply a representation of the orchestra music at the last few rehearsals.

You will see that the orchestra members are given the information and cautions mentioned in the next section, or copies of it.

To the Pit Musicians:

You may be expected to attend dress rehearsals as well as the performances. If you are called for dress rehearsals, you will remember that rehearsals are confidential, and everything that takes place there is impersonal in nature. You should form no opinion then as to the merit of the coming show, for it is possible only after years of experience to judge a production from a dress rehearsal, so much does the effect of a performance depend upon the presence of an audience. With a full house on the opening night, for example, you will sometimes roar with laughter at things that "bored you stiff" at dress rehearsal! Above all else, you will express no opinion on the show to anyone until after you have seen an actual performance. After the opening night, if you watch the complete performance, you are then, like other spectators, at liberty to praise or criticise it. You will ignore all criticism of an actor or technician which you may hear made by the director or anyone else during a dress rehearsal, and will never repeat it, as you would not a criticism the orchestra leader had made of an individual during an orchestra rehearsal.

You may expect a dress rehearsal to begin late and end late, and to contain long delays. Be reconciled to this condition, and do not permit it to annoy you. You may take along a book to read, or provide yourself with something else to do during the waits. Do not talk above a whisper. The actors and the director are already under nervous strain in a rehearsal and are readily irritated by the slightest disturbance that interferes with their work, so don't give them cause for it!

If the orchestra leaves the pit during the performance, it must do so in a body and as inconspicuously as possible. Individual members must not straggle out! If you fail to leave with the other members of the orchestra, you must remain in the pit throughout the scene.

To the Backstage Musicians:

You will receive full instructions from the musical director as to the music you are to play, and from the director or technical director as to its tempo and volume.

You should inspect your position on the backstage before the dress rehearsal and advise the technical director of any changes you want. You may expect to be cramped for room, however, as free backstage space is limited.

You will either pick up your cues from a cue-sheet or you will receive them from a reader. You will receive two cues, a warning cue, which will give you just enough time to get ready, and a cue, which should be your first beat. On a stop cue you will, according to your instructions, either stop instantly or let the music fade away. You usually will be given a stop warning before the actual stop cue.

A hand raised in order to obtain attention is the conventional backstage signal for a warning cue. The hand is dropped for the actual cue.

If offstage applause is supposed to follow your music, you will start it yourselves.

Leave the pit as inconspicuously as possible, and in plenty of time to reach your backstage position for your cue. If it has to be done quickly, see, in advance, that you have everything ready for playing. Either return to the pit inconspicuously, or wait until an intermission to do so.

If you are not a member of the pit orchestra, you will learn when you are to reach the theatre. It may be at a different hour for dress rehearsals and performances. Arrive in ample time and notify the stage manager that you are present. If you want to see the performance after you have played or sung, or before you start, go to the back of the auditorium to do so. Do not obstruct the stage entrances, and do not enter the auditorium by entrances to it that are near the stage.

If you leave instruments backstage, see that they are made safe, either by position, or by putting them into their cases. The theatre is not responsible for instruments left unprotected backstage.

You will be expected to attend dress rehearsals—possibly some of the previous ones.

To The Reader for Backstage Musicians:

In case the backstage musicians are so placed that they cannot hear their starting cues, you will stand where you can hear them and give the musicians hand signals for them. It usually is impossible for musicians to hear their stop cues through their own music, so you almost certainly will have to give these to them by means of another hand signal. In advance of each piece of music you will tell them whether the music is to fade in or start sharply, how loud it should be, and whether it will fade out or come to a sharp stop. Aid them in any other way possible.

You should attend several rehearsals before those attended by the musicians, in order that you may give the signals correctly the first time they appear. Frequently before the regular musicians appear you will be asked to simulate the offstage music. If so, you will play or hum, or obtain someone else to do so. It is best to use the selection that the musicians will play, but this is not essential. It does not matter whether you play well or not. Even chords or one-finger scales on the piano will suffice.

These duties often are assigned to the prompter.

To the Onstage Musician:

The instant you walk on the stage you become an actor, and must act whether you have lines or not. You must listen to all that is said by the actors and react to it, unless you are supposed to be at such a distance that you cannot hear them. You will make no distracting movements. You must learn and rehearse your entrances, exits, and stage movements just as do the actors who have lines to speak. You must attend the rehearsals, although if you have no lines you may not be called until the last few rehearsals. Ordinarily, you will use make-up.

Do not let the audience observe you looking at the orchestra leader as he gives you the tempo. Ignore the audience and play for the benefit of the actors on the stage. If you acknowledge applause, bow to the actors, not the audience. This refers to a play in which there is incidental music, of course. In musical comedy, comic opera, and revue the conventional practice is for the musician to recognize the audience.

CHAPTER XI

THE DIRECTOR AND HIS STAFF

To the Director:

These instructions cover only the handling of the crew of back-stage workers—not your handling of the actors. All your directions to the subordinate workers should reach them through their superior officers; that is to say, if there is a technical director, all comments should be made to him rather than directly to the crew. The exact method for this depends upon the rigidity of the organizational system. With a loosely organized staff, the director, with the knowledge and consent, actual or implied, of the technical director, or in his presence, may deal directly with the members of the crew. In a strictly systematized organization, where each man expects to receive his instructions from his immediate superior, the director should ask permission down the line of officials, through the technical director, stage manager, et cetera, before giving directions to an individual grip. While this seems a needless formality, it is usually advisable in order to preserve the consciousness of full responsibility along the chain of officers. In the end it will save the director time and annoyance, for workers then will not seek to discuss matters with him which should be handled for him by others. Also, in the case of criticisms to be given, assistants may know of extenuating circumstances or of a different responsibility for an error than the director believes to be the case, and so save him the embarrassment and loss of prestige from being wrong and unjust.

The timing of light changes, effects, and curtains, is the responsibility of the director, and should be determined by him at the dress rehearsal. In all other matters, the technical director should have the first opportunity to make corrections and criticisms on the backstage work. For example, a complaint from him about noise on the backstage is far more effective than if it came from you.

Praise of the backstage work by the director, particularly in the presence of the actors, is extremely valuable in creating good feeling, and also in preparing the crew to receive critical comments. Great care should be taken to include praise of the hack jobs as well as of the more important ones, for the less noticeable the job, the more important and the more appreciated can a worker thereby be made to feel. The crew has no opportunity to receive the approval of an audience, as has the actor. Criticism of an executive in the presence of his subordinates is injurious to his authority, and to your prestige, if he is well liked, and especially so when you are judged by the crew to be unjust in your criticism.

If the practice you wish followed in any phase of the backstage work is not the usual one, you should explain it fully well in advance of dress rehearsals to all those affected.

You should be present during any trial set-up of scenery in order to catch errors before the dress rehearsals. Designs are sometimes deceptive as to size and relationship of parts. You also should assist at lighting rehearsals, other than those for drilling the workers after your approval of the lighting has been given.

A suggested list of topics for discussion at dress rehearsal follows, planned to allow the backstage workers, whose work probably will begin early the next day, to leave early after a rehearsal without delaying the departure of the actors or yourself. At the same time it will permit you to criticize the actors in semi-privacy:

TOPIC LIST FOR DRESS REHEARSAL COMMENTS

   I. Make-up (technical director, director, make-up master).
  II. Costumes, and the wearing of them (technical director, director, costume master. It is inadvisable to make comments on costumes which will make the actors self-conscious).
III. General announcements.
     A. Roll call, if needed.

B. Director's announcements for the entire staff:
>   Curtain calls,
>   Flowers,
>   Photographs,
>   Complimentary tickets,
>   Et cetera.

C. Announcements by others.

D. Opportunity for the actors to report any difficulties about scenery, costumes, et cetera.

E. Dismissal of the actors to remove their make-up and costumes, with a definite time set for their return, dressing gowns to be worn if they are not dressed.

IV. Technical comments (technical director, director, and others of the staff).

A. General.

B. Corrections in the scene shifting plots, cue-sheets, et cetera.

C. Technical staff to be turned over to departmental heads for dismissal.

D. Call made for the actors.

V. Actors (director; technical director on the relation of the actors to scenery, properties, and lights).

It is well to urge everyone to make notes of his instructions, as that not only will give him a written record to which to refer, but will aid in remembering them.

Especially important announcements, such as the times of rehearsals, should be posted on a call board in the greenrooms. Delegate someone to keep this board up-to-date by destroying old notices.

To the Assistant to the Director:

There is a wide variety of tasks put upon you according to the practice of different directors. You will follow the instructions of your director.

If you are assigned to conduct partial or complete rehearsals, you will not endeavor to have original ideas adopted unless you have been given specific permission to do so, but will, instead, coach the actors in the readings and business already given them by the director. You will take full authority and enforce the same compliance with direction as would the director, but don't confuse the words "director" and "dictator"! You should not hesitate to answer any unusual question presented to you by saying, "I don't know. I shall have to get the director himself to answer that," or, "I have no authority to make a decision on that." You will lower your prestige, however, if you are not prepared to give the meanings and pronunciations of all words, or are not able to make decisions in all routine matters that arise.

To the Rehearsal Secretary:

You may be called to serve at the preliminary rehearsals, or only at the dress rehearsals. You are to trail the director or technical director, as the case may be, to wherever he goes to watch a rehearsal, and will take notes at his dictation either in longhand or printed script. You will serve also as a messenger.

You may be instructed to make notes in consecutive order, with annotations in the margin of the pages to indicate the scenes and actors or the technical departments to which they refer. Or you may arrange them under a series of headings, such as "Technical Director," "Actors," "Line Slips," "Comments on Make-Up," "Costume Notes," and the like, as instructed by the director. Your notes of his comments should always be definite enough to prevent any misunderstanding of them later, adding identifications of them yourself if the director does not give ones that are specific enough.

If the director seems to be holding a private conversation, or if a member of the staff seems embarrassed by being corrected in your presence, you will retire tactfully to a point from which you cannot overhear the discussion. You will remain near enough to be able to return quickly when called. Under no circumstance will you ever repeat anything you have overheard or anything you are told, whether or not it seems private to you.

Include praise as well as censure in your notes. Include, too, all comments the director makes which he does not instruct you to record, but which you think he might want to use later. Put these in parentheses, and explain the matter when you give him the notes.

If you should hear the director personally deliver a message you have put in his notes, write "Delivered" in front of it.

When the director is ready to make comments to the staff, you will hand him the sheets containing the notes arranged in the order in which he probably will want to deal with them. Follow the discussion carefully, and record any comments by staff members that you think the director will want.

If the director or technical director is in the habit of sending for the electrician or stage manager frequently during dress rehearsals, it may be possible to have a signal device connected to a backstage light, by which means they can be called more quickly than otherwise. A telephone equipped with a very weak buzzer or bell, or with a light, is even better, permitting the electrician or stage manager to ask for approval of effects without leaving his backstage duties.

When serving the technical director, as you make other notes, prepare a check-list of things to be done the next day. A word or phrase indicating the task is all that is needed. Omit all comments, for they are contained in the full notes. Omit, too, anything which can only be checked in rehearsal, or make a separate compilation of them. This list is to be used by the technical director the next day as a memorandum of the things he still must do.

Where very exact lighting of areas is being planned, and changes to fit the actor's movements are expected, provide yourself with detailed floor plans of the settings, and mark them off into small numbered areas, so that exact reference and notations can be made accordingly.

Invoice clip-boards (writing boards with a clamp at the top to hold sheets of paper) are useful for making the notes. You may need a flashlight. Stage supply dealers handle tiny flashlights which may be attached to a pencil, and illuminate only a small writing area.

To the Actors:

During dress rehearsals and performances, you are responsible to the director for the interpretation of your part, but to the stage manager and his assistants for all matters connected with the staging of the play. The stage manager is responsible for the technical phases of the performance—scenery, lighting, costumes, make-up, and the proper entrances of the actors. When you are told to get out of the way of scenery, to come on the stage, or to change your make-up, you are to comply immediately and without question.

You never are to be late to the theatre for dress rehearsal or performance. You should use every possible means to get word to the director or stage manager if for any reason you cannot be in the theatre at least half an hour before your first entrance. "Only death is an excuse for missing a dress rehearsal, and even death is no excuse for missing a performance," Madame Maria Ouspenskaya was accustomed to tell her students at the American Laboratory Theatre.

You must be ready for entrance on cue, even though you have to slight make-up and dressing. When the call boy knocks on your door you have one minute in which to reach the stage. You *must* make it. If he should happen to call you earlier than that one night, do not count on the same thing happening on other nights, for he will vary slightly in the time of his calls from performance to performance.

You will consult the costume master and make-up master or their assistants at least a week in advance of the dress rehearsal. At the first dress rehearsal you will have the costumes and properties you were told to obtain for yourself, and will at that time secure from the wardrobe master all garments the theatre furnishes. You will receive instructions from him as to whether to turn them in each night or only after the last performance. You are financially responsible for the loss or injury of costumes while in your possession, and for any damage to the theatre or theatre property.

Always rest on the days of performances. Preferably, sleep for a short time in the afternoon. You must come to the theatre thoroughly rested. There should be no "partying" on nights preceding perform-

ances. If you are in a school theatre, you must not let a production interfere with class work, and particularly with class attendance, even
to the extent of taking your "legitimate cuts" at this time. You will do
your dramatic organization a great deal of harm by attending classes
irregularly during the production of a play.

You will receive instructions from the make-up master accordingly
if you are to furnish all or part of your make-up. You always will
provide yourself with a smock or other protection for your clothes
or costume when being made up.

You must never allow yourself to be seen in make-up or costume
by a member of the audience. The only exception is in the case of
people who come backstage immediately after the performance. Remove your make-up before leaving the theatre—not to do so is in
bad taste.

The property master is responsible for providing all the hand-
properties, but you are required to see that those not obviously called
for in the script are on his lists, and you should arrange with him to
place them on the stage or give them to you backstage. Personal properties such as watches, handkerchiefs, and the like, used in the business of the play, usually are supplied by the actor, but either are
handled by the property master or checked by him as being in your
hands each night.

To the Prompter:

In the professional theatre the prompting is done by the stage manager or one of his assistants. In the amateur theatre, there usually is
an individual especially assigned to the task. Extremely difficult to do
well, it is one of the most exacting of positions.

No matter how skillfully and conscientiously done, you are likely
to be thought ill of, given "dirty looks," or even openly criticized by
actors for failing to throw them lines, or for throwing them lines
when they think they did not need them. The director, if he will, can
smooth your path by telling you, in the presence of the cast, when and

when not to prompt, so that your instructions may be understood by all. Few directors remember to do this. Under no circumstances allow the criticisms to annoy you.

During rehearsals it is your duty to write into the script all the changes made by the director; all the stage business he gives; and, if he wishes it, all comments he makes on the correct interpretation of the play or of particular characters. This is for his record, and for anyone who wants to study or revive the play. The actors often like to copy the annotated script in case they should ever have occasion to produce the play.

A piece of business that has been given and written into the prompt copy of the play becomes just as important as the lines, and should be prompted in rehearsal just as are the lines. If it is evident that the actor is trying a new piece of business, with or without the permission of the director, do not interrupt the action to report it, but do so at the first pause in the rehearsal. Obviate making enemies among the actors by asking "if the director wants the new business recorded," instead of reporting that the actor is not following the business given him.

You are to hold the actor to perfect line accuracy, *even to the most unimportant words.* A good author chooses all his words carefully, and he probably considered and rejected all substitutions of language the actor is likely to make. Even if he has not done this consciously, an experienced playwright will choose instinctively better words and phrases than will an actor. If a change is necessary in lines, the director is the only one privileged to make it. In the long run it is easier for the actor if he is held to word accuracy, for if he constantly improvises lines, he sometimes makes serious blunders in performance when good substitute words do not come to him. One of the objects of rehearsals is to so drill him on words that he will speak them semi-automatically and not from conscious deliberation. Also, he will learn lines more quickly that he has been allowed to speak only as written, for he then will have no recollection of any other phraseology.

Nevertheless, the first time an actor plays without his book in hand, do not hold him to perfect accuracy. It is far more important at this moment that he become line-sure and free from dependence on the book. He will be conscious that he is not word-perfect and will continue to rehearse the script in private. Too many corrections will drive him back to the use of his book. Hold him to every sentence of the part, but not to every word. If he makes only a few errors, it is helpful to indicate them in the margin of the prompt book and tell him about them after the rehearsal. After the first rehearsal without a book, show no further leniency.

If you are asked to read the part of an absentee, *act* it as he or she does or you will lower the whole tone of the rehearsal. Do not try to be funny. If you are sincere in your acting, no one will be amused, however incongruous you may be in the part as to sex or size.

At the early rehearsals you may sit anywhere in the theatre you choose. The director may want you to sit beside him in order that you may make notes and more easily record the business he gives. During the last week of rehearsals, you should sit in approximately the same location as at the performances, and should experiment until you find the softest voice in which you can successfully throw lines. Remember that individuals vary in their capacity to hear, so all do not require the same voice. A strong whisper often is more satisfactory than a soft voice. The more distinctly you articulate, particularly the consonants, the softer may be the voice. At the final rehearsals and through the performances, you should not interrupt the actors in order to hold them to the book, but make careful notes of errors. Give these to the director, who probably will have the actors repeat scenes where serious ones were made.

At the dress rehearsals and performances you will sit or stand in a position where you can see and easily be heard on the stage. By this time you should know the play so well that you will realize instantly when a pause in the action is dramatic and when it is a lapse of memory on the part of the actor. Nothing drives an actor so frantic as to have a line thrown to him repeatedly when he knows it and is only waiting for the correct moment to say it. However, when in doubt, throw it.

The practice of directors on prompting varies. A few directors require the prompter to read the entire play in a very soft voice just ahead of the actors, and merely increase the volume of a line to be thrown. This is the practice on the Continental stage, especially at the repertory theatres, where an actor has to keep in memory a number of parts at the same time.

The more common method is for the prompter to read the lines to himself just ahead of the actor. When there is a pause, he will look up at the hesitant actor with the next few words, or the next important word, already in mind and will throw it if needed. Never read *with* the actor and look up without the line on the tip of your tongue. At all times follow the lines as they are spoken with your finger or the point of your pencil. Throw a line in a loud enough voice to be heard by the actor the very first time. It is far better for the audience to hear the prompting than to have a doubly long pause. It usually recognizes the need of an actor to be prompted, anyway, even though it does not hear the prompting.

Make notes of serious omissions of lines in the performance and mark the places. If the actors should realize that they have cut a passage and jump back to a section of omitted dialogue, their worst moment will come at the point where they have to skip the dialogue already spoken. You must be ready to give them the line which will bridge over the gap. Give it without waiting to see if they will get it themselves. This bridging-over line is not always the exact speech at which they stopped. There may be a better speech a few lines further on, or a few lines back. Repetition will not be noticed. Do not expect in such circumstances to be able to make the dialogue read perfectly smoothly. It is in such situations that a prompter must show judgment and quick-wittedness in order to obviate blemishes to the performance. If an omission is sufficiently important, the prompter should force the actors back over it by repeatedly giving an essential line, preferable to the nearest actor. You have a far better chance of making a reasoned choice of lines than have the actors, who are under high mental stress trying to straighten out the jumbled lines. Sometimes the prompter can tell an actor about to enter to include in one of his speeches an omitted fact essential to the sense of the scene.

Make a list of the word errors made in performance if the director wants them.

When you are prompting, you *must not* talk to anyone, unless you have to send a message to an actor or to the technical crew. Your duties are so important that your whole and undivided attention should be given to them.

You will know best the psychological moment for a curtain, so you usually will give the cue for it. At a point in the script well in advance of the moment for it, make a conspicuous mark as a warning cue, and then signal the curtain man accordingly. Just before the curtain, raise your hand and keep it suspended. At the exact moment for the curtain, drop the hand as the cue. You may have to give other backstage cues, such as those for the effect master, the switchboard operator, and the musicians. Give them in the same manner. If the cue has to carry far, hold a white handkerchief in your raised hand. If it is dark, use a flashlight.

You may have other duties to perform, such as timing the scenes and the scene changes, for which instructions are given elsewhere. These tasks will be assigned to you by the director. During performance, like the rest of the backstage workers, you are under command of the stage manager.

After the production you will ask the director what portions of the memoranda you have made he wants left in the prompt book, and will erase everything else. Until then you will have used only a pencil in marking the book, but he may ask you to substitute ink for all the comments, business, et cetera, that he wants to remain there permanently. Also obtain the time records on the length of scenes and on the scene changes from whoever has made them, and insert them in the prompt book.

CHAPTER XII

A FINAL WORD

Doubtless some of the readers of the foregoing pages will say that it is impossible to get young people to work as systematically as is here proposed. To them I can only rejoin that, while using the system for a period of several years, I did it repeatedly. Admittedly, young people of high school and college age are not accustomed to work very systematically either in their school work or otherwise, but it is a habit that they should acquire if they are to have the best of success in business or professional work. They seem to realize this subconsciously, and, given even as elaborate a system as this one, they accept it quite willingly, most of them enthusiastically, for they readily see sense in it and quickly appreciate its advantages. They accept it more willingly than much of their other school work that attempts to give the same training.

Some of the readers will say further that workers will rebel against the regimentation and discipline imposed. To them I make a similar answer: I found no opposition on part of the workers, either expressed or reflected in their demeanor. They went about their tasks interestedly, often joyously, entirely indifferent to their state of subordination to a long chain of officers and unresentful of the disciplinary rules governing them. Having been assigned tasks for which they were give detailed personal instruction-sheets, they were subjected to much less "ordering about" that would have been the case had the stage manager or technical director given them these instructions orally during rehearsals.

The regimentation was organizational rather than disciplinary. Inasmuch as each worker had a specific task to do, for which he

202

was responsible and for which he could see a purpose, and which, to a considerable extent, he could do in his own way and at his own pleasure, there was no need for a military-like atmosphere, and it did not exist. The technical director had no cause to complain of too much talking, joking and idling. Instead of declaring, "We will all have to stay until six o'clock," and then trying to get as much work out of the crew as possible before that hour by impromptu directions, and creating dissatisfaction by refusing to allow individuals to leave earlier, his assignment of definite tasks with written instructions implied, "Here is your particular work with full information about it; it must be finished before you leave, and you can leave when you have finished it." The workers applied themselves assiduously not only because they could thus readily do so, but in order to finish and depart as soon as possible. Instead of soldiering on jobs they did not like, in the hope that someone else would be assigned to complete it after they left, they completed it as quickly as possible because they knew that they would not be given help. Where there was the necessity for haste in the work, as at the set-up and during quick changes, it was the students who hurried each other, not the technical director. He appeared in no wise anxious about his time being consumed, and was only concerned with saving it for the workers.

To give just a few personal experiences, I cite the following:

I never had less than five applications each for the positions of stage manager, property master, and electrician for a production, although they require more work than any other backstage positions.

I never had difficulty in getting a crew large enough to handle the most elaborate of productions, for nearly all young people are allured by theatrical work of all kinds, and do not in the least mind its exactions and vicissitudes.

On one set-up day, when the erection of platforms and other work had taken longer than expected, fully half the workers came to me seeking other things that they might be doing in the meantime, instead of sitting around chattering, as is the common condition where this spirit of conservation of time has not been developed.

I never had a crewman fail to appear for a dress rehearsal or performance, or come to one more than a few minutes late—never so late that he could not do all his work.

In two productions the crew volunteered to come for an extra afternoon scenic rehearsal to speed up the changes, and members of the acting cast volunteered to substitute for one or two backstage workers who could not be present.

Some readers will wonder if students given such dictatorial powers will not abuse them and make themselves disagreeable to their associates. In one case that happened, but the crew themselves, without interference by other officials, in the way that young people can do, and without openly resisting his orders, "took it out of him." In all other cases it was a greater problem to induce the students to make sufficient use of the authority accompanying their positions, and to get them to give up enough of the work to their subordinates.

Some readers will say that the system involves an excessive amount of advance planning. In a few exceptional organizations, such as those which put on a play a week, and have a regular backstage staff for at least the directional part of the work, much of it will be unnecessary, and some of it will be a waste of time. In an organization, however, which puts on from two to ten productions a year, and has only a small full-time staff, it will effect actual saving of time. It will entail a greater amount of effort and time on the part of those selected for executive positions, but that will be more than offset by the saving in the effort and time of the crew as a whole. Even did it not save time in the aggregate, it would save time at the strategic moments. Besides, the method gives excellent training in personal efficiency to all the workers.

Some readers will say that the plan requires a larger staff than they can assemble. This is only because the backstage work has been divided into the smallest possible segments and the largest practicable number, for ease of explanation and in order to allow any combination of tasks desired. In practice, the stage manager, for instance, may imitate Mussolini, who holds enough cabinet offices to make a quorem and a majority of his own cabinet. The chief technical assistant might also be the stage manager, head electrician, head property master, superintendent of set-up, curtain man and timer; the property master or the head electrician might do all the work given as duties for his various assistants. Other opportunities for combining tasks are suggested in the preceding chapters. In a one-set show, the performance crew might consist of only three or four workers—the stage manager, the property master, the costume master, and the electrician. One plan of simplified organization is given in Chapter I.

While cogent reasons have been recited for the use of such a system, and important advantages arising from it have been suggested, it is not the intention to present it as a cure-all for every problem incident to the production of a play. Despite its use, difficulties will still arise, accidents will still happen, mistakes will still be made, but it will be found effective in reducing them and in overcoming them when they occur. Its most satisfying effect, however, will be experienced in the smoothness, speed, and technical perfection with which the backstage work will be performed, and the reflection of this in the quality of the performance.

INDEX TO THE PUBLISHED WORKS ON
STAGECRAFT

This index is a compilation of references to all the standard books on the design, the construction, and the handling of the physical elements of a dramatic production. Only those sections and passages that are thought to be of immediate practical value in shop and performance work are included.

Subjects and their related topical items are grouped. All topics related to costumes, such as "armor," "head-dresses," "jewelry," for example, are to be searched for as subtopics under "Costumes." (The general subjects are: Bibliographies, Business Department, Color, Costumes, Design, Effects, Flats, Flying, Lighting, Make-up, Painting, Properties, Supplies.) But such subtopics, except those belonging under Lighting and Make-up, are also given in their own alphabetical order and are there cross-indexed.

Books are referred to by the name of the author. If more than one book by the same author is cited, a word from each title is added in order to distinguish between them, as, for example, "Chalmers *Clothes*" and "Chalmers *Make-up*."

Only one edition of each book has been included in the index, except for Selden and Sellman's *Stage Scenery and Lighting*. For page numbers in other editions, reference must be made to the indexes of those editions. Because this index is intended as a guide to all books that may be available to the reader, many that cannot be recommended for purchase are included.

THE BOOKS INDEXED

Andrews, Harry Lee, and Weirick, Bruce, *Acting and Play Production,* Longmans Green, New York, 1925
Appleton Publishing Co., *Theatrical Scene Painting,* Appleton Publishing Co., Omaha, Nebraska, 1916
Ashton, D. C., *The Art of Directing Plays,* Eldridge, Franklin, Ohio, 1931
Atkinson, Frank H., *Scene Painting and Bulletin Art,* Drake, Chicago, 1927
Baird, John F., *Make-up,* French, New York, 1930

Baker, Blanche M., *Dramatic Bibliography*, Wilson, New York, 1933

Barber, Philip W., *The Scene Technician's Handbook*, Whitlock's Book Store, New Haven, Connecticut, 1928

Barton, Lucy, *Historic Costume for the Stage*, Baker, Boston, 1935

Bax, Peter, *Stage Management*, Lovat Dickson, London, 1936

Bernheim, Alfred L., *The Business of the Theatre*, Actors Equity Association, New York, 1932

Bosserman, F. W., *Masks and Costumes*, South Park Commissioners, Chicago, 1934

Bosworth, Halliam, *Technique in Dramatic Art*, Macmillan, New York, 1926

Brandon-Thomas, Jevan, *Practical Stagecraft for Amateurs*, Harrap, London, 1936

Bricker, Hershel L. (editor), *Our Theatre Today*, French, New York, 1936

Britannica Booklet No. 7, *see* Cox

Brown, Corinne, *Creative Dramatics in the Lower School*, Appleton-Century, New York, 1929

Browne, Van Dyke, *Secrets of Scene Painting and Stage Effects*, Dutton, New York, 1913

Campbell, Wayne, *Amateur Acting and Play Production*, Macmillan, New York, 1931

Cartmell, Van H., *A Handbook for the Amateur Actor*, Doubleday Doran, Garden City, New York, 1936

Chalmers, Helena, *The Art of Make-up*, Appleton-Century, New York, 1925

Chalmers, Helena, *Clothes, On and Off the Stage*, Appleton-Century, New York, 1928

Chalmers, Helena, *Modern Acting*, Appleton-Century, New York, 1930

Cheney, Sheldon, *The Art Theatre*, Knopf, New York, 1917

Clark, Barrett H., *How to Produce Amateur Plays*, new and revised edition, Little Brown, Boston, 1923

Cox, Warren E. (editor), *The Theatre and Motion Pictures; A Selection of Articles from the new 14th Edition of the Encyclopædia Britannica* (Britannica Booklet No. 7), Encyclopædia Britannica, Inc., New York, 1933. (The same references will be found in the full set, but not on the pages cited.)

Crafton, Allen, and Royer, Jessica, *Acting*, Crofts, New York, 1928

Crafton, Allen, and Royer, Jessica, *The Process of Play Production*, Crofts, New York, 1926

Crump, Leslie, *Directing for the Amateur Stage*, Dodd Mead, New York, 1935

Dabney, Edith, and Wise, C. M., *A Book of Dramatic Costume*, Crofts, New York, 1930

D'Amico, Victor E., *Theatre Art*, Manual Arts Press, Peoria, Illinois, 1931

Dayton, Helena Smith, and Barratt, Louise Bascom, *Book of Entertainments and Theatricals*, McBride, New York, 1923

Dean, Alexander, *Little Theatre Organization and Management,* Appleton-Century, New York, 1926

Dolman, John, Jr., *The Art of Play Production,* Harper, New York, 1928

Downs, Harold (editor), *Theatre and Stage,* two volumes, Pitman, London, 1934

Drummond, A. M., *Play Production for the Country Theatre,* Cornell University Extension Service, Ithaca, New York, 1924 (also published by the author as *A Manual of Play Production*)

Dyer, Ernest F., *Producing School Plays,* Nelson, London, 1935

Eastman, Fred, and Wilson, Louis, *Drama in the Church,* French, New York, 1933

Eustis, Morton, *B'way Inc!,* Dodd Mead, New York, 1934

Evans, Mary, *Costume Throughout the Ages,* Lippincott, Philadelphia, 1930

Ewer, Monica, *Play Production for Everyone,* Labour Publishing Co., London, 1924

Exmouth, Charles E. Pellew, *Dyes and Dyeing,* McBride, New York, 1928

Factor, Max, *Hints on the Art of Make-up,* Max Factor Make-up Studios, Hollywood, California, 1930–1931 (a set of nine pamphlets)

Fay, W. G., *How to Make a Simple Stage,* French, New York, 1931

Fitzkee, Dariel, *Professional Scenery Construction,* Banner, San Francisco, 1930

Fuchs, Theodore, *Stage Lighting,* Little Brown, Boston, 1929

Fuerst, Walter René, and Hume, Samuel J., *Twentieth Century Stage Decoration,* Knopf, New York, 1928 (vol. 1, text; vol. 2, illustrations)

Gall, Ellen M., and Carter, Leslie H., *Modern Make-up,* Banner, San Francisco, 1928

Gamble, William Burt, *The Development of Scenic Art and Machinery; A List of References in the New York Public Library,* revised edition, New York Public Library, 1928

Gordon, Leslie Howard, *Play Production and Stage Management for Amateurs,* Mills and Boon, London, 1927

Green, Joyce M. C., *Period Costumes and Settings for the Small Stage,* Harrap, London, 1936

Grimball, Elizabeth B., and Wells, Rhea, *Costuming a Play,* Appleton-Century, New York, 1925

Halstead, William P., *Stage Management for the Amateur Theatre,* Crofts, New York, 1937

Hartmann, Louis, *Theatre Lighting; A Manual of the Stage Switchboard,* Appleton-Century, New York, 1930

Heffner, Hubert C., Selden, Samuel, and Sellman, Hunton D., *Modern Theatre Practice,* Crofts, New York, 1935

Helvenston, Harold, *Scenery, A Manual of Scene Design,* Stanford University Press, Stanford University, California, 1931

Hembrow, Victor, *The Model Theatre,* Studio Publications, New York, 1934

Hinsdale, Oliver, *Making the Little Theatre Pay*, French, New York, 1925

Hobbs, Mable Foote, *Play Production Made Easy*, National Recreation Association, New York, 1933

Hume, Samuel J., and Foster, Lois M., *Theatre and School*, French, New York, 1932

Hynes, Mary Helen, *Practical Stage-Craft*, Baker, Boston, 1930

Isaacs, Edith J. R. (editor), *Architecture for the New Theatre*, Theatre Arts, New York, 1935

Jeffreys, M. V. C., and Stopford, R. W., *Play Production for Amateurs and Schools*, Methuen, London, and Dutton, New York, 1933

Jones, Charles T. H., and Wilson, Don, *Musico-Dramatic Producing*, Gamble-Hinged, Chicago, 1930

Jones, Leslie Allen, *Painting Scenery*, Baker, Boston, 1935

Kelly, Francis M., and Schwabe, Randolph, *Historic Costume*, Scribner, New York, 1925

Knapp, Jack Stuart, *Lighting the Stage with Homemade Equipment*, Baker, Boston, 1933

Kniffen, Herbert R., *Masks*, Manual Arts Press, Peoria, Illinois, 1931

Koch, Frederick H., and others, *Play Production for Amateurs*, University of North Carolina Extension Service, Chapel Hill, North Carolina, 1922

Köhler, Karl, and Sichart, Emma von, *A History of Costume* (translated by Alexander K. Dallas), Harrap, London, and G. Howard Watt, New York, 1928

Krows, Arthur Edwin, *Equipment for Stage Production*, Appleton-Century, New York, 1928

Krows, Arthur Edwin, *Play Production in America*, Holt, New York, 1916

Latham, Jean Lee, *Do's and Don't's of Drama*, Dramatic Publishing Co., Chicago, 1935

Luckiesh, M., *Color and Its Applications*, Van Nostrand, New York, 1915

Luckiesh, M., *The Language of Color*, Dodd Mead, New York, 1918

Luckiesh, M., *Light and Shade and Their Applications*, Van Nostrand, New York, 1916

McCandless, Stanley R., *A Method of Lighting the Stage*, Theatre Arts, New York, 1932

McCandless, Stanley R., *A Syllabus of Stage Lighting*, second revised edition, Whitlock's Book Store, New Haven, Connecticut, 1931

Macgowan, Kenneth, *Footlights Across America*, Harcourt Brace, New York, 1929

Mackay, Constance D'Arcy, *Costumes and Scenery for Amateurs*, Holt, New York, 1915

Meloy, Arthur S., *Theatres and Motion Picture Houses*, Architects' Supply and Publishing Co., New York, 1916

Mitchell, Roy, *The School Theatre*, Coward-McCann, New York, 1925

Mitchell, Roy, *Shakespeare for Community Players*, Dutton, New York, 1919

INDEX TO WORKS ON STAGECRAFT

213

Bibliographies (*continued*)

—pageants: Baker, 151

—scenery: Baker, 85; Bricker, 413; Britannica, 43; Dyer, 190; Gamble, 58, 127; Heffner, 365; Hume, 356; Jeffreys, 193; Ommanney, 415; Perry, 199; Purdom, 220; Selden, 384 (rev. 422); Shay, 138; M. Smith *Guide,* 153; Wilson, 137

—theatre, general: Baker, entire; Bricker, 409; D'Amico, 211; Dolman, 448; Downs, 587; Drummond, 75; Dyer, 190; Eastman, 196; Fuerst, i, 169; Gamble, entire; Heffner, 358; Hobbs, 57; Hume, 354; Jeffreys, 194; C. Jones, 135; Koch, 58; Krows *Equipment,* 141; Krows *Play Production,* 397; Macgowan, 380; Ommanney, 407; Perry, 196; Purdom, 219; Ridge, 194; Selden, 383 (rev. 417); Shay, 19, 135; M. Smith *Guide,* entire; Wells, 146; Wilson, 137

Bins, scenery: Halstead, 38

Blood: *see* Effects

Book: *see* Flats: construction: two-fold *and* Ceiling

—setting: Selden, 198 (rev. 202)

Borders, cloth: Bax, 108; Fitzkee, 29; Halstead, 75, 84, Fig. 20; Heffner, 190; Hume, 261; Selden, 116 (rev. 120); Wilson, 105. *See also* Flying

Borrowing: Halstead, 124, 127, 167

Box office: *see* Business department

Boxes, door and window: Barber, 35; Bax, 119; Downs, 648, 890; Fitzkee, 58; Halstead, 108; Heffner, 178; Jeffreys, 121; Krows *Equipment,* 51; Mitchell *School,* 55; Selden, 102, 107 (rev. 106, 111); M. Smith *Book,* 133; Throckmorton, 23; Webster, 57, 78; Whorf *Runnin',* 21; Wilson, 122

—in a drape setting: Campbell, 184; Downs, 628; Eastman, 156; Green, 150; Mitchell *Shakespeare,* 50; Parsons, *Management,* 34; M. Smith *Book,* 109

Brace, stage: Barber, 60; Bax, 114; Halstead, 63; Heffner, 206; Hume, 326; Jeffreys, 89; Krows *Equipment,* 39 (special methods); Selden, 176 (rev. 180); M. Smith *Book,* 148; Throckmorton, 41; Webster, 50; Wilson, 125. *See also* Jack

Breasting a drop: *see* Flying

Breeze: *see* Effects

Bridles: *see* Flying

Bronzing powders: *see* Painting: metallic paints

Brushes: *see* Supplies

Budget: *see* Business department

Building paper: A. Smith, 86

Bushes: Helvenston, 63; Selden, 130 (rev. 134); A. Smith, 108. *See also* Foliage

Business department: Ashton, 11; Bernheim, 110; Cheney, 188; Crafton *Process,* 25; Crump, 11; Dayton, 21; Dean, entire; Downs, 53; Drummond, 13; Dyer, 145; Eastman, 89; Eustis, entire; Hinsdale, entire; C. Jones, 50; Koch, 13; Krows *Play Production,* 239; Moderwell, 283; Purdom, 147; Shay, entire; M. Smith *Book,* 238

—advertising: Ashton, 11, 99; Bernheim, 112, 147; Cheney, 208; Crafton *Process,* 43; Downs, 439; Eastman, 143; Heffner, 15; Hinsdale, 31; Krows *Play Production,* 293; Shay, 114; M. Smith *Book,* 241; Stanton, 48

—audience: Heffner, 15; Krows *Play Production,* 364, 386; Purdom, 153; M. Smith *Book,* 242

Fields and marshes: Helvenston, 66
Finances: *see* Business department
Fire: *see* Effects
—laws: Cartmell, 83; Dolman, 345; Krows *Equipment,* 11; Stanton, 67. *See also* Lighting: code
Fireplace: Barber, 42; Downs, 697; Heffner, 186; Krows *Equipment,* 55; Selden, 109 (rev. 113); M. Smith *Book,* 135; Somerscales, 28; Throckmorton, 25; Webster, 88
—backing: Downs, 698; Krows *Equipment,* 55; Nesfield-Cookson, 28; Selden, 111 (rev. 115); Webster, 91
Fireproofing: Atkinson, 200; Barber, 30; Bax, 128; Downs, 863; Hume, 290; Jeffreys, 120; Knapp, 85; Latham, 97; Polunin, 8; Selden, 93 (rev. 97); Viola, 41; Wilson, 110
Flap hinges: *see* Boxes
Flats:
—altering: Krows *Equipment,* 35; Mitchell *School,* 54
—construction: Barber, 33; Bax, 111; Crafton *Process,* 126; D'Amico, 122; Downs, 591; Dyer, 98; Fay, 30; Fitzkee, 43; Hume, 290; Hynes, 28; Jeffreys, 117; C. Jones, 42; L. Jones, 33; Koch, 45; Krows *Equipment,* 32; Mitchell *School,* 41; Playground, 18; Purdom, 116; Raine, 228; Selden, 84, 95 (rev. 88, 99); M. Smith *Book,* 115, 123; Viola, 47; Webster, 58; Wilson, 119
—arch: Barber, 48; Fitzkee, 63; Hume, 258; Jeffreys, 124; Krows *Equipment,* 49; Raine, 234; Selden, 111 (rev. 115); Webster, 62
—door: Barber, 36; Bax, 111; Downs, 647; Fitzkee, 56; Heffner, 179; Raine, 229; Selden, 101 (rev. 105); Webster, 61; Wilson, 124. *See also* Boxes
—fireplace: Barber, 42; Downs, 697; Drummond, 41; Heffner, 179; Selden, 101 (rev. 105); M. Smith *Book,* 135
—jog: Heffner, 177; Selden, 99 (rev. 103)
—joints: Barber, 30; D'Amico, 122; Downs, 591; Fitzkee, 41; Heffner, 169; Hume, 291; Jeffreys, 118; Krows *Equipment,* 36; Selden, 85 (rev. 89); Webster, 54
—lips: Halstead, 63; Throckmorton, 7; Webster, 19, 65
—plug: Barber, 35; Halstead, 109; Selden, 128 (rev. 132); Somerscales, 18; Throckmorton, 9; Webster, 65
—three-fold: *see* Dutchman
—two-fold: Barber, 60; Bax, 114; D'Amico, 123; Fitzkee, 33; Halstead, 107; Heffner, 178; Hume, 296; Mitchell *School,* 45; Selden, 99 (rev. 103)
   —arch: Barber, 48; Drummond, 6; Fitzkee, 61; Selden, 111 (rev. 115)
—window: Barber, 37; Bax, 111; Downs, 695; Drummond, 41; Heffner, 179; Raine, 230; Selden, 101 (rev. 105)
—covering: Barber, 31; Crafton *Process,* 129; D'Amico, 122; Downs, 967; Dyer, 98; Fitzkee, 46; Heffner, 171; Hume, 291; Jeffreys, 118; L. Jones, 43; Koch, 48; Krows *Equipment,* 35; Mackay, 67; Mitchell *School,* 45; Playground, 19; Raine, 229; Selden, 82, 89 (rev. 85, 93); M. Smith *Book,* 126; Webster, 63; Wilson, 120
—lashing: *see* Lashing flats
—mending: Hume, 306; Mitchell *School,* 54
—numbering: Barber, 30; Halstead, 46; Heffner, 219; Hynes, 83; Krows *Equipment,* 133; Krows *Play Production,* 94; Webster, 121

Lighting (*continued*)

—glass color slides: *see* Lighting: color: media

—globes, light: *see* Lighting: lamp globes

—ground rows: Bricker, 320; Jeffreys, 103; McCandless *Method,* 84

—grounding wires: Fuchs, 60, 327; McCandless *Syllabus,* 50; Selden, 277 (rev. 298)

—history: D'Amico, 87; Fuchs, 31; Hartmann, 1; McCandless *Syllabus,* 5

—home-made equipment: Campbell, 186; Downs, 715, 761, 809; Eastman, 152; Fuchs, 214, 370, 484; Hobbs, 27; Knapp, 26; Parsons *Management,* 89; M. Smith *Book,* 224; Somerscales, 44

   —border lights: Campbell, 188; Downs, 715; Dyer, 120; Eastman, 152; Fuchs, 250; Hobbs, 28; Knapp, 34; Koch, 41; Raine, 260; Wilson, 69

   —bunch lights: Drummond, 55; C. Jones, 58; Knapp, 26; Mitchell *Shakespeare,* 89; M. Smith *Book,* 225

   —dimmers: Brandon-Thomas, 117; Campbell, 188; Downs, 811; Drummond, 60; Dyer, 124; Eastman, 153; Fuchs, 376, 485; Knapp, 37; Parsons *Management,* 99, 118; Powell, 11; Raine, 262; Ridge, 27; M. Smith *Book,* 230

   —footlights: Downs, 761; Dyer, 120; Fuchs, 228, 484; Hobbs, 28; Knapp, 32; Koch, 40; Raine, 260; Wilson, 73

   —olivettes: Brandon-Thomas, 116; Campbell, 186; Downs, 761; Dyer, 122; Eastman, 153; Fuchs, 272; Hobbs, 29; Knapp, 19; Parsons *Management,* 93, 117; Ridge, 53; M. Smith *Book,* 226; Wilson, 74

   —rheostat: *see* Lighting: home-made equipment: dimmers

   —spotlights: Brandon-Thomas, 116; Downs, 761; Dyer, 123; Fuchs, 256, 485; Jeffreys, 104; Knapp, 26; Parsons *Management,* 91, 115; Powell, 31; M. Smith *Book,* 224; Wilson, 76

   —standards: Knapp, 20

   —striplights: Eastman, 152; Fuchs, 254; Hobbs, 28; Knapp, 34; Parsons *Management,* 90, 114; M. Smith *Book,* 224

   —switchboard: Brandon-Thomas, 118; Dyer, 213; Eastman, 154; Fuchs, 384, 485; Heffner, 338; Knapp, 42; Koch, 42; Nelms, 67; Parsons *Management,* 98; Ridge, 39; Webster, 150

—house lights: Bax, 194; Halstead, 98; Selden, 275 (rev. 296); M. Smith *Book,* 219; Webster, 148

—illuminants, color of: *see* Color: illuminants

—insulation: Bax, 180; Downs, 26; Fuchs, 54; Heffner, 327; McCandless *Syllabus,* 51; Ridge and Aldred, 6; Selden, 217 (rev. 233). *See also* Lighting: wiring

—interiors: Bricker, 292; Crump, 89; Downs, 1060; Hartmann, 79; Heffner, 346; Ridge and Aldred, 107; Selden, 361 (rev. 393). *See also* Lighting: design

—iris shutter: Powell, 5; Selden, 267 (rev. 292). *See also* Lighting: shutter

—lambert: Fuchs, 113; McCandless *Syllabus,* 17

—lamp dips: *see* Lighting: color: media

—lamp globes: Bax, 181; Downs, 176; Fuchs, 154; Heffner, 303; McCandless *Syllabus,* 54; Nelms, 16; Powell, 22; Ridge, 6; Ridge and Aldred, 18; Selden, 265 (rev. 288)

—lamp lighter: Powell, 19

—lamps, ornamental: Heffner, 278; Powell, 19, 31; Whorf *Runnin',* 69

Make-up (*continued*)
—blackface: *see* Make-up: Negro
—blindness: Rodgers, 46; Strauss, 118
—body: *see* Make-up: hands
—Bulgarian: Downs, 1152
—butler: Chalmers *Make-up,* 94; Factor, No. 5; Gall, 72; Strauss, 168
—changes: Downs, 708
—character: *see* Make-up: age
—check-list: Halstead, 180
—cheeks: Downs, 222; Drummond, 70; Russell, 105; James Young, 68. *See also* Make-up: rouge
—Chinese: Baird, 109; Bosworth, 282; Campbell, 167; Chalmers *Make-up,* 111; Downs, 1056, 1202; Factor, No. 5; Gall, 72; Parsons *Make-up,* 77; Redgrove, 111; Rodgers, 64; Strauss, 168; E. Ward, 77; Whorf *Time,* 60; Wolters, 76; James Young, 119
—clergyman: Chalmers *Make-up,* 83; Gall, 74; Strauss, 172
—clown: Baird, 90; Bosworth, 282; Chalmers *Make-up,* 126; Factor, No. 5; Gall, 75; Redgrove, 142; Rodgers, 65; Strauss, 174; E. Ward, 87; Whorf *Time,* 54; James Young, 104
—collodion: Downs, 802; Strauss, 115; Whorf *Time,* 44
—colors: Baird, 42, 67, 77, 84, 115; Chalmers *Make-up,* 155; Downs, 507; Redgrove, 8; Strauss, 45, 51; Wolters, 27, 36. *See also* Make-up: supplies *and* Color: light on make-up
—concert: Baird, 97; Chalmers *Make-up,* 141; Strauss, 131; James Young, 132
—consumptive: Strauss, 176
—cosmetic: Baird, 20; Bosworth, 272; Chalmers *Make-up,* 25; Downs, 127; Rodgers, 29; Russell, 97; E. Ward, 21; Whorf *Time,* 8; Wolters, 20
—Creole: Chalmers *Make-up,* 121; Gall, 76; Strauss, 178
—crêpe hair: Baird, 18, 53; Bosworth, 293; Brandon-Thomas, 142; Bricker, 359; Campbell, 172; Chalmers *Make-up,* 44; Crafton *Acting,* 274; Crump, 190; Downs, 315, 363, 411; Drummond, 69; Eastman, 132; Factor, No. 3; Gall, 35; Gordon, 93; Hobbs, 37; Hume, 241; Jeffreys, 157; Koch, 56; Latham, 20; Mitchell *School,* 72; Mitchell *Shakespeare,* 106; Ommanney, 301; Parsons *Make-up,* 37; Purdom, 129; Raine, 310; Redgrove, 100; Rodgers, 53; Russell, 111; M. Smith *Book,* 190; Strauss, 61; E. Ward, 59; Whorf *Time,* 28; Wise, 91; Wolters, 60; James Young, 51
—Cubans: Chalmers *Make-up,* 121; Redgrove, 121; Strauss, 179
—Cupid's bow: *see* Make-up: lips
—death: Redgrove, 147
—designer: Halstead, 176
—dimple: Rodgers, 28
—doll: Baird, 88
—dope fiend: Chalmers *Make-up,* 82; Strauss, 179
—dress rehearsal: Halstead, 178
—drunkard: Rodgers, 66; Strauss, 179; James Young, 126
—dry: Andrews, 252; Baird, 16, 97; Bosworth, 274; Campbell, 140; Chalmers *Make-up,* 29; Crump, 185; Gall, 47, 53; Hume, 240; Ommanney, 302; M. Smith *Book,* 194; Wolters, 96
—ear: Baird, 41; Brandon-Thomas, 133; Chalmers *Make-up,* 29, 33; Downs,

Make-up (*continued*)

sons *Make-up,* 75; Redgrove, 123; Rodgers, 63; E. Ward, 71; Whorf *Time,* 63; James Young, 115

—Santa Claus: Gall, 91; Strauss, 198; Whorf *Time,* 60

—scars: Baird, 22; Chalmers *Make-up,* 137; Downs, 802; Factor, No. 3; Gall, 23; Hobbs, 38; Latham, 23; Redgrove, 87; Rodgers, 51; Strauss, 114; Whorf *Time,* 44

—Scotch: Baird, 105; Chalmers *Make-up,* 95; Downs, 1098; Gall, 91; Redgrove, 129; Rodgers, 61; Whorf *Time,* 62; James Young, 109

—sea captain: Chalmers *Make-up,* 80; Factor, No. 5

—shadows: *see* Make-up: hollows

—shoulders: *see* Make-up: neck

—skull: Downs, 260, 660; Parsons *Make-up,* 27; Whorf *Time,* 48; James Young, 5

—Southern: Factor, No. 5; Rodgers, 57; James Young, 105

—Spanish: Baird, 107; Chalmers *Make-up,* 100; Downs, 1150; Factor, No. 6; Gall, 91; Parsons *Make-up,* 74; Redgrove, 121; Rodgers, 61; E. Ward, 67; Whorf *Time,* 63; James Young, 114

—spinster: Chalmers *Make-up,* 77; Factor, No. 5; Gall, 89

—statuary: Gall, 91; Rodgers, 65; Strauss, 203; James Young, 96. *See also* Make-up: gold

—statuesque: Baird, 89

—stone age: Strauss, 204

—straight: *see* Make-up: juvenile

—street: Chalmers *Make-up,* 143; Strauss, 140; E. Ward, 56

—superintendent: Eastman, 134; Halstead, 178; Koch, 12

—supplies: Baird, 11, 132; Baker, 123; Bricker, 353; Chalmers *Acting,* 64; Chalmers *Make-up,* 6; Crafton *Acting,* 244; Crump, 177; Downs, 22, 71; Drummond, 64; Eastman, 134; Factor, No. 2; Gall, 11, 125; Gordon, 99; Halstead, 180; Hobbs, 38; Jeffreys, 152; Koch, 52; Parsons *Make-up,* 42; Raine, 306; Redgrove, 77; Rodgers, 16; Russell, 89; M. Smith *Book,* 181; Strauss, 40, 215; Viola, 149; E. Ward, 10; Whorf *Time,* 2, 65, 73; Wolters, 6; James Young, 9

—Swedish: Baird, 106; Chalmers *Make-up,* 101; Downs, 1098; Gall, 92; Parsons *Make-up,* 75; Redgrove, 124; Rodgers, 62; Strauss, 198; E. Ward, 66; Whorf *Time,* 62; James Young, 92

—team: Baird, 17; Downs, 710; Koch, 12; Latham, 24; M. Smith *Book,* 195; Strauss, 191

—teeth: Baird, 20, 37; Bosworth, 286; Chalmers *Make-up,* 69; Crafton *Acting,* 269; Downs, 268; Factor, No. 3; Hobbs, 38; Parsons *Make-up,* 46; Redgrove, 94; Rodgers, 49; Russell, 104; Strauss, 121; E. Ward, 34; Whorf *Time,* 53; Wolters, 101; James Young, 69

—tramp: Chalmers *Make-up,* 81; Factor, No. 5; Gall, 92; Rodgers, 58; James Young, 92

—Turkish: Rodgers, 63

—unshaven: Baird, 60; Crump, 192; Factor, No. 3; Rodgers, 55; Whorf *Time,* 50; James Young, 36

—villain: Gall, 92

—widow's peak: Chalmers *Make-up,* 116

Properties (*continued*)
—ash tray: Halstead, 134
—baskets: Dayton, 280; Halstead, 131; Webster, 137
—borrowing: Eastman, 100, 136; Halstead, 124, 127; Koch, 11; Latham, 87; Webster, 133
—buying: Halstead, 128; Webster, 137
—clearers: Halstead, 132, 135
—construction: Bax, 163; D'Amico, 128; Ewer, 73; Nesfield-Cookson, entire; M. Smith *Book*, 199
—cue-sheets: *see* Cue-sheets
—custodian: *see* Properties: master
—definition: Barber, 4; Bax, 135; Bernheim, 142; D'Amico, 127; Halstead, 103, 131, 136; Krows *Equipment*, 134; Nesfield-Cookson, 11; M. Smith *Book*, 197
—flying: *see* Flying
—food: Bax, 142; Chalmers *Acting*, 120; Downs, 515; Halstead, 134; Mitchell *Shakespeare*, 62; Parsons *Management*, 28; Purdom, 84; M. Smith *Book*, 199; —trick: M. Smith *Book*, 200
—furniture: Barber, 76; Barton, entire (period); Bax, 136; D'Amico, 128; Downs, 472, 987, 1068, 1137; Halstead, 93, 129, 132, 134; Hume, 205; Mackay, 245; Mitchell *Shakespeare*, 60; Nesfield-Cookson, 18; Shipp, 27; M. Smith *Book*, 199; Webster, 137
—hand properties: Bax, 135; Bernheim, 111; Brandon-Thomas, 59; Chalmers *Acting*, 110; Dean, 167; Dyer, 128; Ewer, 71; Halstead, 136; Heffner, 43; Krows *Play Production*, 232; Latham, 86; M. Smith *Book*, 208; Webster, 134
—hanging: D'Amico, 125; Halstead, 125; Hume, 325; Selden, 99 (rev. 103)
—master: Barber, 3, 75; Bax, 52; Campbell, 164; Clark, 12; Downs, 471, 651; Eastman, 139; Ewer, 71; Halstead, 123; Hume, 61; Jeffreys, 22; L. Jones, 95; Krows *Play Production*, 235; Latham, 86, 90; Mitchell *Shakespeare*, 24; Parsons *Management*, 15; Shipp, 26; M. Smith *Book*, 19, 208; Taylor, 33
—mirrors: Bax, 141; Halstead, 126; Latham, 95
—moving draperies: Halstead, 125
—performance: Halstead, 132
—personal: Downs, 473; Halstead, 136
—pictures: Bax, 141; D'Amico, 125; Halstead, 125; Selden, 99 (rev. 103)
—plot: Bax, 165; Bricker, 246; Chalmers *Acting*, 110; Crump, 168; D'Amico, 204; Dolman, 346; Downs, 471, 1137; Dyer, 128; Eastman, 136; Gordon, 53; Halstead, 129; Heffner, 42; C. Jones, 35; Koch, 10; Parsons *Management*, 15; Purdom, 114; Russell, 15; M. Smith *Book*, 208; Stanton, 13; Webster, 134. *See also* Cue-sheets
—rehearsal properties: Bax, 47; Eastman, 139; Halstead, 124; Webster, 137
—renting: Halstead, 127
—scenic references: Halstead, 123
—tables: Chalmers *Acting*, 115; Halstead, 132; Hume, 61; Webster, 136
—weapons: Bax, 143; Mitchell *Shakespeare*, 63. *See also* Costumes: armor
Proscenium, false: Bax, 85, 116; Downs, 292; Dyer, 69; Fay, 18; Hume, 308; Wilson, 27. *See also* Temporary stage
Publicity: *see* Business department
Puddling: *see* Painting

Supplies (*continued*)
venston, 77; Jeffreys, 181; Polunin, 7; Selden, 82 (rev. 85); Throckmorton, 53; Webster, 50. *See also* Costumes: fabrics
—paints: Appleton, 93; Atkinson, 16; Browne, 10; D'Amico, 151; Heffner, 222; Hynes, 17; L. Jones, 54; Mitchell *School,* 59; Polunin, 5; Redgrove, 8 (manufacture); Selden, 141 (rev. 145); M. Smith *Book,* 139; Webster, 72. *See also* Painting: palette
—stage hardware: *see* Stage hardware *and* Supplies: hardware
—tools: Barber, 36; Downs, 545; Halstead, 67; Helvenston, 77; Hynes, 16; Selden, 76 (rev. 81)
Sweeps: *see* Thicknesses: arch
Symbolism: *see* Color: symbolism

Tab curtain: *see* Flying: rigging: French drape
Teaser: *see* Flying
Technical director: Barber, 1; Bernheim, 110, 142; Crafton *Process,* 82; Dolman, 326; Halstead, 18; Heffner, 16; Koch, 10; Shay, 53; W. Ward, 255. *See also index to this book*
Technical rehearsal: *see* Lighting: rehearsals *and* Shifting scenery
Telephone bell: *see* Effects
Template: Selden, 73 (rev. 76)
Temporary stage: Bax, 250; Browne, 55; D'Amico, 111; Dayton, 284; Downs, 291; Drummond, 40, 53; Fay, 7; Hume, 149; Jeffreys, 80; Overton, 219; M. Smith *Book,* 66; Somerscales, 2; Wilson, 21
Terminology, stage: *see* Glossaries
Theatre buildings: Britannica, 1; Cheney, 217; Crafton *Process,* 273; D'Amico, 133; Downs, 711; Eastman, 147; Fuerst, i, 87; Hume, 108; Isaacs, entire; Jeffreys, 76; Krows *Equipment,* 5; Krows *Play Production,* 73; Macgowan, 254; Meloy, entire; Moderwell, 238; Overton, 207; Pichel, entire; Ridge, 95; Ridge and Aldred, 68; Sexton, entire; M. Smith *Book,* 60; M. Smith *Equipment,* entire; Stratton, 1; Wilson, 17
Thicknesses: Barber, 48; Halstead, 58, 108; Mitchell *School,* 54; Selden, 102 (rev. 106); Webster, 71
—arch: Barber, 48; Downs, 957; Jeffreys, 123; Selden, 111 (rev. 115); Webster, 68
Three-dimensional set pieces: *see* Set pieces
Three-fold: *see* Dutchman
Thunder: *see* Effects
Tickets and ticket taker: *see* Business department
Tights: *see* Costumes
Time sheet: Bax, 229; Bernheim, 111; Dyer, 130; Halstead, 121; Krows *Play Production,* 232; Stanton, 47
Toggle-rails: *see* Flats: construction
—independent: Barber, 58; Bax, 138; Halstead, 125
Toggles: Bax, 114
Tools: Halstead, 66. *See also* Supplies
Torches: *see* Effects

INDEX

261

Flying (*continued*)
—trimming: 72
—tripping drops: 87, Fig. 21
Foot irons: 64
Frames, gelatine medium: 150
French curtain: 81, Fig. 19
French drape: 80, Fig. 18
Furniture: 93, 129, 132, 134

Gelatines: 150
Graphing legs and borders: 84, **Fig. 20**
Greenrooms: 17
Grips: 103
Ground cloth: 44, 57
Group leaders: 42

Hardware: 67
Hinges: 59
House lights: 98

Independent toggle-rails: 125
Insets: 108
Intermission length: 14

Jacks: 64, Fig. 13

Keeper hooks: 65, Fig. 14
Knots: 72, 74, 162, Fig. 15

Lashing: 104
Leg drops: 83, Fig. 20
Lighting: 137
—arc-spot: 164
—balcony operator: 163
—batten: 155
—bracket lights: 156
—bridge: 155, 164
—cables: 152
—cellophane: 150
—check-list: 154
—color frames: 150
—color media: 150
—connections: 152, 155, 162
—construction: 148
—cue-sheets: 144, Figs. 25-31
—draughting: 140
—electrician: 137
—fixtures: 156
  —suspended: 93

Lighting (*continued*)
—floor operator: 162
—follow-spot: 163
—gelatine storage: 150
—house lights: 98
—masks or mats: 150
—medium frames: 150
—numbering lights: 142
—performance: 157
—phantom load: 144
—planning: 138
—plot: 140, Fig. 25
—reader: 160, 164
—rehearsal: 164
—set-up: 155
—signal board: 119
—slides: 150
—sound effects: 157
—supplies: 148, 154
—switchboard: 142, 146, 156, **158**
  —light: 157
  —numbering: 142
  —operator: 158
—tormentors: 155
—tower: 155, 164
—wall lights: 156
—wiring: 152
Lines: 72
Lips: 63
Loose-pin hinges: 59

Maker of moving plot: 52
Make-up: 176
—album: 176
—assistants: 181
—check-list: 180
—designer: 176
—dress rehearsal: 178
—form-sheets: 178
—pictures: 176
—superintendent: 178
—supplies: 180
—wig band: 175
—wigs: 170, 174, 175
Marking stage: 100
Masking pieces: 44, 106
Master cue-sheet: 29
Media: 150